D1499397

Great Dates in United States History

General Editor André Kaspi

Facts On File®

AN INFOBASE HOLDINGS COMPANY

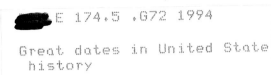
Great Dates in United States History

Facts On File, Inc.
460 Park Avenue South
New York NY 10016

Library of Congress Cataloging-in-Publication Data
Great dates in United States history / general editor, André Kaspi.
    p. cm.—(Great Dates)
    "Some material in this volume was originally published in Les grandes dates des Etats-Unis . . . Librairie Larousse, 1989"—T.p. verso.
    Includes index.
    ISBN 0-8160-2592-4 (alk. paper)
    1. United States—History—Chronology.   I Kaspi, André.
    Grandes dates des Etats-Unis. V. Series.
    E174.5.G72 1994
    973'.02'02—dc20   93-42889

Facts On File books are available at special discounts when purchased in bulk quantities for businesses, associations, institutions or sales promotions. Please call our Special Sales Department in New York at 212/683–2244 or 800/322–8755.

Text design by Robert Yaffe
Jacket design by Catherine Hyman
Printed in the United States of America

RRD FOF 10 9 8 7 6 5 4 3 2 1

This book is printed on acid-free paper.

CONTENTS

LIST OF MAPS

PREFACE

Great Dates in United States History is intended to meet the need for a comprehensive, accessible source of information on the events, people and ideas that have shaped the American experience. As with other volumes in the Great Dates series, it is designed for a wide audience: informed and interested lay readers; students, researchers, and teachers; and professionals in journalism, government, and related fields. The choice of materials reflects a broad view of U.S. history as encompassing science, technology and culture as well as more traditional political, diplomatic, military and economic developments.

The basic structure of the book is a chronology of key dates in U.S. history from earliest times to the present. Each chapter addresses a distinct time period. Within each chapter, chronological entries are organized under such categories as political and institutional life, foreign policy, economy and society, science and technology, and civilization and culture. As appropriate, special categories, such as the Vietnam War or Watergate, are included. Each chapter opens with a synopsis of its time period, and relevant tables and maps are provided throughout the text. The comprehensive index will help to further guide the reader through U.S. history and current events.

Chapter 1

The Discovery of the North American Continent

North America, a huge continent covering approximately 9 million square miles, was "discovered" several times. The people met by the first European explorers were themselves not native to the continent. Indeed, the American Indians came from eastern Asia at various times during the prehistoric period. The chronology of the early civilizations that flourished on the territory now belonging to the United States is still uncertain and the subject of considerable controversy. Although these civilizations never matched those of Mexico or Peru in terms of imperial glory, their social structures are nevertheless immensely interesting, in particular for their extreme linguistic and cultural diversity.

The European discovery of a "New World" dates from roughly the year A.D. 1000. At that time, the Vikings began to follow in the footsteps of predecessors of whom they were unaware, namely Irish monks of the High Middle Ages who traveled west in search of mysterious lands. But only at the end of the 15th century was Europe economically and scientifically mature enough to exploit the New World and its dazzling wealth.

Christopher Columbus landed in the West Indies in 1492, in the first of four voyages that explored these islands and part of the Central American coastline. From 1492 to 1540, a number of other expeditions departed western Europe in search of new lands. Still, it was impossible to foresee in 1500 which European power would rule North America. The Spanish, the Portuguese, then the French and, later, the English started to compete with one another in the waters around Newfoundland and along the coasts of the American continent. Only the Spanish, however, succeeded in establishing a few permanent settlements. The 16th century in North America was the era of exploration, the 17th century the era of colonization. Already, the contacts between American Indians and Europeans were bringing about transformations in the lives of both populations.

Native Tribes in U.S. Territory Prior to European Colonization

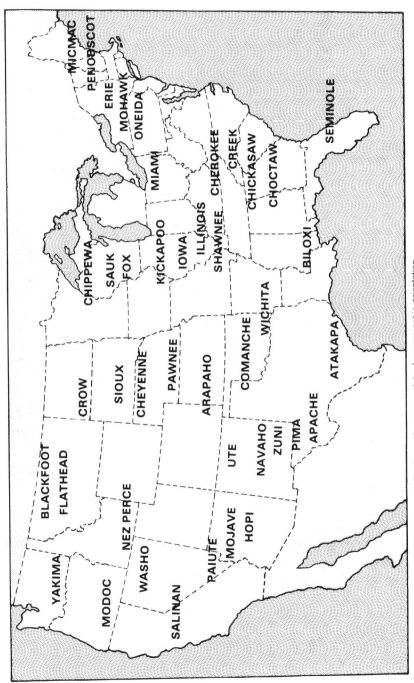

Approximate locations superimposed on map indicating contemporary states for geographic orientation

American Indians Populate the Americas

ca. 50,000–11,000 B.C.
Waves of Mongolian people arrive from Siberia by crossing the Bering Strait.

ca. 35,000–8000 (or 5000) B.C.
The Paleo-Indian era is marked by the hunting of large mammals; the use of stone tools; and the appearance of cultures now named after the archaeological sites where they were uncovered: Sandia, Clovis, Folsom (New Mexico).

ca. 10,000 or 8000 B.C.
End of the Pleistocene epoch: withdrawal of glaciers, global climatic warming; some animal species disappear.

ca. 8000 (or 5000)–1000 B.C.
Archaic period: seminomadic civilizations (hunter-gatherers), then agriculture imported from Central America (ears of corn from approximately 3000 B.C. have been found in Bat Cave, New Mexico). The use of agriculture and pottery spreads throughout North America (ca. 2000 B.C.). Domesticated species include dogs and turkeys.

ca. 300–100 B.C.
Migrations of the Aleutians and the Siberian Eskimos to North America.

ca. 1500 (or 1000) B.C.– A.D. 1000 (or 1500)
Formative era: agriculture, sometimes with irrigation; pottery, sculpture, textiles and, in some places, copper metallurgy. Civilization of the "Mound Builders": Adena (1000 B.C.–A.D. 200 in the Ohio valley) and Hopewell (300 B.C.– A.D. 700 throughout the Midwest) cultures, and the Mississippi civilization (ca.

700–1500). In the Southwest: Mogollon, Hohokam and Ansazi civilizations, the latter being the ancestor of the Pueblo civilization, which experienced its Golden Age from 750–1000 (wealthy and densely populated villages, refined crafts). In Mexico: Maya, Zapotec and Toltec civilizations.

ca. 1025
The territory today constituting the Southwest of the United States is invaded by Navajo tribes from the north.

ca. 1275
Following a period of severe drought, some Pueblo sites are abandoned.

The European Discovery of America

986
Bjarni Herjulfson, a Viking, leaves in search of a colony founded by Erik the Red located southwest of Greenland. Lost, he is probably the first to sight the coast of the North American continent.

ca. 1000
Leif Eriksson, son of Erik the Red, explores the North American coast and names three regions: Helluland, "land of the flat stones" (possibly Baffin Island); Markland, "land of the woods" (possibly Labrador); and Vinland, "land of the vineyards" (Newfoundland: identification confirmed by the archaeological discoveries of Anseaux-Meadows).

1004–1008
Thorwald and Thorstein, brothers of Leif Eriksson, explore the coast, possibly down to New England.

1010–1015
The Icelandic merchant Thorfinn Karlsevni explores possibly as far as Hudson Bay.

ca. 1415
End of the Viking settlements in Greenland.

ca. 1450
Portuguese expeditions probably reach Newfoundland.

1473–1481
English-Danish expeditions (Bristol) search for the legendary islands of "Antilles" and "Brazil."

1492–1493
First voyage of the Genoese Christopher Columbus, hired by Isabella of Castile to reach the legendary island of "Cipango" by a western route. Columbus discovers the islands of San Salvador (Bahamas), Cuba and Santo Domingo (Hispaniola).

1493–1496
Second voyage of Columbus. Puerto Rico is discovered, and a colony is founded on Santo Domingo.

1494
The Treaty of Tordesillas, arbitrated by Pope Alexander VI, establishes a line 370 leagues west of the Cape Verde Islands to divide the areas of Spanish and Portuguese colonization.

1497
First voyage of John Cabot, an Italian explorer in the service of Henry VII of England. Cabot lands on Newfoundland and travels south, perhaps to the coast of Maine.

1498
Second voyage of Cabot, in search of "Cipango." He explores the North American coast (possibly down to the Chesapeake Bay) and then disappears.

1498–1500
Third voyage of Columbus. He reaches Trinidad and sights the Central American coastline.

Amerigo Vespucci, an Italian member of a Spanish expedition, probably sights the South American continent.

ca. 1500
Portuguese expeditions explore Labrador.

1502–1504
Fourth and last voyage of Columbus to the Caribbean.

1506
Christopher Columbus dies, still believing he had reached Asia.

1507
To honor Amerigo Vespucci, the German geographer Martin Waldseemüller suggests the name "America" for the New World.

Explorations and Attempts at Colonization

1508–1513
Spanish explorations are launched from the West Indies.

1513
The Spaniard Juan Ponce de León explores the coasts of Florida (a name that then designated the whole of what is now the southeastern part of the United States).

Vasco Núñez de Balboa succeeds in crossing the Isthmus of Panama and discovers the Pacific Ocean.

1521–1528
The Spanish attempt to colonize Florida.

1524
A French expedition led by the Italian Giovanni da Verrazano is sent in search of a passage to the East Indies. It lands on the continent probably in the area now covered by the Carolinas, travels north and discovers New York Bay and Narragansett Bay (Newport), and then sails along the coast of Maine.

1528
Failure of the Spanish colony that Pánfilo de Narváez had founded at Tampa Bay (Florida).

1534
Jacques Cartier's first voyage to the New World. He explores the straits of Belle Island, the entrance to the St. Lawrence River and Prince Edward Island.

1535
Cartier's second voyage. He sails up the St. Lawrence to the sites where Quebec and Montreal will later be built.

1539–1543
The Spaniard Hernando de Soto sets off from the interior of Florida and reaches the western bank of the Mississippi River, then the Ozark Mountains and eastern Oklahoma. After his death, the survivors of his expedition make it back to the Gulf of Mexico.

1540–1542
Francisco de Coronado sets off from Mexico and discovers Colorado, New Mexico and Texas.

1541
Third voyage of Cartier to Canada and Newfoundland.

1542
Exploring the Pacific Coast, Juan Cabrillo claims California for the king of Spain. After Cabrillo's death, Bartolomeo Ferrero continues north to the coast of Oregon.

1562–1565
A colony of French Huguenots is founded in Florida.

The first descriptions of American Indians are published in Europe by J. Lemoyne.

1565
The Spaniards found St. Augustine in Florida and then massacre the French Huguenots.

1579
Sir Francis Drake explores the coast of California and San Francisco Bay.

1583
In the first British attempt at colonization in America, Sir Humphrey Gilbert establishes a short-lived settlement in Newfoundland; he disappears on his return voyage to England.

1584
Sir Walter Raleigh, resuming the endeavor of his half-brother Gilbert, discovers Roanoke Island (North Carolina) and names the region Virginia, in honor of Queen Elizabeth.

1585–1586
The colony of Roanoke is founded and then quickly abandoned.

1587

A new expedition to Roanoke includes the painter John White. A settlement is founded but will disappear three years later.

1588

The first description of North America written in English is provided by Thomas Harriot, a member of Raleigh's expedition to Roanoke.

1589

In London, Richard Hakluyt publishes several narratives of British explorers; watercolors by John White also appear.

1598

The Spanish begin colonizing the southwest.

1603–1606

Samuel de Champlain explores the St. Lawrence River and establishes trading posts in Canada.

1605

The French found the colony of Port Royal in Acadia.

Economy and Society

ca. 1500

The American Indian population of North America is variously estimated to be 1 million to 10 million.

ca. 1520

The first epidemics of European origin (smallpox, measles, influenza and others) appear among the Indians.

1520

The first shipment of furs (primarily beaver) leaves for Europe.

ca. 1525

The cultivation of sugarcane begins in the West Indies.

1540

The expedition of Coronado introduces the first horses into the southwest.

ca. 1550

A new way of drying fish is developed (it will lead to an increase in the consumption of cod in England).

1565

The Spanish introduce sheep into New Mexico. Indians begin using weaving looms.

1577

Around Newfoundland, 150 French, 100 Spanish, 50 Portuguese and 15 English fishing boats work the waters.

ca. 1580

Produce from the New World appears in Europe: tobacco, tapioca, tomatoes, potatoes.

1587

Virginia Dare, granddaughter of the painter John White, is the first British child born in North America (in Roanoke).

ca. 1600–1700

Horses that escape from the Spanish colonies in the southwest transform the way of life of the Plains Indians.

1603

Henry IV of France grants a monopoly of the fur trade to Pierre du Gast, Sieur de Monts, a member of Champlain's expedition.

Chapter 2

British Colonization

At the dawn of the 17th century, England, ruled by the Stuarts, was ready to take part in the colonization of North America, which would also provide her with a safety valve for her social and religious problems.

At first, England's colonial endeavors were entrusted to merchant companies chartered by the Crown. Each of the two Virginia Companies, of London and of Plymouth, was given control over a geographical area on the North American coast. After several failures, the first permanent settlement was founded in Virginia in 1607 and named Jamestown, in honor of King James I. A few years later, New England was formed around the first settlements at Plymouth and on Massachusetts Bay.

While the French and Dutch adventures in North America continued, the British Crown, after the English Civil War and the restoration of the Stuarts in 1660, became increasingly involved in developing its colonies, especially through the gift of American territories to high-ranking personalities of the kingdom. Thus the mid-Atlantic colonies (New York, New Jersey, Pennsylvania) came into being, as did the southern colonies (Carolina and, much later, Georgia in 1732). The colonies were increasingly differentiated by their economies. In the south, Virginia and Maryland flourished, thanks to the single-crop farming of tobacco; after 1750, the plantation system encouraged the importation of slaves from Africa. In the north and in the mid-Atlantic region, a combination of shipping and diversified agriculture prevailed. The variety of institutional means employed to start the colonies (chartered company, territorial grant by the Crown, direct royal rule) was soon counterbalanced by a trend toward uniformity of provincial governments. Indeed, all of the colonies would eventually be ruled by a council of notables or an assembly of colonists in association with a governor appointed by London.

The Founding of the Colonies

1606–1607
The first attempts at colonizing New England, made by the Virginia Company of Plymouth, end in failure.

1607

May. Jamestown is founded in Virginia by approximately 100 colonists led by Captain John Smith under the patronage of the Virginia Company of London. This is the first permanent English settlement in the New World.

1608

Quebec is founded by Samuel de Champlain.

1609

The English explorer Henry Hudson makes his first voyage on behalf of the Dutch East India Company. He sails up the Hudson River and reaches the site of present-day Albany.

Santa Fe (New Mexico) is founded by the Spanish.

1611

Set adrift by his own rebellious crew on a subsequent voyage, Hudson perishes after having explored the bay that will later bear his name.

1613

The first Dutch trading post is established on the island of Manhattan.

A Dutchman, Adrian Block, explores Manhattan and Long Island, and establishes Fort Nassau, near Albany. The area becomes the colony of New Netherland around this time.

1620

The Pilgrims, English Calvinists seeking religious freedom, set off on the *Mayflower* with a patent from the Virginia Company of Plymouth to settle in America; they establish the colony of Plymouth (Massachusetts).

1622

The Council for New England, the successor to the Plymouth Company, grants Maine to John Mason and Ferdinando Georges.

1624

The Dutch West India Company establishes Fort Orange, near Albany.

1626

Peter Minuit, governor of the Dutch colony of New Netherland, buys Manhattan Island from the Indians for 60 guilders ($24), paid in kind, and names it New Amsterdam.

1630

John Winthrop establishes a colony at Salem, on Massachusetts Bay. The town of Boston will soon be established, leading to a major migration of Puritans (former members of the Church of England).

1631

Portsmouth (New Hampshire) is founded.

1632

Charles I grants a charter to George Calvert (Lord Baltimore), a Catholic nobleman. This charter allows Calvert to establish a colony in Virginia north of the Potomac River.

1634

Maryland is founded by Leonard Calvert, son of George; 50 percent of the colonists are Catholic.

1635

New Hampshire is founded by John Mason.

1636

Providence (Rhode Island) is founded by Roger Williams, who was expelled from Massachusetts after having protested against the policy of religious intolerance that prevailed there.

Connecticut is founded by colonists from Massachusetts.

1638

Delaware is founded by Swedes of the New Sweden Company, which is backed by private investors in Holland.

1653–1654

Colonists from Virginia settle north of Albermarle Sound, in what will become North Carolina.

1663

Charles II grants a charter to a group of eight proprietors, allowing them to colonize the area between 31 and 36 degrees north latitude, comprising the present-day Carolinas and Georgia.

1664

The English capture New Amsterdam and rename it New York. The Duke of York, the new owner of the former Dutch colony, sells New Jersey to Sir William Berkeley and George Carteret.

1670

Charleston (South Carolina) is founded by English colonists from Barbados.

1673–1674

Two Frenchmen, Louis Jolliet and Jacques Marquette, explore the Mississippi Valley.

1676

New Jersey is divided into two parts; one part is given to a group of Quakers.

1682

Pennsylvania is founded by a Quaker, William Penn, on the basis of a royal charter.

French Louisiana is founded after the expeditions of Robert Cavelier de La Salle.

Spanish colonists settle in Texas.

Delaware, which is not owned by the Duke of York, is nonetheless sold by him to William Penn.

The Government of the Colonies

1608

Captain John Smith is elected president of the Council of the Virginia Company of London.

1609

Internal turmoil in Virginia leads to the granting of a new charter.

1611

Sir Thomas Dale, governor of Virginia, imposes severe penalties to halt internal disorder (the Dale Code).

1618

The fourth charter for Virginia is granted.

1619

The first meeting of the General Assembly of Virginia is held: the 22 burgesses, elected by landowners, will sit with the governor and his council.

1620

On Cape Cod, 41 Pilgrims sign the Mayflower Compact, establishing a contractual government in the future colony of Plymouth.

1621
William Bradford becomes governor of Plymouth.

1623
James I establishes the Council for New England, which will demarcate areas for colonization.

1624
The Crown revokes the charter of Virginia, which becomes a royal colony (its form of government remains the same).

1630
The General Court (assembly) of Massachusetts meets for the first time and organizes an autonomous government.

1631
In the Massachusetts Bay Colony, only members of the Congregationalist Church have voting rights.

1632
Proprietary government is established in Maryland.

1635
The House of Representatives of Maryland meets for the first time.

1636
The Plymouth Colony breaks with its London sponsors and forms a government with a governor and a general assembly.

1639
The Fundamental Orders of Connecticut establish a government similar to that of Massachusetts.

1641
The first compendium of the laws of Massachusetts appears.

1643
The New England Confederacy, a defensive alliance of Massachusetts, New Haven, Plymouth and Connecticut, is created; its aim is to achieve military coordination in the face of Indian and Dutch threats.

1644
Roger Williams is granted a charter for Rhode Island. The new colony institutes a complete separation of church and state.

1649
Charles I of England is executed.

1652
Massachusetts annexes Maine.

1654–1655
Clashes between Catholics and Puritans occur in Maryland.

1655–1658
British ruler Oliver Cromwell deprives Lord Baltimore of his proprietary authority in Maryland.

1660
The Restoration of the Stuarts occurs in Great Britain with the accession of Charles II to the throne.

1662
A new royal charter is granted to Connecticut.

1664
Charles II grants a huge territory, including New Netherland, to his brother, the Duke of York.

1665
New Haven is united with Connecticut.

1669

The Fundamental Constitution of the Carolinas is written by John Locke; it will not be put into effect.

1680

New Hampshire becomes a royal colony distinct from Massachusetts.

1682

William Penn establishes the form of government of Pennsylvania (governor, council and assembly).

1683

The provincial assembly of New York meets for the first time.

1684

Charles II revokes the charter of Massachusetts and dissolves the New England Confederacy.

1685

With the accession to the throne of James I, the Duke of York, New York becomes a royal colony.

Relations with Indians and Other European Colonists

1607

In Virginia, Captain John Smith is captured by the Indian chief Powhatan; he is freed thanks to the intercession of the Indian princess Pocahontas.

1613

Colonists from Virginia launch a raid against the French settlements of Port Royal (Acadia) and Mount Desert (Maine).

1614

Powhatan and the colonists of Virginia sign a treaty. Pocahontas, baptized in 1613, is married to John Rolfe.

1616

Pocahontas is introduced to the Court of James I.

1616–1618

Chickenpox decimates the Indian tribes of New England.

1621

A treaty creates a defensive alliance between the Pilgrims of Plymouth and the Wampanoag Indians against the Narragansett Indians.

1622

The Powhatan Confederacy (six Algonquin tribes), led by Chief Opechancanough, attacks Virginia; the colonists at Jamestown are massacred.

1637

A war is waged against the Pequot Indians in the Connecticut River valley.

1644

In Virginia, the second Powhatan War results in the death of Opechancanough.

1646

A treaty is signed by Virginia and the Powhatan Confederacy; the latter yields large territories.

1655

New Netherland captures New Sweden (Delaware), ending Swedish efforts to colonize North America.

1664

New Amsterdam (New Netherland) surrenders to the English, who rename it New York.

1673–1674

The Dutch recapture New York for a few months.

1675

The Susquehannock Indians attack Virginia.

1675–1676

In King Philip's War, the Wampanoag Indians of New England, led by Metacom (whom the British call King Philip), wage an unsuccessful effort to halt British subjugation of the Indians of the region.

1677

In Virginia, the government signs a treaty with the Indians, who lose more territory.

1680

In New Mexico, the Pueblos, led by Popé, revolt against the Spanish, who are driven out of Santa Fe.

Population, Economy and Society

1607–1609

Famine, scurvy and dysentery afflict the colonists at Jamestown; the population falls from 105 to 32.

1609

First harvest of corn in Jamestown.

1610

Population of Virginia: 350.

1612

First harvest of tobacco in Jamestown; the first cargo of tobacco will be sent to England in 1614.

1617

Land is distributed to the Virginia colonists: 50 acres of land per person brought over to America.

1619

A Dutch ship brings 20 Africans to Jamestown as indentured servants.

1627

The first gristmills appear in Manhattan.

1629

Large land grants are given to New Netherland colonists ("patroons").

1630

Population of the British colonies: 4,646, including 50 blacks in Virginia.

Virginia exports 1.5 million pounds of tobacco.

1641

The first official mention of slavery in the colonies is provided in a Massachusetts law.

1644

Shipbuilding and textile industries appear in Massachusetts.

1652

The first American coins are minted in Boston, despite a British ban.

Rhode Island becomes the first colony to outlaw slavery.

1660

Population of the British colonies: 75,058, including 2,920 blacks.

1664

A Maryland law specifies that blacks who convert to Christianity will nonetheless remain slaves for life.

1675–1677

In western Virginia, Nathaniel Bacon leads a revolt against the colonial government, which he views as failing to protect colonists from the Indians and as levying unfair taxes. After seizing control of the colony for a time, the revolt ends when Bacon dies of dysentery and his followers are captured by British troops.

1677–1680

John Culpeper leads a revolt in Carolina against major landowners.

1680

Population of the British colonies: 151,507, including 6,971 blacks.

1683

The first German colonists (Mennonites) arrive in Philadelphia.

Religion, Education and Culture

1607–1655

Franciscan missions are established in Spanish Florida; approximately 25,000 Indians are converted.

1609

The Anglican Church is established in Virginia.

1620

The first Congregationalist church is founded in Plymouth.

1624

In London, John Smith publishes his *History of Virginia*, which strongly encourages emigration.

1628

The Dutch Reformed Church is established in New Amsterdam.

1630

The first Congregationalist church is founded in Boston.

1634

The first Catholic church is established in Maryland.

1636

Boston Latin School, a secondary school, and Harvard College are founded in Boston.

Providence (Rhode Island) is the first colony to allow religious freedom.

1638

Anne Hutchinson is banished from Massachusetts.

The first printing press appears in Massachusetts (Cambridge).

1640

The *Bay Psalm Book* is the first full-length book printed in the British colonies.

1647

A Massachusetts law makes it compulsory for each settlement of over 50 families to organize a school.

1649

Maryland ratifies the Toleration Act, which applies to Christians of all denominations.

1656–1659

Quakers are violently persecuted in Massachusetts.

1663

The first Bible is printed in America; translated by John Eliot, a minister, it is in the Algonquin language.

1664

In Massachusetts, a synod relaxes the requirements for those wanting to join the Congregationalist Church (Halfway Covenant).

1665

A law on religious tolerance is passed in New York.

1682

Town planning commences for the city of Philadelphia.

1685

Huguenots driven out of France by the revocation of the Edict of Nantes arrive in America.

Chapter 3   1685–1763

The Emergence of British America

Colonial struggles, echoes of the numerous wars between the European powers, dominated the end of the 17th and much of the 18th centuries. In particular, the rivalry between England and France grew more intense and culminated in the Seven Years' War (1756–1763). In America, the Indians were invariably drawn into these conflicts, with the English finding an ally in the Iroquois, the everlasting enemies of the French. These wars resulted in the French being eliminated from North America and the English achieving mastery beginning in 1763.

The wars and the growth of the colonies forced the British government to increase the political centralization of its empire. By 1760, for example, 8 of the 13 colonies had come under the direct rule of the Crown. But the colonists actually enjoyed considerable autonomy, which enabled them to proceed with their training in self-government.

Despite political turmoil, physical insecurity and the mercantilist policy of Great Britain, the colonial economies blossomed. The Chesapeake colonies, the Carolinas and Georgia were almost exclusively devoted to the commercial farming of produce for export to England—tobacco, rice, indigo. The mid-Atlantic colonies of Pennsylvania, New Jersey and New York provided grain, meat and leather, while New England flourished thanks to fishing, shipbuilding and trade with the West Indies (even though the latter was illegal). However, since the laws of the empire required the colonies to import from England virtually all manufactured products, the balance of trade was always in deficit.

Colonial society also underwent change. French Huguenots, Scotch-Irish and, above all, Germans from the Rhine valley joined the English immigrants in America. In addition, the natural increase of the colonial population was impressive, even among those involuntary immigrants, the Africans. Indeed, on the plantations, black slaves replaced indentured European servants who had repaid with several years labor the employers who funded their passage to America. Religious, economic and political factors, meanwhile, produced mounting tensions among the white colonists. Although the colonies had by now produced what could be termed an "American" culture, they still retained close ties to the mother country.

Colonial and Indian Wars

1689–1697

King William's War (in Europe, War of the League of Augsburg). The English and Iroquois battle the French and their Indian allies in the Hudson Bay region, the St. Lawrence and upper Hudson valleys, and Acadia.

1690

February. Schenectady (New York) is burned by the French and their Indian allies.

May. The English capture Port Royal (Acadia).

October. Governor Frontenac drives back the English before Quebec.

1691

The French take back Port Royal.

1697

The Treaty of Ryswick reestablishes the status quo ante in the colonies.

1702–1713

Queen Anne's War. A conflict between British and French forces in North America and the Caribbean is waged at the same time as the War of the Spanish Succession (1701–1714) in Europe.

1702

The English capture St. Augustine and several other Florida missions from the Spanish.

1704

French Acadia is attacked by colonists from New England. The French destroy Deerfield in Massachusetts.

1710

Port Royal is captured by the English.

1711

The English fail to capture Quebec.

1711–1713

The Tuscarora War (North Carolina) between Lower Tuscarora Indians and English colonists erupts over territorial expansion and the enslavement of the native population. The defeated Tuscarora move north and join the Iroquois Confederacy.

1713

Treaty of Utrecht: France cedes the Hudson Bay Territory, Newfoundland and Acadia (Nova Scotia) to Britain.

1715–1728

Yamassee War between Yamassee Indians and South Carolina colonists. Despite Spanish backing, the Yamassee are defeated.

1718

New Orleans is founded by the French.

ca. 1720

French forts are built in the Mississippi and Ohio valleys.

1721–1725

In Dummer's or Lovewell's War, French and English colonists skirmish in northern Maine and Vermont.

1722

The Iroquois Confederacy and Virginia enter into a treaty.

1739–1743

War of Jenkin's Ear. The British and the colonists battle the Spanish, who are accused of mistreating English sailors. The Spanish are driven back to Florida.

1744–1748

In King George's War (War of the Austrian Succession), the British and colonials fight the French.

1744

The French are defeated by the British at Port Royal (Nova Scotia). A treaty is entered into by the English and the Iroquois, who give up territory in the Ohio valley.

1745

French-Indian raids are launched into Maine.

The fortress of Louisbourg, on Cape Breton Island, is captured by an English expedition from New England.

1748

In the Treaty of Aix-la-Chapelle, the French regain Louisbourg, and the status quo prevails in the other colonial territories. Great Britain retains its monopoly on the transportation of slaves to the Spanish colonics.

1748–1755

The British and French struggle for control of the Ohio valley.

1753

Lieutenant Colonel George Washington, 21 years old, is sent by the governor of Virginia to demand that the French leave the Ohio valley.

1754–1763

The French and Indian War (in Europe, the Seven Years' War, 1756–1763).

1754

The French build Fort Duquesne at the confluence of the Allegheny and Monongahela Rivers. Washington is defeated by the French at Fort Necessity.

1756–1757

French general the Marquis de Montcalm captures Fort Oswego and Fort William Henry in New York.

1758

July 8. The British are defeated by Montcalm's forces at Fort Ticonderoga (New York).

July 27. The British capture Fort Louisbourg.

November. Fort Duquesne is surrendered to the British; it will become Pittsburgh.

1759

September 18. The French are defeated on the Plains of Abraham at Quebec; both Montcalm and the British commander, General James Wolfe, are killed.

1760

Montreal and then Detroit are surrendered to the British.

1763

February 10. The Treaty of Paris is signed by Great Britain, France and Spain. France relinquishes Canada and the territories east of the Mississippi River (except New Orleans) to Great Britain, and cedes New Orleans and Louisiana, the vast territory between the Mississippi and the Rocky Mountains, to Spain. In America, France retains only the islands of Saint Pierre and Miquelon. Spain yields Florida to Great Britain.

Indians under the leadership of the Ottawa chief Pontiac stage an uprising. Several forts (Detroit, Michilimackinac) are attacked, and British settlers are massacred. Pontiac is defeated at Bushy Run, near Pittsburgh.

The Thirteen Colonies, 1750

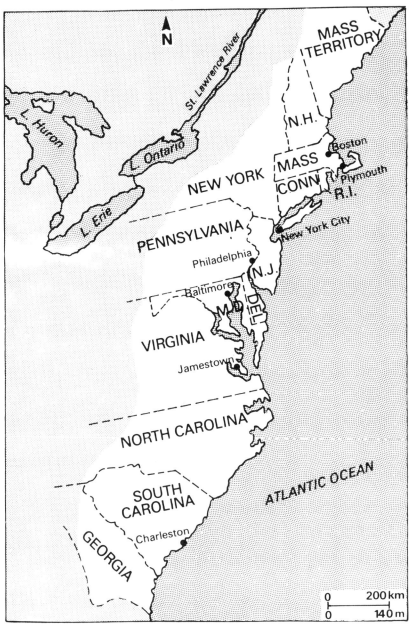

Political Life in the British Empire

1685
The Stuart James II, a Catholic, becomes king of England; he intends to reorder the administration of the colonies.

1686–1689
The Dominion of New England, which includes the colonies of New York and New Jersey, is created.

1687
The governor of the Dominion, Sir Edmund Andros, revokes the colonial charters and dissolves the colonial assemblies.

1688
James II is dethroned in the "Glorious Revolution." He is replaced by his daughter Mary and his son-in-law William of Orange. The people of Boston imprison the unpopular Governor Andros.

1689–1691
Jacob Leisler leads a rebellion in New York and Long Island. Lieutenant Governor Francis Nicholson is driven away. Leisler, after proclaiming loyalty to William and Mary, forms a new government. He surrenders to a superior English force and is tried and hung. The unpopular Andros, expelled from New England, will be tried in England.

1689
In Maryland, the Protestants revolt against the Catholics.

1696
The Board of Trade for the Plantations, a governmental institution, is created; its decisions will be submitted to the Privy Council of the king.

1702
New Jersey becomes a royal colony.

1712
Each of the Carolinas is given its own governor.

1719
The colonists of South Carolina revolt against their governor, who is accused of not protecting them against the Indians.

1729
Both Carolinas become royal colonies.

1732
In order to create a buffer against the Spanish in Florida, a royal charter granted to the philanthropist James Edward Oglethorpe allows him to found a colony, Georgia, which will also be a refuge for debtors.

1733
Savannah is founded in the new colony of Georgia.

1739
Oglethorpe signs a peace treaty with the Creek Indians.

1749
King George II grants a charter to the Ohio Company.

1752
Georgia becomes a royal colony.

1754
At the Albany Congress, Benjamin Franklin proposes a plan to unite the colonies. The plan is rejected by both the colonists and the Crown.

1760

George III, 22 years old, succeeds George II.

1763

Lord Grenville becomes prime minister of England.

In order to avoid conflicts with the Indians, a royal proclamation prohibits colonization beyond the sources of the rivers running down the Appalachian Mountains to the Atlantic Ocean.

Economy and Society

1690

Whaling begins in Nantucket.

Paper money (notes of hand) is issued in Massachusetts.

1695

In New York, the first measures are taken to assist paupers.

1696

A new Navigation Act creates admiralty courts in the colonies. These courts are to try, without a jury, maritime and commercial cases.

The cultivation of rice begins in the Carolinas.

1698

The Royal African Company's loss of its monopoly of the slave trade benefits New England traders.

1699

The Wool Act forbids the export of woolen fabric from New England to Europe or the other colonies.

1700

Population of the British colonies: 250,888, including 27,817 blacks.

1703

The use of paper money is allowed by North Carolina.

1705

A law adds several products (rice, molasses, shipping stores) to the list of products that can be exported only to Great Britain.

A Massachusetts law forbids interracial marriages.

1709–1710

Large numbers of Swiss and German immigrants arrive in North Carolina, where the port of New Bern is founded.

1712

Slaves revolt in New York.

1713

The first American schooner is built in Gloucester, Massachusetts; this marks the beginning of a flourishing shipbuilding industry in New England.

1717

Colonial merchants are allowed to trade molasses with the French West Indies.

1721

The first vaccinations against smallpox are given in Boston.

1729

Franklin publishes his *Inquiry on the Nature and Necessity of Paper Money*.

1731–1732

Smallpox kills 6 percent of the population of New York.

1732

The Hat Act prohibits colonial hatmakers from having more than two apprentices; American beaver furs must be worked in England.

18th-Century Colonial Trade Routes

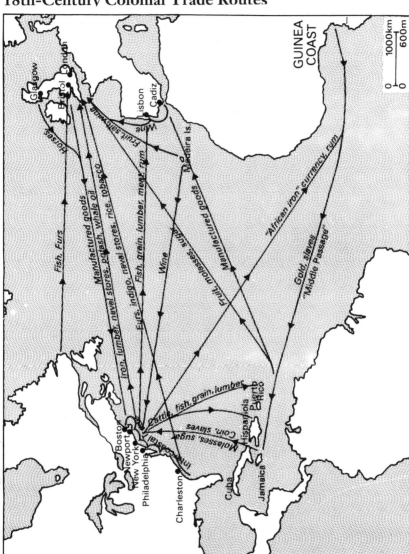

1733

The Molasses Act imposes a prohibitive tariff on imported sugars in order to protect the planters in the British West Indies.

1739

Slaves wishing to flee to Florida stage a revolt in the Stono Valley (South Carolina). A wave of panic spreads among slaveholders.

ca. 1740

The cultivation of indigo begins in North Carolina.

1741

The "Negro Conspiracy" occurs in New York. Whites, fearing crime allegedly committed by blacks, flee the city; the militia is called in to restore order, and 21 blacks are killed.

1746

Small landowners stage a revolt in New Jersey.

1750

The Iron Act encourages the production of pig iron but bans its transformation into manufactured products.

There are 50 rum distilleries in Massachusetts.

ca. 1750

Coffee houses multiply; Americans meet in them to debate the problems of the hour.

1751

The Currency Act forbids the use of banknotes in the colonies.

1752

The first public hospital is established in Philadelphia.

1753

The first steam engine is imported for use in a copper mine in New Jersey.

1756

A regular stagecoach line is established between New York and Philadelphia.

1760

Population of the colonies: 1.6 million, including 326,000 blacks.

1763

The Paxton Boys, frontiersmen from western Pennsylvania, march on Philadelphia, demanding that help be provided in case of an Indian attack. They are persuaded to withdraw in return for greater representation in the legislature.

BLACK POPULATION IN BRITISH COLONIES

	1680	1700	1720	1740	1760
Total	6,971	27,857	68,839	150,024	325,806
Massachusetts	170	800	2,150	3,035	4,566
New York	1,200	2,256	5,740	8,996	16,340
Virginia	3,000	16,390	26,559	60,000	140,570
North Carolina	210	415	3,000	11,000	33,554

POPULATION OF MAJOR CITIES IN BRITISH COLONIES, 1760

Boston	New York	Philadelphia	Charleston
16,000	18,000	23,000	8,000

Religion, Education and Culture

1685

The first printing press in Philadelphia is established.

1686

Governor Edmund Andros forces the Anglican denomination on the people of the Dominion of New England.

1688

The Germantown Quakers denounce slavery for the first time.

1692

Witchcraft trials are held in Salem, Massachusetts: 20 persons are executed.

1693

The Anglican College of William and Mary is founded in Williamsburg, Virginia.

George Keith, a Quaker, issues a written protest against slavery.

1695

The first synagogue is founded in New York.

1697

An official Day of Atonement in Massachusetts commemorates the Salem witchcraft trials.

1701

The Congregationalist College of Yale is founded in Connecticut.

The Society for the Propagation of the Faith, an Anglican organization, is created to evangelize in the colonies.

1702

The Anglican Church is established in Maryland.

1704

The *Boston News Letter* is the first newspaper published in the colonies.

The Anglican Church is established in the Carolinas.

1711

There are 30 bookshops in Boston.

1716

The colonies' first theater is founded in Williamsburg, Virginia.

1719

Two new newspapers begin publication: the *Boston Gazette* and the *Mercury* (Philadelphia).

1721

An anonymous artist executes the oldest portrait known to have been painted in the colonies (Ann Pollard is the subject).

1727

A chair in mathematics is established at Harvard College.

1728

The *Pennsylvania Gazette* is founded in Philadelphia.

1729

Benjamin Franklin buys an interest in the *Pennsylvania Gazette*.

1731

In Philadelphia, Franklin founds the first library to lend books to the public.

1732

Franklin publishes the first edition of *Poor Richard's Almanac*.

1734

John Edwards preaches in Northampton, Massachusetts.

1735–1736

The Great Awakening, a Protestant revival, spreads throughout New England: The Old Lights, who support tradition, are opposed by the New Lights, who support the Great Awakening.

1735

The Westover mansion is built in Virginia.

The Moravian Brethren, Pietists from Germany, arrive in Georgia.

In New York, the journalist John Zenger is accused of libeling British governor Cosby and put on trial; Zenger is acquitted. Freedom of the press is officially recognized.

1736

John Wesley preaches in Georgia, marking the beginning of Methodism.

1738

The first Masonic lodge is founded in Massachusetts.

1739–1740

The Great Awakening continues: The English preacher George Whitefield tours the colonies.

1741

In Pennsylvania, Bethlehem is founded by the Moravian Brethren.

1742

In New England, Unitarianism is established in reaction to the sentimentalism of the Great Awakening.

1743

The American Philosophical Society is founded in Philadelphia.

1746

The Presbyterian College of New Jersey is founded in Princeton.

1750–1760

In Virginia, the Great Awakening leads to clashes between the Baptists and the Anglican aristocracy.

ca. 1750

Works of the architect Peter Harrison appear in New England (Newport, Boston).

1751

The nondenominational Franklin Academy, which will become the University of Pennsylvania, is founded.

1752

Franklin conducts his experiments with electricity.

1754

In New York, the Anglican King's College is founded; it will become Columbia University in 1784.

1755

Quakers who import slaves are excluded from the Society of Friends.

The first school for black children is founded in Philadelphia.

Chapter 4 1764–1776

The Origins of the American Revolution

With the end of the French and Indian War (1754–1763), the British colonies entered a new period in their history that would lead them to independence.

While the colonists looked forward to settling in the territories between the Appalachians and the Mississippi that the French had relinquished, the British government, fearing conflict with the Indians, tried to close those territories to settlement. Since the British treasury had been exhausted in part by the military campaigns to defend the colonies, the king and his ministers decided that America should refund approximately a third of the cost of its defense. The money would be raised through a more rigorous enforcement of tariff regulations and through new taxes imposed on the colonies. The colonists saw in all this a plot by Parliament and the Crown to ruin America, and they rebelled. Indeed, the measures taken by London beginning in 1764 weighed heavily on an economy already depressed at the end of the war. Each new law from Parliament was answered with a wave of protests in the colonies. The colonists signed petitions, refused to comply with royal directives, and boycotted taxed products. In 1764, 1765, 1767 and 1773, there were acts of violence against officers of the Crown.

Beginning in 1770, skirmishes took place between colonists and British soldiers. Newspaper articles, pamphlets and tracts denounced the absolutism of the king and maintained that citizens who were not represented in Parliament could not be taxed by it. In order to coordinate their resistance, the colonists created a Continental Congress that met in Philadelphia in 1774 and again in 1775.

Although the break between the colonies and the mother country had in fact already been finalized in the clashes between local militias and British soldiers, nobody dared to speak of independence before the beginning of 1776, when *Common Sense* was published in Philadelphia. Thomas Paine's pamphlet promoted in fierce language both independence and the establishment of a republic in America. It acted as a catalyst, and soon Congress adopted Thomas Jefferson's Declaration of Independence.

Imperial Policy and Colonial Resistance

1764

April. Lord Grenville, chancellor of the exchequer, presents in Parliament a set of measures aimed at raising at least £45,000. The Revenue Act (the "Sugar Act") increases the tariff on foreign sugar and imposes new tariffs on other non-British products: molasses, foodstuffs, rum and lumber. The Currency Act forbids colonists to issue paper money. Violators will be tried before an admiralty court sitting in Halifax (Nova Scotia).

May. In Boston, James Otis denounces "taxation without representation."

June. Protests against the Sugar Act, asking in vain for its repeal, take place throughout the colonies.

August. The first agreements to boycott British products are reached by Boston and New York merchants.

1765

March. The Stamp Act requires the payment of a tax on every contract, publication, official document and set of playing cards. It is the first tax ever levied by the Crown in the colonies.

The Quartering Act requires the colonies to provide housing and provisions for two years to the British troops stationed in America.

May. Patrick Henry protests against royal policy in the House of Burgesses of Virginia.

Summer. Secret associations, the "Sons of Liberty," are formed in several cities to organize resistance to the Stamp Act.

October. The Stamp Act Congress, a gathering of delegates from 9 of the 13 colonies, meets in New York. A petition against the enforcement of the act is adopted, and it is decided to boycott British products and to refuse to use stamps. The Congress also opposes taxation without representation and trial without jury.

November. A riot against the Stamp Act occurs in New York.

1766

March. Pressured by London merchants hurt by deteriorating commercial relations with America, Parliament repeals the Stamp Act but adopts the Declaratory Act affirming the right of Parliament to legislate for the colonies.

November. The tariff on foreign molasses is reduced.

1767

June. Charles Townshend, chancellor of the exchequer, has new measures voted to extract money from the colonies. They include new customs duties on numerous products, including glass, lead, paint, paper and tea.

October. Merchants in the major American ports reach new agreements not to import British products. A boycott of British goods will spread to other colonies.

The Assembly of New York is suspended after refusing to pay for the quartering of British troops.

November. John Dickinson, in his "Letters from a Pennsylvania Farmer," declares that the Townshend duties are unconstitutional.

1768

February. Samuel Adams of Massachusetts sends the other colonies a circular letter denouncing the Townshend duties.

June. In Boston, customs agents seize a ship belonging to John Hancock, who had refused to pay import duties on Madeira wine. After a crowd attacks the agents, military reinforcements arrive to restore order.

1769

May. The Assembly of Virginia denounces Parliament's taxes and votes to prohibit the importation of British goods. The governor dissolves the Assembly.

1770

January. A skirmish between soldiers and a crowd at Golden Hill, in New York, leaves many wounded.

March 5. In the "Boston Massacre," British soldiers kill five demonstrators, including Crispus Attucks, a black man.

April. Lord North, the prime minister, proposes to repeal the Townshend duties, except those on tea. The colonists are pacified and end their boycott of British goods.

1772

In Providence, Rhode Island, a customs ship, the *Gaspee*, is set on fire; new tensions arise.

November. The first of the "committees of correspondence," instigated by Samuel Adams of Boston, is created to establish communications among the assemblies of the colonies.

Ships of the East India Company carrying tea are turned back at Boston, New York and Philadelphia.

1773

May. To assist the East India Company, Parliament passes the Tea Act, which relieves the company of import duties on tea from the Orient and gives it a monopoly on the sale of that tea in America. American importers protest against this cheap competition.

December. The Boston Tea Party: Bostonians dressed as Indians throw overboard three shiploads of tea belonging to the East India Company.

The Break

1774

March–May. In London, Parliament passes the "Intolerable Acts" to punish Boston: the harbor is closed to all ocean-going ships; the culprits of the "tea party" are to be tried in England; the charter of Massachusetts is repealed.

May. The Quebec Act establishes a centralized government in the Canadian province and extends its borders to enclose the Mississippi and Ohio valley regions and Labrador. The Act is seen by the American colonists as a threat.

June. A new act permits the quartering of troops in private homes.

September. The First Continental Congress, gathering delegates from all the colonies except Georgia, meets in Philadelphia. The Intolerable Acts are declared illegal and the colonists are asked to form militias. The Congress will meet again in May 1775.

1775

February. Lord North proposes a compromise on the problem of taxation, but an act forbids New England to trade with countries other than Great Britain and the British West Indies.

March 23. Patrick Henry says, "Give me liberty or give me death" in an address to the Virginia Convention.

April 18. Paul Revere rides to warn the Americans that British troops are approaching Concord, Massachusetts.

April 19. In Lexington and Concord, the first clashes between the British army and the Minutemen, the militia of Massachusetts, take place after the British try to destroy an arms depot belonging to the latter. Both sides suffer dozens of casualties. The British withdraw to Boston, and are besieged by the Americans.

May. British reinforcements arrive in Boston. Fort Ticonderoga, on Lake Champlain, is captured by the Americans, led by Ethan Allen.

The Second Continental Congress meets in Philadelphia.

June 15. The Congress names George Washington commander in chief of the Continental Army. Troops are levied throughout the colonies.

June 17. The Americans are defeated in the Battle of Bunker Hill, near Boston, after twice repulsing the British under General William Howe. The British suffer heavy casualties.

July 5. In the Olive Branch Petition, written by John Dickinson, the Continental Congress asks George III to suspend hostilities.

July 6. The Continental Congress adopts the "Declaration of the Causes and Necessity of Taking Up Arms" but does not yet contemplate independence.

August 23. George III rejects the Olive Branch Petition and declares the colonies to be in a state of rebellion.

POPULATION OF THE THIRTEEN COLONIES, 1770

Colony	Total Population	Black Population
New Hampshire	62,396	654
Massachusetts	235,308	4,754
Rhode Island	58,196	3,761
Connecticut	183,881	5,698
New York	162,920	19,112
New Jersey	117,431	8,220
Pennsylvania	240,057	5,761
Delaware	35,496	1,836
Maryland	202,599	63,818
Virginia	447,016	187,605
North Carolina	197,200	69,600
South Carolina	124,244	75,178
Georgia	23,375	10,625
(Maine)	31,257	458
(Vermont)	10,000	—
(Kentucky-Tennessee)	16,700	2,725
Total	2,148,076	459,805

SOURCE: *Historical Statistics of the United States.*

August–December. American expeditions against Canada succeed in occupying Montreal (November 13) but are defeated at Quebec (December 31).

October–December. The Congress organizes a navy by outfitting some fishing vessels with cannons.

November 29. The Congress appoints a committee to oversee the establishment of relations with foreign governments.

1776

January. Thomas Paine publishes *Common Sense* in Philadelphia. In it, he calls George III a "royal brute" and advocates independence and the establishment of a republic.

March 17. General Howe, commanding the British forces, abandons Boston and withdraws to Halifax.

May. The Congress recommends that the colonies adopt representative governments.

June 7. Richard Lee drafts a resolution proclaiming independence. The Continental Congress appoints a committee of five members (including Thomas Jefferson, Benjamin Franklin and John Adams) to draw up a declaration justifying American independence.

June 12. Virginia drafts its Bill of Rights, which will serve as a model for all others.

June 28. British forces are defeated at Charleston, South Carolina.

July 2. The Congress adopts Lee's resolution.

July 4. The Congress adopts, with amendments, the Declaration of Independence written by Jefferson. Copies are sent to the various "states," or former colonies.

Society and Population in the West

1764

Chartered companies are created for the colonization of the West. George Washington heads the Mississippi Company.

1766

The Indian chief Pontiac signs a peace treaty with the British.

1768

The British sign a treaty with the Iroquois, who give up territory west of the colony of New York and between the Ohio and Tennessee Rivers. The Treaty of Hard Labor is signed with the Cherokees. Indian tribes withdraw to the west. The Indiana Company, created in 1766, buys from the Iroquois 1.8 million acres southwest of the Ohio River.

1768–1769

Daniel Boone explores Kentucky.

1769

The Grand Ohio Company is created; it purchases 20 million acres of land.

1769–1771

Pioneers on the western frontier of the Carolinas take the law into their own hands. In South Carolina, the Regulators, a movement of farmers and shopkeepers, protests against inadequate representation in the colonial assembly and against the excessive power of the colonists in the east. Several leaders of the movement are executed.

1773

The president of Yale College initiates the idea of returning freed blacks to western Africa.

1774
Rhode Island abolishes slavery.

1775
In Philadelphia, the first abolitionist society is founded by Benjamin Franklin.

The Continental Congress creates a postal service to replace the Imperial Post. Franklin is named postmaster general.

Boonesborough, a fort in Kentucky, is founded by Daniel Boone.

Religion, Culture and Technology

1764
Rhode Island College, the forerunner of Brown University, is founded in Providence.

James Otis publishes *Rights of the British Colonies Asserted and Proved.*

1765
Portrait of the merchant John Hancock, by John Singleton Copley of Boston.

The first medical school in America is founded at the College of Philadelphia.

Consideration Upon the Rights of the Colonies to the Privileges of British Subjects, by John Dickinson.

1766
St. Paul's Chapel is built in New York.

In New Jersey, Queen's College is founded; it will become Rutgers University.

The first permanent theater in the colonies is founded in Philadelphia by the American Company of Comedians.

1767
The first American planetarium is built by David Rittenhouse, a Philadelphia clockmaker.

1768
Paul Revere, a silversmith from Boston, engraves a silver bowl in honor of the resistance to the Stamp Act.

"The Liberty Song," the first American patriotic song, is published in the *Boston Gazette.*

The first Methodist church is consecrated in New York.

1769
Dartmouth College, a Congregationalist school devoted to the education of young Indians, is founded in New Hampshire.

ca. 1770
Street lights begin appearing in cities.

1770
In Virginia, Thomas Jefferson begins building Monticello, his home.

1771
Benjamin Franklin begins writing his *Autobiography.*

1772
Benjamin West of Philadelphia becomes George III's history painter in London. Charles Willson Peale paints the first full-length portrait of George Washington.

Chapter 5   1776–1789

From Independence to
the Constitution

The years 1776–1789 mark the first time in world history that former colonies succeeded in having their independence recognized and building an entirely new political system.

At first sight, the Americans had little chance of winning the Revolutionary War. Compared with the British forces (supplemented by German mercenaries), the Continental Army was small in number and weak in organization. Moreover, General George Washington had difficulty keeping his soldiers in the army and equipping them properly. At sea, British superiority was crushing, and only the assistance of the French made possible the final victory at Yorktown. The British also relied on the Indians and on some slaves, to whom freedom had been promised. The loyalists among the colonists probably never numbered more than a fifth of the total population, and many of them, once their property was confiscated, fled to Canada or elsewhere. Confident in their strength, the British nevertheless lost the war, having underestimated the intensity of American nationalism.

The Americans did not wait for the end of the struggle to begin building a new political system organized around the principle of popular sovereignty. As early as 1776, the states began writing republican constitutions. In 1777, the Continental Congress drafted the Articles of Confederation, which left considerable autonomy to the states because the patriots feared above all a strong central government.

Despite their weakness, the former colonies not only won the war but solved the delicate problem of the western territories between the Appalachians and the Mississippi. This land, formally acquired in the Treaty of Paris, would eventually be divided into states and incorporated into the Confederation. But the young Republic faced difficulties in those areas where the Confederation Congress was entirely powerless. The monetary system was in chaos, international trade was disorganized, and the war had provoked social turmoil. A growing portion of the population came to believe that a stronger national government was indispensable to the survival of the new nation.

The Philadelphia Convention in 1787 drafted an entirely new constitution, one organized around federalism and including a system of checks and balances among the branches of the central government. After protracted debate, the Constitution was finally ratified in 1789, and George Washington was elected the first president of the United States. But the Founding Fathers did not solve all the problems facing the new nation: neither slavery nor coexistence with the Indian tribes was dealt with. Still, their work is remarkable, for the Constitution they devised 200 years ago to govern a small republic of 4 million inhabitants remains the supreme law of the largest Western democracy in the world.

The Revolutionary War

1776

June. A British fleet and its commander in chief, Admiral Lord Richard Howe, arrive in New York.

June 28. Attacking from the sea, the British are defeated at Charleston, South Carolina.

August 27. The Americans, under George Washington, are defeated at the Battle of Long Island.

September 15. The Continental Army abandons New York City.

September 22. The British execute Nathan Hale for spying.

November 16. Washington's army, having lost its positions north of Manhattan, withdraws into New Jersey and then onto the western bank of the Delaware River, in Pennsylvania.

December 25–26. Washington recrosses the Delaware. In the Battle of Trenton, the Americans, after a surprise attack, capture a thousand Hessian mercenaries.

1777

January 3. Washington is victorious against General Lord Charles Cornwallis at Princeton, New Jersey.

June. The British launch an invasion from Canada.

July 6. The British general John Burgoyne captures Fort Ticonderoga in northern New York.

July 27. The Marquis de Lafayette arrives as a volunteer in the Continental Army.

September 11. Washington is defeated along Brandywine Creek in Pennsylvania.

September 26. The British occupy Philadelphia; the Continental Congress flees.

October 4. Washington is defeated at Germantown, Pennsylvania.

October 17. Burgoyne surrenders his army at the Battle of Saratoga, in New York.

December 17. Washington withdraws to Valley Forge, northwest of Philadelphia. Hunger and cold inflict many casualties on the Continental Army.

France agrees to recognize the United States.

1778

February 6. France enters into a treaty of alliance with the United States.

February 17. British prime minister Lord North proposes a compromise.

April. After harassing British shipping in the Irish Sea, John Paul Jones, commander of the *Ranger,* lands at Whitehaven, England, and spikes the guns of the local fort; he then seizes the residence of an earl on St. Mary's Island. Jones's raids provoke outrage among the British.

June 6. North's proposal is rejected by the Continental Congress.

June 18. The British, fearing a naval blockade by the French, give up Philadelphia.

June 28. Washington defeats the British at Monmouth, New Jersey.

July 10. France declares war on England. French admiral Conte d'Estaing's fleet reaches the mouth of the Delaware.

August 30. The Americans, together with the French fleet, fail to take Newport, Rhode Island.

December 29. The British occupy Savannah, Georgia, seeking to shift the theater of operations to the south.

1779

June 19. Spain declares war on England.

September 23. The American warship *Bonhomme Richard*, under the command of John Paul Jones, defeats the British frigate *Serapis*.

September 27. The Congress appoints John Adams to negotiate peace.

October 9. The French fleet is held in check outside Savannah.

October 17. Washington sets up winter quarters in Morristown, New Jersey. During the harsh winter, his army suffers numerous desertions.

1780

May 12. Charleston, South Carolina, is captured by the British.

July 11. A French army and its commander in chief, the Comte de Rochambeau, arrive in Newport, Rhode Island.

August 16. The Americans are defeated at the Battle of Camden, in South Carolina.

September 23. The American officer Benedict Arnold, who was discovered to be a traitor and was taken into custody, escapes and joins the British.

October 7. The British are defeated at King's Mountain, North Carolina, by militia.

1781

January. Mutinies occur in the American army in Pennsylvania.

January 17. The Americans are victorious at Cowpens, South Carolina.

August 4. The army of British general Lord Cornwallis occupies Yorktown, Virginia, and awaits reinforcements from New York.

September 5–9. In the Second Battle of the Capes (in Chesapeake Bay), the French fleet commanded by Admiral François de Grasse prevents the British fleet from reaching Yorktown.

September–October. Yorktown is besieged by the combined American and French forces.

October 19. Cornwallis surrenders his army at Yorktown; the war is largely over.

1782

February 27. In London, the House of Commons refuses to pursue the war, but fighting will continue in the south.

March 20. Lord North resigns as prime minister.

April 12. Peace negotiations begin in Paris.

July 11. The British abandon Savannah.

November 30. A preliminary treaty of peace with England is signed in Paris by John Adams, Benjamin Franklin and John Jay.

December 14. The British leave Charleston.

1783

April. The Continental Congress proclaims the end of hostilities and approves the preliminary peace treaty.

September 3. The Treaty of Paris is signed by England and the United States, officially ending the Revolutionary War. The Treaty recognizes the United States as an independent nation and defines its borders (Great Lakes, Mississippi River, Spanish Florida).

November 25. The British leave New York.

December 23. Washington resigns as commander in chief.

1784

January 14. Congress formally ratifies the Treaty of Paris.

Creation of a New Nation

1776

June–December. Republican constitutions are adopted in New Hampshire, New Jersey, Pennsylvania, Delaware, Maryland and both Carolinas.

July 4. The Declaration of Independence is approved by the Continental Congress.

August 2. The text of the Declaration of Independence is signed by 55 delegates to the Congress.

September 26. The Congress appoints Silas Deane and Benjamin Franklin to seek financial and military assistance from France.

October 3. The Congress authorizes a loan of $5 million at 4 percent interest to finance the war.

1777

The states of New York, Vermont and Georgia adopt their constitutions.

June 14. The Congress adopts the American flag with 13 stars and 13 red and white stripes signifying the 13 original states.

November 15. After lengthy debate, the Congress adopts the "Articles of Confederation and Perpetual Union," the nation's first constitution.

1778

July. The Congress returns to Philadelphia. Conrad Alexandre Gerard, the French ambassador named by Louis XVI, is the first foreign diplomat accredited to the United States.

1779

The Congress issues $10 million worth of paper money.

1780

February 1. The state of New York grants its rights to western territories to the Congress.

June. Massachusetts adopts its constitution.

1781

A new issue of paper money, worth $191 million, will soon become valueless.

January 2. Virginia relinquishes its rights to western territories.

March 1. The Articles of Confederation, ratified at long last by the states, enter into force.

1784

April 23. Jefferson drafts an ordinance on the government of the western territories (it will be the basis for the text adopted in 1787).

1785

February 24. John Adams is named U.S. minister to the British government.

March 10. Jefferson is named U.S. minister to France.

May 20. An ordinance regulates the sale of land in the western territories. The territories are divided into townships of 6 square miles, and lots will be sold for $1 per acre.

1786

January 16. The Virginia legislature adopts the Ordinance of Religious Freedom, which was initially drafted by Jefferson.

August. The Congress debates the revision of the Articles of Confederation.

September 11–14. The Annapolis Convention meets to amend the Articles of Confederation. Only five states send delegates, who decide to meet again in 1787 in Philadelphia.

1787

May 25–September 17. The Philadelphia Convention, presided over by George Washington, drafts a new constitution, which is signed by 39 of 42 delegates. James Madison's ideas exert a powerful influence on the convention.

July 13. The Congress adopts the Northwest Ordinance, creating a territorial government and providing for the formation of three to five new states.

September 28. The Constitution is sent to the states for ratification.

December. Delaware, Pennsylvania and New Jersey ratify the Constitution.

1788

January–May. Georgia, Connecticut, Massachusetts, Maryland and South Carolina ratify the Constitution.

June 21. The Constitution is formally adopted by the United States when New Hampshire becomes the 9th state to ratify it.

June–July. Virginia and New York ratify the Constitution.

1789

The Federalist Party is formed.

February 4. The Electoral College (presidential electors chosen by popular vote or appointed by the legislatures of 10 of the states that have ratified the Constitution) casts ballots for president in New York, the nation's temporary capital.

March 4. The Constitution goes into effect. The first Congress elected under the new Constitution is convened.

April 6. The votes of the Electoral College are counted in the Senate: George Washington is unanimously elected the 1st president of the United States; John Adams is elected vice president.

April 30. Washington takes the oath of office in New York.

July. The Department of State is created; Thomas Jefferson is named secretary of state.

September. The Department of the Treasury is created; Alexander Hamilton is named secretary of the treasury.

The Supreme Court is established.

September–December. To pacify the Antifederalists, Congress drafts a Bill of Rights to be added to the text of the Constitution.

November 21. North Carolina ratifies the Constitution.

Economy and Society

1776

September 21. A fire in New York destroys all buildings dating back to the Dutch occupation.

1779

November 19. The Continental Congress advises the states to adopt a policy of price and wage controls.

1780

Slavery is abolished in Pennsylvania.

The Constitution of Massachusetts proclaims that "all men are born free and equal."

1781

December 31. The Congress creates the Bank of the United States, a national bank with a capital of $400,000. Allowed to discount notes as well as to take deposits, the bank will loan money to the Confederation and reintroduce coin currency.

1783

April. Seven thousand loyalists leave New York for Canada.

July. The Massachusetts Supreme Court declares slavery unconstitutional, in accordance with the state's constitution.

1784–1788

The nation endures a serious economic depression.

1784

Slavery is abolished in Connecticut and Rhode Island.

1785

Primogeniture is abolished in Virginia.

Slavery is abolished in New York State.

The first free health clinic is opened in Philadelphia by Benjamin Rush.

1786

Slavery is abolished in New Jersey.

Journeymen printers go on strike in Philadelphia.

July 1786–February 1787

Farmers dissatisfied with the increasing taxes imposed by the state government stage an armed rebellion in western and central Massachusetts under the leadership of Daniel Shays. Shays's Rebellion worries the supporters of a strong national government.

1787

The Northwest Ordinance forbids slavery in the territories between the Ohio and Mississippi Rivers.

The first textile mill for spinning cotton is established in Massachusetts.

The Pennsylvania Society for the Encouragement of Manufactures orders carding and spinning machines from England.

1789

May 12. In New York, the Tammany Society, named after an Indian chief, is founded; it is a political club sympathetic to the Federalists.

July 4. The first protectionist tariff is voted by Congress.

November 26. The first official celebration of Thanksgiving as a national holiday occurs.

Religion, Education and Culture

1776

December. Thomas Paine publishes *The Crisis.*

1779

Jefferson proposes an ambitious scheme for public education in Virginia.

1782

The American Academy of Arts and Sciences is founded in Boston.

The Skater, a painting by Gilbert Stuart, who settled in London.

Harvard's medical school opens.

Hector St. John (Michel-Guillaume Jean de Crèvecoeur) publishes his *Letters From an American Farmer* in London.

1783

The Society of the Cincinnati, a gathering of ex-officers of the Revolutionary War, is established under the leadership of George Washington.

The first American daily newspaper, the *Pennsylvania Evening Post*, appears.

Publication of *The American Speller*, by Noah Webster.

1784

The Methodist Church is organized in the United States.

1785

The Unitarian Church is established.

1787

The State University of Georgia is founded.

Benjamin Rush publishes *Thoughts on Female Education*.

The Federalist Papers are published in New York. These articles, signed "Publius," advocate the adoption of the proposed Constitution; they are actually written by Hamilton, Madison and John Jay.

1788

Philip Freneau's poetic works are published.

1789

The Capitol of the state of Virginia is built in Richmond; it follows the design of the Maison Carrée in Nîmes sent by Jefferson from France.

The University of North Carolina at Chapel Hill is founded.

Noah Webster defines the "American republican" language in his *Dissertations on the English Language*.

Chapter 6   1790–1815

The Young Republic

The years 1790–1815 were devoted to the development of new political structures and to the strengthening of national unity. But the new republic also faced difficult internal and external problems.

Henceforth, elections would lend a rhythm to American political life: Congress would be renewed every two years, and the president would be elected every four years. Born during the debate over the ratification of the Constitution, the two major parties—the Federalists and the Anti-federalists (or Democratic-Republicans)—clashed over the role of the federal government, economic policy, currency issues and foreign policy. During the presidency of George Washington, these clashes remained muted and a national identity began to emerge. At the end of his second term, Washington retired, thus setting an example for his successors; until Franklin Roosevelt in 1940, no American president ran for a third term.

Thomas Jefferson's election in 1800 marked the coming to power of the Democratic-Republican opposition, and despite the fears of some, the transition was smooth. In contrast with the French Revolution, which, through a succession of violent upheavals, ended with the restoration of an authoritarian regime, the American Revolution succeeded in consolidating its gains.

Foreign affairs were dominated at first by efforts to maintain America's neutrality in the face of the Napoleonic wars in Europe. The subsequent War of 1812 against Great Britain was of dubious value because it resulted only in the continuation of the territorial status quo. The most important event of the period, however, was America's purchase of Louisiana from France in 1803. The acquisition of this huge area, extending from the Mississippi River to the Rocky Mountains, doubled the territory of the United States and opened the door to the Pacific Ocean.

The economy, still wholly agricultural, began to lessen its dependence on England as new commercial links were developed, especially with the Far East. And as industry appeared in New England, Americans also began to recognize the importance of developing a transportation network.

Political and Institutional Life

1790

March 26. A law on naturalization permits immigrants to become citizens after two years residency.

May 29. Rhode Island is the 13th and last original state to ratify the Constitution.

June. Philadelphia becomes the federal capital until the completion of a new capital on the banks of the Potomac River.

1791

March 4. Vermont becomes the 14th state to join the Union.

December 15. The Bill of Rights is officially added to the Constitution (the first 10 Amendments).

1792

The Democratic-Republican Party, headed by Thomas Jefferson, is founded.

April. A law on currency is adopted: bimetallism (gold and silver) becomes the basis for currency, which will be minted in Philadelphia.

June 1. Kentucky secedes from Virginia and becomes the 15th state in the Union.

December 5. George Washington re-elected president and John Adams vice president by electors representing the 15 states (the electoral votes will be officially tabulated on February 13, 1793).

1795

A law on naturalization extends to five years the residency requirement for citizenship.

1796

June. Tennessee joins the Union as the 16th state.

September 17. Washington issues his Farewell Address, which will be published in the *American Daily Advertiser* (Philadelphia) on September 19.

December 7. Presidential electors select John Adams, a Federalist, as the 2nd president, and Thomas Jefferson, a Democratic-Republican, as vice president.

1797

March 4. John Adams takes office as the 2nd president.

1798

January. The 11th Amendment to the Constitution is ratified: federal courts cannot try cases brought by a citizen of one state against another state of the Union.

June–July. Congress passes the Alien and Sedition Acts, which modify the rules for naturalization (14 years residency) and allow the president to arrest or expel any individual "dangerous to the welfare of the country." The Democratic-Republicans are furious.

1799

December 14. George Washington dies.

1800

November. Congress and President Adams move to the new federal capital, Washington, located in the District of Columbia.

December 3. After a stormy political campaign, electors meet to select the next president: Jefferson and his fellow Democratic-Republican, Aaron Burr, each receive 73 votes, resulting in a tie, and the election is thrown into the House of Representatives.

1801

January 20. President Adams appoints the Federalist John Marshall chief justice of the Supreme Court.

March 4. Elected by the House of Representatives, Jefferson, the first Democratic-Republican president, takes office, with Burr as vice president.

1802

March. Congress establishes the U.S. Military Academy at West Point.

1803

February. The Supreme Court, in *Marbury v. Madison*, rules unconstitutional a law passed by Congress. The ruling establishes the precedent that federal courts can review the constitutionality of laws (judicial review).

March. Ohio joins the Union as the 17th state; it is the first state created from the Northwest Territory, where slavery is forbidden.

1804

July 11. Vice President Aaron Burr mortally wounds Alexander Hamilton in a duel in Weehawken, New Jersey; Hamilton will die the next day.

September 25. The 12th Amendment to the Constitution is ratified: it requires presidential electors to differentiate between their votes for president and vice president.

December 5. Jefferson is reelected president.

1806

November. General James Wilkinson alleges that Burr is plotting to create a kingdom in the southwest (with himself as king) and to invade Mexico.

1807

February. Burr is arrested and indicted for treason.

September. Burr, declared not guilty, leaves for Europe.

1808

December 7. James Madison, a Democratic-Republican, is elected the 4th president (Jefferson refused to run for a third term).

1809

March 4. Madison takes office with George Clinton of New York as vice president.

1812

Louisiana joins the Union as the 18th state.

December 2. Madison is reelected president despite the unpopularity of the war against England.

Foreign Policy and Territorial Expansion

1790

March. Jefferson returns from France to take office as secretary of state in Washington's cabinet.

October. A war against the Indians in the Northwest Territory begins.

1793

April. Washington proclaims American neutrality in the war between France and England.

December. Jefferson resigns as secretary of state.

1794

August 20. General Anthony Wayne defeats the Maumee Indians near present-day Toledo, Ohio.

United States Expansion, 1783–1898

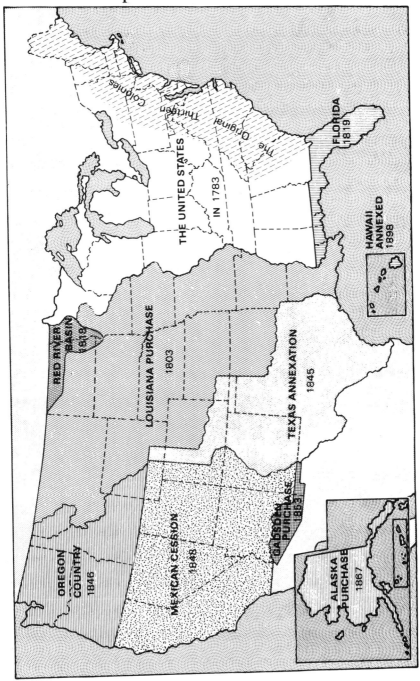

November 19. "Jay's Treaty" is signed by Great Britain and the United States. Britain gives up its forts in the Great Lakes region but retains the right to search American vessels for deserting British sailors.

1795

October. Pinckney's Treaty with Spain defines the borders of the United States to the west and south.

1796

July. France declares that it will seize any vessel destined for England from a neutral country (316 American vessels will be seized from July 1796 to June 1797).

November. In a treaty with Tripoli, the United States pledges to pay a tribute in exchange for protection against acts of piracy in the Mediterranean.

December. The new American minister to Paris, Charles Pinckney, is poorly received by the French government.

1797

October. In the "XYZ Affair," three agents of the French government demand an American loan to France and a bribe for the French foreign minister, the duc de Talleyrand, as prerequisites for a treaty of amity and commerce. The demand is rejected.

1798

April. President Adams discloses the XYZ Affair to Congress. Anti-French feeling spreads among the American public.

July. Congress repudiates the treaty of 1778 with France. An undeclared naval war follows. U.S. Navy ships and privateers will capture French ships.

1799

December. Adams sends a new delegation to France in order to negotiate a treaty.

1800

March. Napoleon Bonaparte, first consul, stops French attacks on U.S. shipping and receives the American delegation.

September. The Treaty of Morfontaine (Convention of 1800) ends the quasi war with France.

1801

May. The Tripolitan War begins after the United States refuses to increase its tribute to the Barbary pirate state.

1802

April. President Jefferson, worried by a secret French-Spanish agreement giving Louisiana to Bonaparte, orders American ambassador Robert Livingston to negotiate the sale of the port of New Orleans to the United States.

1803

April 30. Bonaparte agrees to sell to the United States the entire territory of Louisiana for $15 million. The Louisiana Purchase doubles the territory of the United States. The formal transfer of the territory will take place on December 20.

1804–1806

Jefferson sends Meriwether Lewis and William Clark to explore the northwest of the country, from the Mississippi to the Pacific Ocean.

1805

April 26. An American military expedition is victorious at Derna, in Tripoli.

June 4. A peace treaty is signed with Tripoli, which gives up its claims to tribute. Acts of piracy will continue, however.

1806

The trade and diplomacy of the United States suffer as a result of England's blockade of European ports controlled by France, and Napoleon's Berlin Decree, which blockades English ports. The United States cannot bring either France or England to recognize its neutrality.

December 1807–February 1809

Under the Embargo Act Americans are prohibited from trading with European ports, and vice versa. Neither France nor England, both smuggling through Canada, is hurt; by contrast, New England traders suffer badly.

1809

March 1. The Embargo Act is replaced by the Non-Intercourse Act, which forbids trade only with France and England.

July 2. Tecumseh, chief of the Shawnees, forms a confederacy of the Indian tribes of the Northwest and the South.

1810

American settlers in Florida revolt against the Spanish government and proclaim the Republic of West Florida.

1811

April. The first American trading post on the Pacific Coast, Astoria in Oregon, is founded by the trapper John Astor.

May. Incidents occur between British and American vessels in the Atlantic.

November. General William Henry Harrison is victorious over Tecumseh's Confederacy at Tippecanoe Creek, in the Indiana Territory.

1812

May. President Madison issues a proclamation annexing West Florida.

June 18. Congress, invoking the doctrine of "freedom of the seas," declares war on England, which had been impressing American merchant sailors (the British in Canada had also been supporting the Indians in their resistance to American settlement of the territories). Opponents of the War of 1812 will call it "Mr. Madison's war."

August 16. Detroit is surrendered to the British without a fight.

October 13. An American invasion of Canada is repulsed at the border.

1813

April–May. An American force captures York (Toronto), the capital of the province of Upper Canada, and burns its public buildings.

August. The Creek Indians, allied with the British, attack in Alabama.

September 10. In the Battle of Lake Erie, Americans under Captain Oliver Perry defeat a British fleet.

September 29. General Harrison retakes Detroit.

September–November. An American force captures Montreal.

October 5. General Harrison defeats the British in the Battle of the Thames, in Canada. Tecumseh, allied with the British, is killed in the battle.

December 29–30. The British burn the city of Buffalo, New York.

1814

March 9. General Andrew Jackson is victorious over the Creek Indians at Horseshoe Bend, Alabama.

August 24–25. Landing in Chesapeake Bay, a British force captures Washington, D.C., and burns the Capitol and the White House in retaliation for the burning of York; the American government had already fled the capital.

September 11. A British naval squadron is defeated on Lake Champlain during the Battle of Plattsburgh.

September 13–14. A British fleet shells Fort McHenry, in Baltimore. Francis Scott Key writes the words to "The Star-Spangled Banner" during the bombardment.

December 24. The Treaty of Ghent is signed by Great Britain and the United States, officially concluding the war; news of the signing will not reach the United States until February 11, 1815, and fighting will continue until then.

1815

January 8. General Jackson defeats the British in the Battle of New Orleans.

March 3. War is declared on Algiers because of the Barbary pirate states' continuing demands for tribute.

March–June. Commodore Stephen Decatur is victorious over Algiers, Tunis and Tripoli.

June 30. Treaties with Algiers, Tunis and Tripoli end the Barbary Wars.

Economy and Society

1790

March–August. The first federal census sets the population at 3.9 million, including 697,000 slaves.

December. In Rhode Island, Samuel Slater establishes a cotton-spinning mill

(the machines were imported from England).

1791

February. On the initiative of Treasury Secretary Alexander Hamilton, legislation is enacted to create a federal bank, the Bank of the United States. Jefferson and Madison debate the constitutionality of the act.

March. The Whiskey Act imposes a tax on distilled liquors.

December. Hamilton's *Report on Manufactures* recommends protectionism to help young American industry; Jefferson has reservations.

1792

The New York Stock Exchange opens.

1794–1795

The Whiskey Rebellion occurs in western Pennsylvania: farmers opposed to the federal tax on alcohol are suppressed by a militia.

1800

A slave rebellion is suppressed in Virginia.

1805

The religious community of Harmonie, Indiana, is founded by German Pietists led by George Rapp.

1806

In New York, strikes break out in the shoemaking industry.

1808

January 1. Congress makes the importation of slaves illegal throughout the territory of the United States.

American trade is hurt by the Embargo Act.

1810

In New York, members of the rope-makers' union are found guilty of "conspiracy" (i.e., of going on strike).

1811

January. In Louisiana, a slave revolt sparks a wave of panic.

March. The charter of the Bank of the United States expires, and the bank is dissolved.

1812–1815

Creation of 120 new private banks.

1814

In Waltham, Massachusetts, Francis Cabot Lowell establishes the nation's first mill to produce cloth from cotton.

1815

The whaling industry flourishes.

Technological Progress

1790

The first federal legislation on patents is enacted, creating the U.S. Patent Office.

1792–1800

The first canals in Massachusetts are dug.

1793

Eli Whitney invents the cotton gin.

1796–1797

Philadelphia: First attempts at gas lighting and creating a central water supply.

1798

Eli Whitney perfects the principle of interchangeable parts and applies it to the manufacture of firearms.

David Wilkinson patents his screw-threading machine.

1807

The *Clermont*, a steamboat designed by Robert Fulton, makes its first trip on the Hudson River, from New York to Albany.

1811

The construction of the Cumberland Road, the most important route to the West, is begun at Cumberland, Maryland.

The first steam-powered ferryboat, built by John Stevens, links Hoboken, New Jersey, and Manhattan.

1812

The first steamboat appears on the Mississippi.

1814

Fulton builds the first steam-powered warship.

Religion, Education and Culture

1790

John Carroll is appointed the first Catholic bishop in the United States.

1791

President Washington selects the site of the federal district that will become the nation's capital. Pierre-Charles L'Enfant, a Frenchman, will design the city of Washington, D.C.

1792

The cornerstones of the White House and the new Capitol building (William Thornton, architect) are laid.

1793

First American publication of Michel-Guillaume Jean de Crèvecoeur's *Letters From an American Farmer.*

1794

In Philadelphia, the painter Charles Wilson founds a public museum.

1795

In Boston, Charles Bulfinch designs the Massachusetts State House.

1796

Portrait of Washington, by Gilbert Stuart.

1797–1801

Religious awakening in the West (Kentucky).

1799

In Philadelphia, the Bank of Pennsylvania, built by Benjamin Henry Latrobe, is the first American building in the Greek Revival style.

1800

The Library of Congress is created.

1803

Benjamin Henry Latrobe takes over the management of the construction of Washington, D.C.

1804

The New York Historical Society is founded.

1807

The Boston Athenaeum is founded.

1809

Under the pseudonym "Diedrich Knickerbocker," Washington Irving publishes his humorous *History of New York.*

1813

First recorded appearance of the character "Uncle Sam" (from the initials stamped on military stores).

1814

The report of Lewis and Clark's western expedition, with a foreword by Thomas Jefferson, is published.

"The Star-Spangled Banner" is composed by Francis Scott Key during the British bombardment of Fort McHenry in Baltimore. This patriotic song will become the national anthem in 1931.

1815

First issue of the *North American Review*, a journal intended to promote American literature.

Chapter 7 1816–1840

Nationalism and the Development of Democracy

Alexis de Tocqueville's America of the 1830s was no longer the one that had come into being at the time of the Revolution. Wide-ranging transformations were taking place in American society. The population had doubled, topping 17 million inhabitants in 1840; cities were growing and multiplying; industry was developing rapidly and already changing social relationships. These changes, encouraged by the supporters of national modernization, frightened the advocates of agrarian democracy and led to harsh political and ideological conflicts.

The majority of the states substituted universal male suffrage for the more restrictive electoral eligibility rules of the early Republic. The result was an increasingly animated political life. Under the presidency of James Monroe, a Democratic-Republican, the weakening of federalism was translated into a kind of national consensus, which a journalist derisively baptized the "Era of Good Feelings." As early as 1824, a new party system was emerging. Whereas the Democratic-Republicans (later the Democrats) were loyal to the Jeffersonian heritage, the National Republicans (later the Whigs) wanted to reinforce the political and economic powers of the federal government.

A spirit of reform swept the nation. The second religious Awakening was accompanied by movements in favor of temperance, the abolition of slavery, women's suffrage and educational reform. Other groups manifested their opposition to new immigrants (Catholics from Germany or Ireland) or to Freemasons, who were denounced as a clique hostile to democracy.

In foreign affairs, the United States continued to assert its independence with respect to Europe, and it assumed the role of self-appointed guardian of democracy in the Western Hemisphere in accordance with the principles of the Monroe Doctrine. The nation also continued its territorial expansion: Florida was annexed, Texas was eyed with increasing interest, and most of all the Indians were brutally driven off their land.

Already throughout much of this period, the problem of slavery was becoming a divisive backdrop to every political, ideological and moral debate, even though few were yet willing to address the issue head-on.

Political and Institutional Life

1816

March 14. The Second Bank of the United States is created, chartered by Congress for twenty years.

December. Indiana, a territory without slaves, becomes the 19th state of the Union.

December 4. James Monroe, a Democratic-Republican, is elected the 5th president; Daniel Tomkins, of the same party, is elected vice president. The Federalists lose many seats in Congress.

1817

March 3. In his last official act as president, James Madison vetoes a major program of public works (highways and canals) voted by Congress; he argues that the Constitution does not give the federal government the power to implement such a program.

March 4. Monroe takes office with a political program inspired by the nationalist principles of the Federalists.

December. Mississippi, a slave territory, becomes the 20th state of the Union.

1818

April. The design of the American flag is officially chosen: 13 red and white stripes representing the original states, and stars on a field of blue representing each state.

December. Illinois, a free (non-slave) territory, becomes the 21st state of the Union.

1819

March. The Supreme Court rules in *McCulloch v. Maryland* that a state cannot tax a federal agency. This establishes the supremacy of federal power over the states.

December. Alabama, a slave territory, becomes the 22nd state of the Union.

1820

March 3. The Missouri Compromise, crafted by Senator Henry Clay, maintains a balance between slave states and free states. Both Missouri (slave) and Maine (free) join the Union, and slavery is henceforth prohibited in the Louisiana Purchase north of 36° 30′.

December 6. Monroe is reelected president.

1824

November 9. Andrew Jackson finishes first and John Quincy Adams second in the first presidential election in which the popular vote is tabulated. Because none of the four candidates, all of whom are Republicans, receives a majority of the votes of the electoral college, the election is thrown into the House of Representatives in accordance with the Constitution.

1825

February. The House elects John Quincy Adams the 6th president, and John Calhoun vice president. Jackson's supporters are furious; they form the Democratic Party to oppose the National Republicans.

1826

Freemasons are accused of kidnapping and murdering William Morgan, former member of a New York lodge. The resulting furor brings about the creation of the Anti-Masonic Party.

1828

November 4. Jackson is elected the 7th president after a stormy campaign.

John Calhoun of North Carolina is elected vice president.

December. Invoking states' rights, Calhoun drafts his *Exposition and Protest*, which argues against the increase in tariffs that was approved in May.

1829

March. Jackson takes office with a program of administrative reform.

1830

January. In the Senate, Robert Hayne and Daniel Webster debate states' rights and the nature of the Union.

1831

Political differences between Jackson and Calhoun increase.

1832

July 10. Jackson vetoes the renewal of the charter of the Second Bank of the United States.

November 24. South Carolina declares null the federal tariff acts of 1828 and 1832 (the Nullification Crisis).

December 10. Triumphantly reelected, Jackson declares that South Carolina does not have the right to secede from the Union.

December 28. Calhoun resigns as vice president.

1833

January. South Carolina levies troops.

February–March. Congress approves the so-called Force Bill, which authorizes the use of the military to collect the federal tariff; on March 2, a compromise tariff act is signed by Jackson, ending the Nullification Crisis.

Jackson announces that the federal government will withdraw its funds from the Bank of the United States and transfer them to 23 banks of its choice.

1834

The National Republicans adopt the British name Whigs. Henry Clay and Daniel Webster lead the party.

1835

December. Following the death of John Marshall, Jackson nominates Robert Taney chief justice of the Supreme Court.

1836

May. Amidst a wave of antislavery petitions, Congress votes the Gag Rule to avoid debating them.

June. Arkansas, a slave territory, becomes the 25th state of the Union.

December. Martin Van Buren, a Democrat, is elected the 8th president, defeating three Whig candidates.

1837

Michigan, a free state, becomes the 26th state of the Union.

March 4. Van Buren takes office; Richard Johnson is vice president.

1839

With the formation of the Liberty Party, the abolitionists officially enter the political arena.

1840

July. An independent federal Treasury is created.

November 10. The Whig William Henry Harrison is elected the 9th president, and John Tyler is elected vice president.

Year of Admission of States to the Union

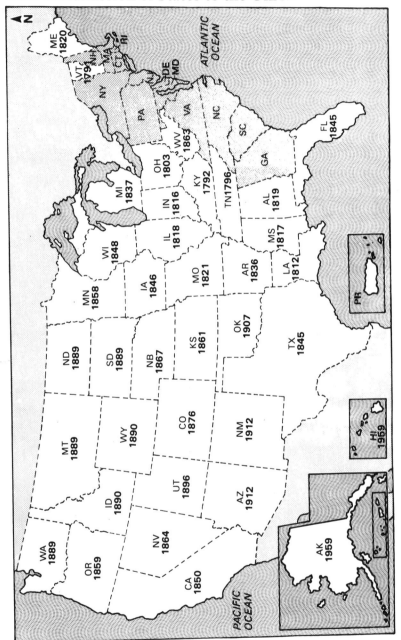

Foreign Policy and Territorial Expansion

1817

April. The Rush-Bagot Agreement between the United States and Great Britain demilitarizes the Great Lakes.

1817–1818

General Andrew Jackson leads a military expedition against Spanish Florida, a refuge for runaway slaves and hostile Seminole Indians. The fort of Pensacola is captured.

1818

A treaty confirms the U.S.-Canadian border along the 49th parallel from the Lake in the Woods to the Rocky Mountains. The Oregon territory is opened to both British and American settlers.

1819

February 22. In the Adams-Onís Treaty, Spain cedes Florida to the United States, which relinquishes its claim to Texas.

1821

January. Moses Austin receives from the Spanish government a land grant in Texas and the authorization to settle 300 American families there.

February. Mexico proclaims its independence.

September. The czar of Russia claims the whole of the Pacific Coast north of the 51st parallel, including part of the Oregon territory.

1822

Monroe asks Congress to recognize the new republics in Latin America.

1823

February. The Mexican government confirms to Stephen Austin, son of Moses, the latter's land grant in Texas.

December 2. The Monroe Doctrine is presented to Congress: The United States will view as an "unfriendly" act any further European colonization in the Americas or any European intervention in the affairs of the nations of the hemisphere (excluding existing colonies and dependencies). American neutrality in European conflicts is also proclaimed. The author of the doctrine, which went largely unnoticed at the time, was John Quincy Adams, the secretary of state.

1826

Jedediah Smith leads the first expedition to reach California from the interior of the continent.

1829

The expedition of Jedediah Smith crosses the Rockies at South Pass and reaches Oregon. A trapper, Jim Bridges, discovers the Great Salt Lake. Mexico refuses to sell Texas to the United States.

1835

American settlers in Texas begin their revolt against the Mexican government of General Antonio López de Santa Anna, which seeks to restrict American immigration into the province.

1836

February–March. Santa Anna besieges Fort Alamo, in San Antonio. Despite their heroic resistance, approximately 200 Texans, including Davy Crockett, are killed.

April–May. The Texans are victorious over the Mexicans at San Jacinto. Texas is proclaimed an independent republic, and its constitution authorizes slavery.

1837

Congress recognizes the independence of Texas but refuses to annex it despite the wishes of the Texans.

1837–1839

Serious tensions arise along the Canadian border. Some U.S. citizens lend support to a Canadian revolt, and a dispute erupts over the boundary between Maine and Canada. President Van Buren reaffirms the neutrality of the United States.

Indian Affairs

1816–1818

The first war against the Seminole Indians, who had sided with the British in the War of 1812 and use Florida as a base for attacks against the United States.

1817

The Indians in Ohio give up 4 million acres by treaty.

1818

By treaty, the Chickasaws relinquish the territory lying between the Mississippi and Tennessee Rivers.

1824

The Bureau of Indian Affairs is created within the War Department.

1825–1827

By treaty, the Creeks give up all of their lands in the state of Georgia.

1828

The Cherokees devise a constitution; adopt an alphabet of 86 signs, developed by Sequoia; and publish a newspaper in their own language.

1829

The Chippewas, Ottawas and Pottawatomies give up large territories in Michigan.

1830

May. President Jackson signs the Indian Removal Act, which compels all Indians to resettle west of the Mississippi.

July. In the Treaty of Prairie du Chien (Wisconsin), the Sioux, Fox and Sauk give up their lands in present-day Iowa, Minnesota and Missouri.

1831

In *Cherokee Nation v. Georgia*, the Supreme Court defines the Indian tribes as "domestic dependent nations."

1832

Chief Black Hawk leads the Fox and the Sac tribes in a war in Illinois to regain their lands. Colonel Zachary Taylor will defeat the Indians in the Battle of the Bad Ax on August 2.

1835

The Cherokees give up by treaty all of their lands east of the Mississippi in exchange for territories in Oklahoma.

1835–1837

In the Second Seminole War the Seminoles and Creeks of Florida, Alabama and Georgia who refuse to move west are defeated by troops commanded by General Zachary Taylor in the Battle of Lake Okeechobee (Florida) on December 25, 1837. The Indians will continue waging guerrilla warfare for another four years.

1838

The forced exodus to Oklahoma of the last Cherokees of Georgia takes place under escort of the federal army (Trail of Tears).

Economy and Society

1816

April. Tariffs are raised on cotton, textiles, iron, leather and other materials.

December. The American Colonization Society, which seeks to send blacks back to Africa, is founded.

1819

January. A financial panic is caused by a contraction of credit.

March. An immigration law requires captains of ships to maintain lists of passengers.

1820

Eighty-six freed slaves leave for Sierra Leone on the west coast of Africa. Nearby, Liberia will be founded as a place of settlement for freed slaves in 1821.

1822

The conspiracy of Denmark Vesey and 35 other slaves to launch a rebellion is discovered in Charleston; all the participants are hung.

1824

Women weavers go on strike in Pawtucket, Rhode Island.

March. In *Gibbons v. Ogden*, the Supreme Court rules that only the federal government has the power to regulate interstate commerce.

May. Federal tariffs are increased to protect American industry.

1826

The American Society for the Promotion of Temperance is founded.

1828

May. President John Quincy Adams signs a new protectionist tariff considered unfair by the South (the "Tariff of Abominations").

1830

President Jackson vetoes the construction of a federal road in Kentucky, but approves an extension of the Cumberland Road Act, which funds the construction of a road that crosses several states.

1831

January. In Boston, the radical abolitionist William Lloyd Garrison launches a newspaper, *The Liberator.*

August. Nat Turner leads an unsuccessful slave revolt in Virginia; 57 whites are killed. Turner is tried and executed.

1832

Jackson signs a new protectionist tariff act that fails to please the South.

1834

June. Financial crisis occurs when silver is devalued relative to gold.

July. In New York, pro- and anti-slavery groups clash.

1835

In Charleston, a crowd burns abolitionist pamphlets.

In Boston, the Society for the Prevention of Poverty is founded.

1836

Jackson issues the Specie Circular, which makes compulsory the use of gold or silver to purchase federal lands, in order to prevent speculation.

1837

March. A financial panic occurs.

May–November. An economic depression occurs, resulting in numerous bank failures.

November 7. The abolitionist editor Elijah Lovejoy is murdered in Illinois.

1838

The Underground Railroad, a support network for slaves escaping to the northern states, is organized by abolitionists.

1839

The nation suffers another economic depression, which will last until 1843.

1840

A world antislavery congress is held in London. When American women are not allowed to take their seats, William Lloyd Garrison, in a sign of solidarity, joins them in withdrawing from the congress.

The Washington Temperance Society is founded; the temperance movement spreads.

Technological Progress and Transportation

1816

In Baltimore, gas is used for street lighting.

1817

The first steamboat line is established, running from Louisville, on the Ohio River, to New Orleans.

1819

The *Savannah* becomes the first steamship to cross an ocean, traveling from Savannah, Georgia, to Liverpool, England, by steam and by sail.

1820

In New York, first fish cannery is founded.

1825

July. The Cumberland Road is extended farther west.

October. The Erie Canal, which links Buffalo (on Lake Erie) to Albany (on the Hudson River), is opened, making possible the transportation of goods by water from New York to the Midwest.

A trial run of the first steam locomotive is made by John Stevens on his property in Hoboken, New Jersey.

1828

The Delaware and Hudson Canal is opened.

1829

The Delaware and Chesapeake Canal is opened.

1830

The Baltimore and Ohio Railroad, the first passenger railroad in the United States, is opened. Robert Stevens develops the T-rail.

1832

In New York, the first horse-driven omnibuses appear.

1834

Cyrus McCormick patents his horse-driven harvester, which he developed in 1831.

1835

Samuel Morse develops the telegraph, which he will patent in 1840.

BANKING ACTIVITY, 1829–1837
(in millions of dollars)

	Number of Banks	Capital Stock	Species Circulating	Loans
1829	329	$110.0	$48.0	$137.0
1834	506	$200.0	$95.0	$324.0
1837	788	$290.0	$149.0	$525.0

SOURCE: Albert Shannon, *America's Economic Growth* (New York, 1951).
Note: Beginning in 1834, threats to the Federal Bank resulted in a proliferation of state banks.

1836
Samuel Colt patents his revolver.

1837
John Deere opens a factory for farm machinery in Vermont.

1839
Charles Goodyear discovers a process for vulcanizing rubber.

Education, Religion and Culture

1816
The first black church in Philadelphia is founded.

1817
The poet William Cullen Bryant publishes *Thanatopsis.*

1818
John Trumbull paints *The Declaration of Independence.*

1819
The University of Virginia at Charlottesville is founded according to a plan elaborated by Thomas Jefferson.

William E. Channing founds the Unitarian Church.

1821
Emma Willard founds the nation's first seminary (secondary school) for young women in Troy, New York.

The nation's first Catholic cathedral is built in Baltimore.

1824
The Rensselaer Institute is founded in Troy, New York; it is devoted to the teaching of natural sciences and technology.

The Marquis de Lafayette makes a triumphant tour of the United States.

1825
In Indiana, the Welsh socialist Robert Owen purchases George Rapp's lands and founds New Harmony, a utopian community.

The Hudson River School of landscape painters (romanticism) appears.

1826
Daniel Webster gives the funeral orations for Thomas Jefferson and John Adams, who both die on July 4th, the fiftieth anniversary of the Declaration of Independence.

The Last of the Mohicans, by James Fenimore Cooper.

1828

After 20 years of research, Noah Webster publishes his *American Dictionary of the English Language*, which contains a number of new, "American" words.

The University of Indiana is founded.

John James Audubon publishes the first volume of *Birds of America*.

1830

Joseph Smith publishes the *Book of Mormon* and founds the Church of Latter-day Saints (Mormons) in Fayette, New York.

1831

The Mormons settle first in Ohio, then in Independence, Missouri.

The Frenchman Alexis de Tocqueville begins a nine-month visit to the United State; he will record his observations on the American character and political system in *Democracy in America*, which will be published in 1835 and 1840.

1832

Horatio Greenough is commissioned to sculpt a statue of George Washington for the rotunda of the Capitol, in Washington.

1833

The first issue of the *Sun*, a popular New York daily, appears.

Oberlin College opens in Ohio. Women and Blacks are admitted, making it the first U.S. coeducational college.

1834

The first issue of the *New York Herald* is published.

The first volume of George Bancroft's *History of the United States* is published; the tenth and last volume will be published in 1874.

1836

Ralph Waldo Emerson publishes *Nature*, marking the birth of the Transcendentalist movement in New England. (Transcendentalists believe there is a body of moral truths that is intuitive and transcends any proof derived from the senses; one such truth—that God and Nature are benevolent, and that humans are divine—led many to view slavery as immoral, and ignorance and poverty as wicked.)

1837

Horace Mann, secretary of the Committee of Education of the State of Massachusetts, launches an educational reform.

Mount Holyoke Female Seminary (Mount Holyoke College), the nation's first college for women, is founded in South Hadley, Massachusetts.

1839

The Mormons settle in Nauvoo, Illinois.

The American Art Union is founded in New York; it circulates reproductions of classical works of art to the general public.

In Cooperstown, New York, Abner Doubleday sets down the rules for baseball.

1840

Edgar Allan Poe publishes *Tales of the Grotesque and the Arabesque*, a collection of stories.

Chapter 8   1841–1860

Slavery, Territorial Expansion and Internal Conflict

Slavery continued to spread as the nation expanded. Slaves were no longer confined to the former southern colonies: Now they were to be found wherever "King Cotton" ruled, in particular in the so-called New South, from Mississippi to Texas. The legalization of slavery in the western territories that achieved statehood raised serious political problems. Slavery began to dominate every aspect of American life, from the formation of political parties and their programs to the interpretation of the Constitution, from economic development to religious and ideological debates. A clash between North and South, between the abolitionist and slave states, seemed unavoidable. In 1860, the splintering of the Democratic Party enabled the antislavery Republican Abraham Lincoln to win the presidency, resulting in the secession of South Carolina from the Union.

As the great debate over slavery and the Union intensified, the United States continued its westward expansion. In 1846, a journalist found a theory to justify the expansionist fever: The "Manifest Destiny" of America, according to John L. O'Sullivan, was to extend its dominion over the "whole continent Providence gave it." Thus, after a war criticized by some, the United States captured much-coveted Mexican territories from Texas to California.

The nation, apparently wholly preoccupied with its internal political crisis, was nonetheless exhibiting an astonishing economic, social and cultural vitality. Industry was developing at an impressive rate. Textile-producing cities such as Lowell, Massachusetts, attracted first young people from the countryside, then, after 1850, Irish immigrants. Urbanization accelerated, bringing with it a host of social ills that reformers tried to eradicate. Women played an increasing role in abolitionist movements, in temperance societies, and as social workers, and they soon felt strong enough to demand civil equality with men. The growing number and variety of utopian communities was another feature of mid-19th-century America, which itself was the embodiment of Utopia for so many disaffected European immigrants.

Political and Institutional Life

1841

April 4. Thirty-one days after taking office, President William Henry Harrison dies of pneumonia.

April 6. Vice President John Tyler becomes the 10th president; he will complete Harrison's term.

September. A conflict between Tyler and the Whigs over banking policy leads to the resignations of five members of his cabinet.

1842

The Supreme Court declares unconstitutional a law of the state of Pennsylvania that forbids the capture of fugitive slaves.

The xenophobic Native American Party is founded.

In Rhode Island, Thomas Dorr leads a rebellion demanding more liberal voting rights.

1844

November. James Polk, a Democrat with expansionist views, defeats Henry Clay, the Whig candidate, and is elected the 11th president; James Dallas is elected vice president. They will assume office on March 4, 1845.

1845

January. Congress passes a law establishing the Tuesday after the first Monday in November as election day for president in all states.

February. Congress votes to annex Texas.

March. Florida, a slave state, becomes the 27th state of the Union.

December. Texas, a slave state, becomes the 28th state of the Union.

1846

August. The House of Representatives adopts David Wilmot's "Proviso" forbidding slavery in any territory acquired from Mexico. The measure is defeated in the Senate.

December. Iowa, a free state, becomes the 29th state of the Union.

1848

May. Wisconsin, a free state, becomes the 30th state of the Union.

August. The antislavery Free Soil Party is founded.

November 7. The retired general Zachary Taylor, a Whig, is elected the 12th president; Millard Fillmore is elected vice president. They will assume office on March 5, 1849.

1849

The Bureau of Indian Affairs is attached to the newly created Department of the Interior.

1850

July 9. President Taylor dies of cholera; he will be succeeded by Vice President Fillmore the following day.

September. Congress approves the Compromise of 1850 on the problem of slavery. California, a free state, is admitted into the Union as the 31st state. Slavery will not be forbidden in New Mexico and Utah, the remaining territories acquired from Mexico. The slave trade is forbidden in the District of Columbia, but the legislation permitting slaveholders to recover fugitive slaves is toughened, despite the protests of the abolitionists.

November. At the Nashville Convention, delegates from seven southern states denounce the Compromise and affirm the right to secede from the Union.

1852

November 20. Franklin Pierce, a Democrat, is elected the 14th president; William King is elected vice president (they will assume office on March 4, 1853). Whigs and Free Soilers are weakened by the election, whereas the anti-Catholic and xenophobic Native American Party gains strength (the latter, nicknamed the Know-Nothing Party because of the secrecy of its members, who claim to "know nothing" of its activities, will rename itself the American Party).

1854

May 30. Pierce signs the Kansas-Nebraska Act. The people in these new territories will themselves decide whether or not to allow slavery. The act voids the Missouri Compromise of 1820, which forbade slavery north of 36°30′, because both Kansas and Nebraska are north of this parallel.

July. Opponents of the Kansas-Nebraska Act (ex-Whigs, Free Soilers, antislavery Democrats) form the Republican Party.

1855

In Kansas, clashes occur between pro- and anti-slavery activists. Each group drafts its own state constitution.

1856

May. In the Senate, South Carolina Representative Preston Brooks uses his cane to physically assault Senator Charles Sumner of Massachusetts, who had just delivered an impassioned anti-slavery speech.

May–June. New violent clashes over slavery occur in Kansas.

November 4. James Buchanan, a Democrat from Pennsylvania, is elected the 15th president; John Breckinridge

of Kentucky is elected vice president (they will take office on March 4, 1857). Buchanan, sympathetic to the South, will refuse to intervene against slavery.

1857

March. In *Dred Scott v. Sandford*, the Supreme Court rules that slaves have no right to sue in federal court, and that the Missouri Compromise is unconstitutional. Sharp protests are issued by the Republicans and the Northern states.

December. In the territory of Kansas, the Lecompton constitution favoring slavery is adopted in a referendum boycotted by antislavery voters. Abolitionists are furious.

1858

February. Buchanan submits the Lecompton constitution to Congress and recommends the admission of Kansas to the Union as a slave state.

March. The Lecompton constitution is rejected by a new referendum boycotted by proslavery voters in Kansas Territory.

April–June. The Mormon government in Utah is declared to be in rebellion.

May. Buchanan signs the English Act, which provides for a popular vote in Kansas on the Lecompton constitution; the constitution will be rejected on August 2, and Kansas will remain a territory.

Minnesota, a free state, becomes the 32nd state in the Union.

August–October. Senatorial candidates in Illinois hold a series of public debates. The Republican candidate, Abraham Lincoln, declares that slavery is an evil, while the Democrat Stephen Douglas maintains that the people

EVOLUTION OF SLAVERY, 1800–1860				
	1800	1820	1840	1860
Number of slaves	893,602	1,538,022	2,487,355	3,953,760

themselves must choose in each state whether they want to legalize slavery or not. Although Douglas will win the senatorial race, Lincoln will win national recognition.

1859

February. Oregon, a free state, becomes the 33rd state of the Union.

October. In western Virginia, the radical abolitionist John Brown attacks the federal arsenal at Harper's Ferry as part of an effort to create a refuge for fugitive slaves in the Appalachians.

December. John Brown is tried and hanged, becoming a martyr of the abolitionist movement.

1860

May. The Democratic Party breaks up over the question of slavery.

November. After a campaign devoted to the question of slavery and the continuation of the Union, the Republican candidate Abraham Lincoln is elected the 16th president, defeating Stephen Douglas, the candidate of the Northern Democrats, and Vice President Breckinridge, the candidate of the Southern Democrats. Hannibal Hamlin is elected vice president.

December 20. South Carolina, unwilling to accept the Republican Party's program, becomes the first state to secede from the Union.

Foreign Policy and Territorial Expansion

1842

The explorer John Frémont makes his first expedition into the Rockies.

The Webster-Ashburton Treaty with Great Britain defines the Northeast border with Canada.

1843

The great migrations westward along the Oregon Trail begin.

Frémont makes his second expedition into the Rockies.

The second war against the Seminole Indians in Florida, which began in 1835, ends.

1844

In the Treaty of Wanghia, China opens five ports to American trade.

1845

March. Mexico protests against the vote of Congress to annex Texas, and it breaks diplomatic relations with the United States.

May. A detachment of the U.S. Army is sent to the border of Texas and Mexico in order to "protect" the new state, which will not be formally admitted to the Union until December.

July. John O'Sullivan's article in *The U.S. Magazine & Democratic Review* evokes the Manifest Destiny of the American people.

December. President Polk reaffirms the principles of the Monroe Doctrine.

1846

February. John Slidell's mission to negotiate with Mexico the purchase of Texas, New Mexico and California ends in failure.

April 25. Hostilities between the United States and Mexico commence.

May 13. Congress declares war on Mexico; it also authorizes the enlistment of 50,000 volunteers and a credit of $10 million. The North is not in favor of the Mexican War.

June. A treaty with Great Britain sets the northern boundary of Oregon at the 49th parallel. In California, the American colonists proclaim their independence from Mexico.

June–December. The Americans occupy New Mexico and claim California.

1847

March. General Winfield Scott's troops make an amphibious landing at Veracruz and begin their march on Mexico City.

September 14. Scott occupies Mexico City.

1848

February 2. In the Treaty of Guadalupe Hidalgo, Mexico gives up all its territory north of the Rio Grande (California, Nevada and Utah, and parts of Arizona, New Mexico, Colorado and Wyoming) in exchange for $15 million.

1849

A treaty of friendship and commerce is signed with Hawaii.

1850

April. In the Clayton-Bulwer Treaty, the United States and Great Britain pledge that they will cooperate in building any canal across the Isthmus of Panama, and that the canal will have a neutral status.

1853

December. In the "Gadsden Purchase," the United States buys from Mexico a strip of land south of New Mexico in order to build a transcontinental railroad.

1853–1854

Commodore Matthew C. Perry's expedition to Japan opens the long-isolated island empire to American trade.

1858

Treaties of commerce are signed with China and Japan.

Buchanan considers buying Cuba from Spain after Americans supported an attempted rebellion on the island.

Economy and Society

1841

Brook Farm, a utopian community, is founded near Boston by a group of intellectuals.

1842

A protectionist tariff is voted by Congress.

In Massachusetts, a trade union is given legal status.

1843

The North America Phalanx, a socialist community modeled after the French Fourierists, is founded.

1844

May. Anti-Catholic riots occur in Philadelphia, marking the beginning of the xenophobic nativist movement.

1845

A massive wave of Irish immigrants, fleeing the potato blight in Ireland, begins arriving in the United States.

Lawrence, Massachusetts, a textile-producing center, is founded.

1847

In Chicago, Cyrus McCormick opens a factory for farm machinery.

1848

A massive wave of German immigrants begins arriving in the United States after the failure of a revolution in Germany.

January. Gold is discovered near Sacramento, California.

July. A convention in Seneca Falls, New York, marks the beginning of the women's rights movement.

In New York, the first department store opens on Broadway.

1849

In San Francisco, the first gold diggers arrive by boat; they will number 100,000 by the end of the year.

1850–1851

In the northern states, many refuse to enforce the laws on fugitive slaves.

1851

Maine is the first state to prohibit the consumption of alcohol.

1854

More than 400,000 immigrants land in New York.

1857

A financial panic sparked by the failure of a branch of a life insurance and trust company begins an economic depression that will last 18 months.

1858

Gold is discovered in Colorado, resulting in another gold rush.

1859

Silver is discovered in Nevada (Virginia City), and oil is discovered in Pennsylvania (Titusville).

1860

February. Journeymen shoemakers stage a strike in Lynn, Massachusetts.

March. Elizabeth Stanton asks the New York State Assembly to grant voting rights to women.

Technological Progress and Transportation

1844

The first telegraphic link is established between Washington and Baltimore (Samuel Morse's system).

1846

Elias Howe patents his sewing machine.

1850

The American Collins Line places four steamboats into service to compete with those of the British Cunard Line across the Atlantic.

1851

Isaac Singer patents his sewing machine.

Europeans discover American ingenuity at the World Exposition of the Crystal Palace in London.

1852

A railroad links Chicago to the East Coast.

1853

In New York, a Crystal Palace is constructed for a World's Fair that meets with little success.

1855

The German-born John Roebling builds a suspension bridge over the Niagara River.

1856

The Western Union Telegraph Company is founded.

1857

In New York Elisha Otis installs the first passenger elevator.

1858

The first transatlantic telegraph cable is laid; President Buchanan exchanges greetings with England's Queen Victoria (the cable will not begin operations until 1866).

John Appleby patents his harvester-binder.

In Chicago, George Pullman begins building railroad sleeping cars.

1860

The Pony Express is established; it links St. Joseph, Missouri, to Sacramento, California, in eight days.

Religion, Education and Culture

1841

Horace Greeley begins publishing the *New York Tribune*.

The philosopher Ralph Waldo Emerson publishes his *Essays*.

1842

P. T. Barnum opens his American Museum in New York.

1843

Dorothea Dix issues her report on insane asylums.

Hiram Powers sculpts *A Greek Slave*, which will receive great acclaim at the World Exposition in London in 1851.

1844

Joseph Smith, the founder and leader of the Mormon Church, is murdered in Nauvoo, Illinois. Brigham Young, his successor, will lead the Mormon migration to Utah in 1846.

1844–1845

The Baptist and Methodist Churches split over the issue of slavery.

1845

John Frémont reports on his explorations in the Rockies.

Margaret Fuller publishes *Woman in the Nineteenth Century*, a book of essays.

Edgar Allan Poe publishes *The Raven and Other Poems*.

The U.S. Naval Academy opens in Annapolis, Maryland.

1846

Articles by James Russell Lowell against the Mexican War appear in the *Boston Courier*.

The Smithsonian Institution, a museum and research center, is founded in Washington.

1847

The Mormons reach the Great Salt Lake and found the state of Deseret, the future Utah.

The poet Henry Wadsworth Longfellow publishes *Evangeline*.

1848

In New York, James Bogardus constructs the first building with a cast-iron facade.

1849

Henry David Thoreau publishes *On Civil Disobedience*.

A riot in the Astor Theater in New York results in numerous casualties.

1850

Nathaniel Hawthorne publishes *The Scarlet Letter*.

The first issue of the magazine *Harper's Monthly* appears.

1851

The first issue of the *New York Times* appears.

Lajos Kossuth, hero of the Hungarian Revolution, makes a triumphal tour of the United States.

A fire in the Library of Congress destroys two-thirds of its books, including those donated by Jefferson in 1815.

Herman Melville publishes *Moby Dick*.

1852

Harriet Beecher Stowe publishes *Uncle Tom's Cabin*, which is an instant success; 1 million copies will be sold within a year.

Massachusetts passes the first law making school attendance compulsory (for those 8 to 14 years old).

1854

Two important public libraries open: the Boston Public Library and the Astor Library in New York.

Thoreau publishes *Walden, or Life in the Woods*, a collection of essays on nature.

1855

Frederick Douglass, a former slave, publishes his *Autobiography*.

1856

Cooper Union, a center for popular education that provides evening courses and a library, is founded in New York.

1857

The white southerner Hinton Helper publishes *The Impending Crisis of the South*, in which he claims that the South's society, founded on slavery, cannot survive. George Fitzhugh publishes *Cannibals All!* a defense of slavery.

The first issues of the *Atlantic Monthly* and of *Harper's Weekly* appear.

1858

Frederick Law Olmsted supervises the initial construction of Central Park in New York (it will be completed in 1876). Other cities will follow this example.

Chapter 9   1861–1865

The Civil War

The issue of slavery at last came to a head in the Civil War. The South could not accept a Republican president whose program was clearly aimed at preventing the spread of slavery in the western territories. Feeling threatened, five states followed the example of South Carolina and seceded from the Union at the beginning of 1861. Together they formed the Confederacy, with its own president and government institutions. Texas soon joined the Confederacy, as did four other states after the attack on Fort Sumter, which marked the opening of hostilities. Only four slave states remained loyal to the Union: Maryland and Delaware, at Washington's doorstep, and Kentucky and Missouri farther west. Throughout the war, President Abraham Lincoln took great pains to avoid offending these four states in order to prevent them from switching sides.

Indeed, for Lincoln, at least until 1862, the aim of the war was not the abolition of slavery but the preservation of the Union. As soon as he took office, he found himself between the "copperheads," Northern Democrats who opposed the war and supported a conciliatory attitude toward the South, and the Radical Republicans and abolitionists, for whom the war was an antislavery crusade. Lincoln's difficulty in finding a competent military commander for the Union Army compounded his political troubles. Moreover, he could not hope for any foreign support because the European powers had quickly proclaimed their neutrality.

The war, which was fought on three fronts (in Virginia, the Mississippi valley, and along the coast of the Confederacy), traumatized the entire country. It was the first "modern" war employing the telegraph, railroads, aerial reconnaissance, armored ships and photography. It was also extraordinarily lethal and destructive: More than 600,000 died, at least as many were wounded, and whole regions were devastated.

Immediately after the South's surrender, Lincoln sought to apply a moderate policy of political "reconstruction" involving the reintegration of the rebel states into the Union. He was prevented from achieving his plan by an assassin's bullet. His death would be a disaster for both the North and the South.

Secession of the Southern States, 1860–1861

Map legend:
- Slave states which did not secede
- States seceding after Fort Sumter
- States seceding prior to Fort Sumter

Map labels: MD; DE; VA April 17, 1861; WV; NC May 20, 1861; SC Dec. 20, 1860; FL Jan. 10, 1861; GA Jan. 19, 1861; KY; TN June 8, 1861; AL Jan. 11, 1861; MS Jan. 9, 1861; MO; AR May 6, 1861; LA Jan. 26, 1861; TX Feb. 1, 1861; N

Political and Institutional Life

1861

January. Mississippi, Florida, Alabama, Georgia and Louisiana secede from the Union.

January 16. The Crittendon Compromise is rejected in the Senate. Drafted by Senator John J. Crittendon, the measure was a last attempt at preserving the Union; it would have prohibited slavery north of 36° 30′ (the Missouri Compromise line) while allowing its expansion into territories south of that line. President-elect Abraham Lincoln opposed the Crittendon Compromise.

January 29. Kansas, a free state, becomes the 34th state of the Union.

February 9. At a convention of seceding states held in Montgomery, Alabama, a new nation, the Confederate States of America, is formed, with Jefferson Davis as its president and Montgomery as its provisional capital.

February 23. Texas secedes from the Union.

March 2. The territories of Nevada, Colorado and North and South Dakota are created.

March 4. Lincoln takes office.

April 17–June 8. Shortly after Fort Sumter is attacked, Virginia, Arkansas, North Carolina and Tennessee secede from the Union.

May 21. Richmond, Virginia, becomes the capital of the Confederacy.

July 2. Lincoln suspends the writ of habeas corpus, which permits courts to inquire into the detention of persons claiming to be illegally held.

1862

April 16. Lincoln signs acts abolishing slavery in the District of Columbia.

September 22. Lincoln announces that all slaves in the Confederate states will be freed as of January 1, 1863.

1863

January 1. The Emancipation Proclamation comes into force. Drafted by Lincoln as early as July 1862, it frees slaves only in the rebel states. It displeases both the abolitionists and the slaveholders.

June. West Virginia, a free area, is detached from Virginia and becomes the 35th state of the Union.

1864

The Republican Party nominates Lincoln again as its candidate for president, and picks a Democrat from Tennessee, Andrew Johnson, as its candidate for vice president. The Democratic Party nominates General George McClellan as its candidate for president.

July. Lincoln vetoes the Wade-Davis Bill for radical reconstruction of the South.

October 31. Nevada becomes the 36th state of the Union.

November 8. Lincoln is reelected president by a slim margin of votes.

1865

February 1. Congress submits the 13th Amendment to the Constitution, which would abolish slavery, to the states for ratification.

February 3. Lincoln meets with Confederate peace commissioners on a ship near Hampton Roads, Virginia. The talks fail because the commissioners insist that the independence of the South be recognized.

March. Congress creates the Freedmen's Bureau to help freed slaves.

March 4. Lincoln takes the oath of office for the second time. In his Inaugural Address, he calls for reconciliation.

April 14. Five days after the South surrenders, Lincoln is shot by John Wilkes Booth, a Southern actor sympathetic to slavery, while attending a play at Ford's Theater in Washington. One of Booth's co-conspirators wounds Secretary of State William Seward.

April 15. Lincoln dies. Andrew Johnson takes the oath of office as the 17th president.

April 26. Lincoln's assassin is killed while resisting arrest.

Military Operations

1861

April 12–14. The Civil War begins when Fort Sumter, a federal arsenal at Charleston, is attacked by forces of South Carolina commanded by General Pierre Beauregard; the fort surrenders.

April 15. Lincoln decrees a state of insurrection in the South and calls for

75,000 volunteers to enlist for three months.

April 19. Lincoln decrees a blockade of Southern ports.

April 20. General Robert E. Lee resigns from the Union Army and enters the service of the Confederacy.

July 21. In the First Battle of Bull Run, near Manassas, Virginia, a Union army is defeated. The Confederate general Thomas "Stonewall" Jackson plays a key role in the battle.

October 21. The Union Army suffers another defeat at Ball's Bluff, Virginia.

November. Lincoln names General George McClellan commander in chief of the Union Army.

November 8. In the *Trent* Affair, a Union warship intercepts the *Trent*, a British ship carrying Confederate diplomats to London; this unauthorized action nearly precipitates a war with England.

1862

February. In the Mississippi Campaign, General Ulysses S. Grant attempts to take the Confederacy from the rear and meets with some success.

March 9. The first battle between ironclad ships, the Union's *Monitor* and the Confederacy's *Merrimack* (renamed *Virginia*), takes place off Hampton Roads, Virginia; the battle ends inconclusively.

April. The Union's Peninsular Campaign begins in Virginia.

April 7. Grant is victorious over General Albert Johnston's Confederate forces at Shiloh, Tennessee.

April 25. Union forces occupy New Orleans.

May 11. The Confederacy's *Merrimack* (*Virginia*) is scuttled by its crew.

June–July. In the Seven Days' Battles, Lee prevents McClellan's army from capturing Richmond, Virginia.

July. Lincoln names Henry W. Halleck general in chief, leaving McClellan commander of the Army of the Potomac.

August 30. In the Second Battle of Bull Run, in Virginia, the Southern generals Lee and "Stonewall" Jackson are victorious over the Union general John Pope.

September 17. Lee, having crossed the Potomac River to invade Maryland, is repelled at the Battle of Antietam (the bloodiest one-day battle of the war), but McClellan fails to pursue him.

November 24. Lincoln replaces McClellan as commander of the Army of the Potomac with General Ambrose Burnside.

December 13. Burnside is defeated at Fredericksburg, Virginia.

December 31. The *Monitor* is shipwrecked.

1863

January. Lincoln replaces Burnside with General Joseph Hooker as head of the Army of the Potomac.

March. In the North, all men 20 to 45 years old are drafted (the hiring of substitutes is permitted).

May 2–4. Lee defeats the Army of the Potomac at Chancellorsville, Virginia.

May 22. Grant lays siege to Vicksburg, on the Mississippi River.

June. Lee, set to invade Pennsylvania, crosses the Potomac.

July 1–3. In one of the bloodiest and most decisive battles of the war, Lee's army is defeated at Gettysburg, Pennsylvania, and forced to retreat to Virginia.

July 4. Vicksburg surrenders. The Confederacy looses control of the Mississippi and is split into two parts.

Free and Slave Areas, 1861

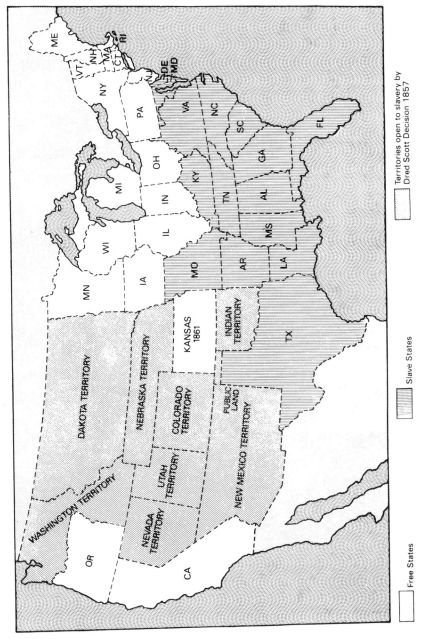

Territories open to slavery by Dred Scott Decision 1857

Slave States

Free States

NORTH AND SOUTH IN 1861		
	North	**South**
States	19 free, 4 slave	11 slave
Territories	6	2
Population	22 million	9 million, including 3.5 million slaves
Men of arms-bearing age	4 million	1.14 million
Railroads	21,900 miles	9,000 miles

Note: When these disparities are taken into account, Southern resistance was unexpected and remarkable in its intensity.

September 20. A Union army is defeated at Chickamauga, Georgia.

November 19. Lincoln delivers his Gettysburg Address at the dedication ceremonies for a military cemetery.

November 25. Grant drives the Confederates out of Chattanooga, a major railroad junction in Tennessee.

1864

March. Lincoln names Grant general in chief of the Union forces.

April 12. In the Battle of Fort Pillow, on the Mississippi, Confederate soldiers slaughter black Union soldiers after they had surrendered.

May 4. The Union general William Tecumseh Sherman leaves Chattanooga and marches toward Atlanta, Georgia.

June 3. Lee scores the last major victory over the North at Cold Harbor, Virginia.

June 15. The Union Army's siege of Petersburg, Virginia, begins.

June 19. The *Alabama*, a Confederate ship, is sunk by the Union fleet off Cherbourg, France.

September 1. Sherman captures Atlanta; the city will be burned on November 15.

November 16. Sherman starts his March to the Sea, destroying everything in his path through Georgia.

December 22. Sherman enters Savannah, Georgia.

1865

February 1. Sherman's army begins its march through the Carolinas, again destroying everything in its path.

February 17. Sherman burns Columbia, South Carolina; he will occupy Charleston the next day.

March. A desperate South promises freedom to all slaves enlisting in the Confederate Army.

April 2–3. Besieged by Union forces for nine months, Petersburg, Virginia, falls; Richmond is captured by Grant.

April 9. Lee surrenders the Army of Northern Virginia to Grant at Appomattox Courthouse, Virginia.

April 18. The Confederate general Joseph E. Johnston surrenders to Sherman in North Carolina. The war ends.

Economy and Society

1861

Congress creates an income tax to finance the war.

1862

May 20. Lincoln signs into law the Homestead Act, providing a virtually free gift of 160 acres of federal land to any head of family or adult over 21 years of age who resides on the land for five years.

August–September. The Minnesota Sioux (Little Crow) Indians stage a revolt.

1863

A locomotive drivers' union is founded.

February 25. Lincoln signs the National Banking Act, which reorganizes the banking system.

July 13–16. Draft riots occur in New York; 105 persons are killed and many more are wounded.

1864

In Colorado, a revolt by the Cheyenne Indians is crushed.

A cigar-makers' union is founded.

July 4. A new immigration act allows foreigners possessing a work contract to enter the country.

1865

In Chicago, the Union Yards slaughterhouse opens.

Technological Progress and Transportation

1861

The first transcontinental telegraph line is completed.

Thaddeus Lowe's experimental balloon flight demonstrates for the first time the military import of this new means of reconnaissance.

1862

The Department of Agriculture is created; its mission is to spread technical knowledge among farmers.

The Pacific Railway Act grants federal funds for the building of a transcontinental railroad.

Religion, Education and Culture

1861

Romantic historical landscape paintings by George Inness and Albert Bierstadt.

Yale University awards the first Ph.D. in America.

1862

The Morrill Act grants to each state in the Union federal lands to be used for agricultural colleges. These land grant colleges will become the forerunners of many state universities.

1863

The National Academy of Science is founded in Washington.

James Whistler exhibits his painting *Little Girl in White* at the "Salon des refusés" in Paris.

Herman Melville and William Cullen Bryant publish war poems. Walt Whitman writes about his experience as a military nurse.

Olympia Brown becomes the first American woman ordained a minister by an official ecclesiastical body.

1865

Winslow Homer, a war correspondent for *Harper's Weekly*, paints *Prisoners on the Front.*

The first issues of the liberal weekly *The Nation* and of the San Francisco dailies the *Examiner* and the *Chronicle* are published.

Chapter 10   1865–1877

Reconstruction

The political, moral and social reconstruction of the nation was led first by Andrew Johnson, who succeeded Lincoln, then by the Radical Republicans in Congress. The result was a difficult reunification and a total failure of racial integration.

Johnson, a Democrat elected on the Republican ticket in 1864, wanted a conciliatory program that included amnesty for the rebels and the reintegration of the secessionist states into the Union without requiring them to give equal rights to blacks. Unable to accept such a program, Congress imposed its own plan. The secessionist states were to remain under the military rule of the Union Army until they agreed to ratify the 14th and 15th Amendments, which entitled blacks to civil rights. This clash between Johnson and the Radicals was also a clash between the executive branch and Congress. It reached its climax in 1868, when a procedure of impeachment was begun against the president; although the Senate failed by a narrow margin to impeach Johnson, the affair weakened the power of the presidency.

In the South, Radical Reconstruction met with fierce resistance from former Confederates and racist whites. Gathered in secret societies such as the Ku Klux Klan, the opponents of Reconstruction terrorized blacks and their supporters, including well-intentioned Northerners who sought to educate or otherwise help the freedmen in the South, adventurers looking for lucrative opportunities (bundled together under the scornful name of "carpetbaggers") and Southerners who had opposed secession and were looking for revenge ("scalawags"). The last Union soldiers did not leave the South until 1877, the date officially marking the end of Reconstruction. But as early as the beginning of the 1870s, most Southern states had taken back their seats in Congress, at the same time hastening to deprive blacks of their constitutional rights and instituting segregation in all public places.

The country was too preoccupied with economic issues to give much thought to the treatment of blacks. The growth of industrial capitalism coincided with serious monetary problems linked to the massive issue of greenbacks during the war. Beginning in 1873, a lengthy economic depression, punctuated by violent labor strikes, worried businessmen and weighed heavily on the working class.

Political and Institutional Life

1865

May 10. The fleeing Jefferson Davis, president of the Confederacy, is captured and imprisoned.

May 29. President Andrew Johnson begins his restoration program by offering amnesty to those rebels who request it (former government and military officials are excluded).

July 7. Four persons charged with participating in John Wilkes Booth's conspiracy to assassinate President Lincoln are hanged.

November 24. In Mississippi, the first Black Code limiting the rights of freedmen is enacted.

December 1. Johnson restores the writ of habeas corpus.

December 4. Congress meets for the first time since Lincoln's death. All of the former Confederate states save Mississippi have accepted reintegration into the Union. But the House of Representatives refuses to allow Southern delegates to take their seats and names a Committee for Reconstruction headed by the Radical Republican Thaddeus Stevens.

December 18. The 13th Amendment, abolishing slavery, is ratified.

1866

February 19. Despite President Johnson's veto, Congress renews and extends the powers of the Freedmen's Bureau.

April 9. Despite the president's veto of March 27, Congress passes the Civil Rights Act, which gives equal rights to blacks.

June 16. The 14th Amendment is submitted to the states for ratification; it extends civil rights to blacks, prohibits ex-rebels from holding public office and declares all debts of the Confederacy to be "illegal and void."

July 24. Tennessee, having ratified the 14th Amendment, is readmitted to the Union.

November. Anti-Johnson Republican majorities are elected to both houses of Congress.

1867

January 7. Members of Congress begin efforts to impeach Johnson; the House of Representatives will reject a resolution of impeachment on December 7.

January 8. Despite Johnson's veto, Congress enacts legislation giving blacks in the District of Columbia the right to vote.

March–July. Congress passes three Reconstruction Acts over Johnson's vetoes. The South is divided into five military districts under federal control; whites who took part in the rebellion are disenfranchised; and states will be readmitted to the Union only if they ratify the 14th Amendment. Military governors are put in charge of the organization of elections in the South and required to ensure that blacks have the opportunity to vote and to be elected.

March 1. Nebraska becomes the 37th state of the Union.

March 2. Two acts limiting presidential powers are passed. The Tenure of Office Act (passed over Johnson's veto) takes away from the president the power to dismiss a cabinet officer whose nomination was approved by the Senate. A law on military command requires the president to issue orders through the general of the army, thus preventing him from dealing directly with military governors in the South.

August 5. Johnson requests the resignation of Secretary of War Edwin Stanton, who refuses to resign.

August 12. Johnson issues an executive order suspending Stanton; General Ulysses S. Grant is appointed acting secretary of war.

1868

January 13. The Senate refuses to accept the replacement of Stanton. Grant and Stanton accept the Senate's decision as lawful.

February 21. Johnson again removes Stanton from office. A motion is made in the House to impeach the president on the grounds that he has violated the Tenure of Office Act.

March–May. Johnson is tried by the Senate, which fails to reach the two-thirds majority vote required for impeachment. He is allowed to finish his term.

June. Arkansas, Alabama, Florida, Georgia and Louisiana are readmitted to the Union.

July. The Wyoming Territory is created.

July 28. The 14th Amendment is ratified by the states.

November 3. Ulysses S. Grant, a Republican, is elected the 18th president; Schuyler Colfax is elected vice president.

December 25. Johnson proclaims an unconditional pardon and amnesty for all rebels, including Jefferson Davis, whose treason trial had begun on December 3.

1869

February. Congress, concerned about violence against blacks in the South, approves the 15th Amendment, which specifies that no state has the power to deprive a citizen of the right to vote because of race; the Amendment is sent to the states for ratification.

March 4. Grant takes office.

December. Georgia, having prevented blacks from voting as soon as Union troops were withdrawn, is prohibited from sending representatives to Congress.

Congress demands that Southern states ratify the 15th Amendment.

1870

January–February. Virginia and Mississippi are readmitted to the Union. Acts of violence occur in Mississippi.

February 23. Republican Hiram Revels of Mississippi, the first black senator, takes his seat.

March 30. The 15th Amendment is ratified. Texas is readmitted to the Union.

May. Congress passes a law directed against the Ku Klux Klan, providing for harsh penalties on those who infringe the voting rights of blacks.

August–November. The Democrats regain control of several Southern states.

Acts of terror are perpetrated against blacks in the South.

1871

The *New York Times* denounces the political corruption surrounding Boss Tweed in New York.

October 17. Federal troops are sent to South Carolina to enforce a proclamation ordering the Ku Klux Klan to disband and surrender its arms.

1872

June 30. The Freedmen's Bureau is closed.

September. The Crédit Mobilier scandal is exposed. The company, involved in the construction of the Union Pacific Railroad, had bribed members of

The End of Reconstruction

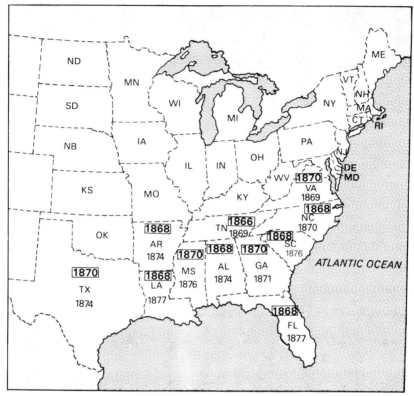

Dates in bold—Readmission to the Union
Dates in light—End of Carpetbagger Government

Congress, including Vice President Colfax when he served in the House.

November. In New York, Boss Tweed is sentenced to 10 years in prison.

November 5. Grant is reelected president; Henry Wilson is elected vice president.

1873

Grant sends federal troops to quell unrest in Louisiana.

March 4. Grant takes the oath of office to begin his second term.

1874

The Greenback Party, made up primarily of pro-inflationist western farmers, is created.

1875

March 1. Grant signs a civil rights act aimed at preventing segregation in public places.

May. The Whiskey Ring scandal is exposed. The proceeds of federal taxes on alcohol were embezzled. Grants's entourage is directly implicated.

1876

March. William Belknap, the secretary of war, is implicated in corruption and forced to resign.

March 27. The Supreme Court rules in *U.S. v. Cruikshank* that the 14th Amendment protects blacks against violations of their rights by states but not by individuals; this means the Ku Klux Klan's activities can go on with impunity.

August 1. Colorado becomes the 38th state of the Union.

November 7. In the presidential election, the Democrat Samuel Tilden receives a majority of the votes over the Republican Rutherford B. Hayes. Because of electoral fraud in the South, however, the election will be decided by Congress.

1877

March 2. The committee of Congress charged with deciding the presidential election rules in favor of Hayes, who will take office as the 19th president on March 4, with William Wheeler as vice president.

April. The last federal troops leave the South (New Orleans).

December. The Socialist Labor Party is founded.

Indian Affairs

1866

The Sioux go to war to defend their "holy lands" in the Black Hills of South Dakota and Wyoming.

December. The Sioux chief Red Cloud is victorious at Fort Kearney, Wyoming.

1868

April. The Treaty of Fort Laramie brings an end to the First Sioux War.

The U.S. Army gives up three forts, and the government pledges to provide food for the Indians if they remain on their reservations.

1871

March 3. President Grant signs the Indian Appropriation Act, which nullifies all treaties with the Indians, who are declared wards of the federal government.

1872–1873

The Modocs of Oregon are defeated and their chiefs hanged at Fort Klamath.

1874–1875

After gold is discovered in the Black Hills, waves of settlers move in. The Sioux refuse to move to their reservations, and the Second Sioux War begins.

1876

March. General George Crook battles the Sioux, led by Chief Crazy Horse, to a draw at Rosebud Creek, in the territory of Montana.

June 25. In Montana, General George Armstrong Custer and his 212 men are massacred by the Sioux, led by Crazy Horse, on the Little Big Horn River. American public opinion is outraged by Custer's defeat.

1877

Starvation forces Crazy Horse to surrender, and he is killed. The Sioux are forced onto their reservations, and the Sioux Wars end. Sitting Bull, another Sioux chief, flees to Canada.

June–October. The Nez Percés attack the army in Oregon and Montana. Chief Joseph, defeated while trying to flee to Canada, is sent to a reservation in Oklahoma, where he will die of malaria.

Foreign Policy

1866

February 12. William Seward, the secretary of state, sends an ultimatum to Napoleon III, ordering him to withdraw his troops from Mexico. The French emperor had taken advantage of the Civil War to invade Mexico and make Maximilian of Austria emperor of Mexico, in violation of the Monroe Doctrine.

1867

February. Napoleon III withdraws his troops from Mexico. Maximilian, left alone to face the revolution led by Benito Juárez, will be executed in June.

March 30. Alaska is bought from Russia for $7.2 million. Public opinion is critical of the negotiation, which was led by William Seward. The only known resources of the territory are furs and fish.

August. The Midway Islands, in the Pacific, are annexed.

1868

The Burlingame Treaty with China guarantees to the Chinese unrestricted immigration into the United States and commercial benefits.

1870

The Senate rejects President Grant's proposal to annex the Dominican Republic.

1871

May. In the Treaty of Washington, the United States and Great Britain settle claims concerning the damage done to the Union fleet by British-built Confederate ships during the Civil War (the *Alabama* Claims).

1875

January. A treaty of commerce is signed with Hawaii, which also agrees to concede no territory to any other power.

Economy and Society

1865

July 1. All Southern ports blockaded by the North during the Civil War are reopened to commerce.

December 24. The Ku Klux Klan is founded in Pulaski, Tennessee.

1866

July. Race riots occur in New Orleans: 48 blacks are killed.

August. The National Labor Union, a nationwide trade union, is founded.

1867

The first housing law is passed in New York.

A secret society of farmers is founded; it will give birth to the Granger movement.

1868

The eight-hour workday is established for employees of the federal government.

1869

January. Blacks organize politically: The National Convention of Colored Men is founded, with Frederick Douglass as president.

The American Equal Rights Association is founded, with Susan B. Anthony as president.

February. A federal tariff increases protection for industry.

March. The Public Credit Act allows treasury bonds to be redeemed in gold.

Paper money (greenbacks) remains legal tender.

May. The National Woman Suffrage Association is founded, with Elizabeth Stanton as president.

The Noble Order of the Knights of Labor, an industrial union, is founded (it will remain a secret society until 1878).

July. A riot against Chinese workers breaks out in San Francisco.

September 24. "Black Friday" occurs on Wall Street: A stock market crash and numerous bankruptcies result from the manipulation of stocks by the financier Jay Gould.

December. Wyoming Territory passes the first law giving women the right to vote.

1870

January. A nationwide strike of telegraph operators occurs.

John D. Rockefeller founds the Standard Oil Company.

February. Women's suffrage is granted in Utah Territory.

1871

July. Brawls between Irish Catholics and Protestants occur in New York leaving 52 dead.

October 8–11. A huge fire breaks out in Chicago.

October 24. Anti-Chinese riots take place in Los Angeles; 15 are lynched.

1872

March. The first nature reserve, Yellowstone National Park, is established.

1873

February 12. Grant signs the Coinage Act, which demonetizes silver; gold becomes the sole monetary standard.

Opponents of the Act will later call it "the Crime of '73."

August. A terrible drought forces many indebted farmers to sell their land. Farmers' Alliances, which will support an inflationist monetary policy, trace their origins to this period.

September 18. The Panic of 1873 begins following the bankruptcy of Jay Cooke's banking firm. The New York Stock Exchange will close for 10 days. The resulting economic depression, caused by years of excessive speculation and lax financial policies, will last until 1878.

1874

March. The Granger movement succeeds in having legislation regulating railroad rates passed in Wisconsin and Iowa.

June. The Legal Tender Act, enacted over Grant's veto, allows an increase in the circulation of greenbacks.

1875

The Molly Maguires, a terrorist group that originated in Ireland, employs violence in an effort to improve the working conditions in the Pennsylvania coal mines.

1877

April. An agreement among the four major eastern railroad companies ends a price war and leads to a reduction of employee wages.

June. Ten Molly Maguires accused of murder are hanged.

July. A huge railroad strike begins. Violent clashes occur in Baltimore and Chicago. Solidarity strikes take place in mines and some other businesses.

September. Thousands of Southern blacks (Exodusters) leave for Kansas in the hope of founding a colony where they may be accepted without discrimination.

Technological Progress and Transportation

1866

The first transatlantic telegraph cable begins operation.

1867

The first "elevated railroad" is constructed in New York.

1868

George Westinghouse perfects the air brake. William Davis perfects the "ice box on wheels," the first refrigerator car. James Oliver patents his tempered steel plow, which will prove to be highly effective in cultivating the virgin soils of the West.

1869

May 10. Two locomotives traveling in opposite directions meet at Promontory Point, Utah, marking the completion of the first transcontinental railroad.

1870

Celluloid is invented.

1873

The first cable cars appear in San Francisco.

1874

Joseph F. Glidden, an Illinois farmer, invents barbed wire to prevent horses from encroaching on cultivated areas; his invention will transform the landscape of the Great Plains.

1876

March. Alexander Graham Bell patents his telephone.

May. The Centennial Exposition, celebrating the nation's first one hundred years of independence, opens in Philadelphia. Its main attraction is a Corliss steam machine. Ten million people will visit the Exposition.

1877

Thomas Edison invents the phonograph.

Religion, Education and Culture

1866

The first architecture course is taught at an American university, the Massachusetts Institute of Technology.

1867

The first novels by Horatio Alger appear. His heroes embody the ideology of the self-made man.

In Washington, D.C., Howard University, a school for blacks, is founded. In Baltimore, Johns Hopkins University is founded.

1868

The University of California at Berkeley is founded.

1869

Mark Twain achieves fame with the publication of *Innocents Abroad*.

1870

The Corcoran Art Gallery is founded in Washington.

1871

In Philadelphia, James Whistler exhibits a portrait of his mother, *Arrangement in Grey and White.*

1872

The Jehovah's Witnesses, a religious group, is founded.

1874

Mark Twain's *The Gilded Age* describes the corruption of America after the Civil War.

1875

Thomas Eakins exhibits *The Clinic of Dr. Gross.* The realism of this painting shocks the public.

Archbishop John McCloskey, the first American Catholic cardinal, is anointed in St. Patrick's Cathedral in New York. Dwight L. Moody leads a religious revival.

1876

Mark Twain publishes *The Adventures of Tom Sawyer.*

Frederick Law Olmsted completes Central Park in New York.

The centennial of America's independence is celebrated in Philadelphia.

1877

Henry James's *The American* is published.

Chapter 11   1878–1890

The Gilded Age and the Triumph of Capitalism

The nation once again regained the optimism and rapid growth of the early 19th century, but the framework for economic expansion was now considerably different. Railroads gave a continental dimension to the national economy; heavy industry, especially iron and steel, replaced small craftsmen; and the population, increasingly heterogeneous because of the ceaseless influx of immigrants (over 5 million from 1881 to 1890), was increasingly concentrated in the large cities. New York, with a population of 3 million in 1890, was still the largest American metropolis, but Chicago, a city that was not even founded a century before, was a close second.

Industrial capitalism found hospitable soil in America. The ideology developed by the British philosopher Herbert Spencer and inspired by Charles Darwin's research in the animal kingdom was greeted enthusiastically. "Social Darwinism" asserted that life was as much a struggle in human society as it was in nature, and would end with the victory of the fittest and the elimination of the weak, to the benefit of the entire society. Thus was justified the individual success of a poor but courageous immigrant and the concentration of power in the trusts, which brought about the destruction of small family businesses.

Protest against this unfair and undemocratic system was rare and without much effect. The relationships between workers and employers were extremely tense. The former, poorly housed in urban slums, badly paid for long workdays, and without security of employment or protection against accidents or sickness, began to organize. But the ethnic diversity of the working class, as well as the prevailing ideology, favored a moderate trade unionism.

A strong protest movement did, however, spread throughout the countryside. With agriculture suffering from low prices, indebted farmers turned to the federal government, asking that it increase the money supply and put an end to the abuses of the railroads, which secretly fixed prices for their own benefit. Farmers' Alliances soon succeeded the Granger movement and the Greenback Party. Local and national political life was poisoned by irresponsibility and corruption.

This "Gilded Age" (Mark Twain), in which quickly made fortunes could not mask the ever-present poverty, ended in 1890 with three significant events: the first attempt to restrain the power of the trusts, the end of Indian resistance, and the observation made by the Census Bureau that the Frontier, as a area for settlement, no longer existed.

Political and Institutional Life

1878

The Greenback-Labor Party demands the free minting of silver, the continuation of the status of greenbacks as legal tender, the limitation of Chinese immigration, and a shorter workday. Fourteen of its members are elected to Congress.

1880

April. The national Farmers' Alliance is organized.

November 2. Republican James Garfield is elected the 20th president; Chester Arthur is elected vice president.

1881

March 4. Garfield takes office.

July 2. Charles Guiteau, a dissident Republican, shoots Garfield in the back in a train station in Washington.

September 19. Garfield dies of the wounds he suffered on July 2. Chester Arthur will become the 21st president the following day.

1883

January. The Pendleton Civil Service Act becomes law. It provides for the recruitment of civil servants according to their qualifications, as measured in competitive examinations, rather than their political connections.

1884

June. The Republican Party is divided over its nominee for the upcoming presidential election. James Blaine, who is suspected of corruption, is nominated. Liberal Republicans will support the Democratic candidate, Grover Cleveland, in the election.

November 4. Cleveland is elected the 22nd president; he will become the first Democratic president since James Buchanan, who was elected in 1856. Thomas Hendricks is elected vice president.

1885

March 4. Cleveland takes office.

1886

April. Cleveland proposes to mediate a nationwide railroad strike.

1887

March. The Tenure of Office Act, which was the basis for President Johnson's impeachment in 1868, is repealed.

1888

November 6. The Republican Benjamin Harrison is elected the 23rd president; Levi Morton is elected vice president.

1889

The states of Montana, Washington and North and South Dakota join the Union.

March 4. Harrison takes office.

1890

The states of Idaho and Wyoming join the Union.

Indian Affairs

1878

The Cheyennes, who wish to leave their reservation in Oklahoma, stage a revolt.

1879

The Utes stage a revolt in Colorado.

1885

In defiance of President Cleveland's ban, settlers intrude on Indian lands in Oklahoma.

1886

The Apache chief Geronimo surrenders to General Nelson Miles.

1887

February 8. President Cleveland signs the Dawes Severalty Act, which orders the breakup of reservation lands and the distribution of 160-acre lots to each Indian family, in the hope of turning Indians into farmers. The act will actually facilitate the purchase by white settlers at a low price of lands without value in the Indians' eyes.

1889

Oklahoma is officially opened to white settlers.

1890

A revival movement spreads among the Sioux who follow the preaching of the medicine man Wowoka.

December 15. The old Sioux chief Sitting Bull is killed while attempting to escape capture at Standing Rock, South Dakota.

December 29. In the Battle of Wounded Knee, 300 Sioux led by Chief Big Foot are killed in South Dakota while resisting the army's effort to return them to their reservation. This battle marks the end of the Indian wars.

Foreign Policy

1880

March. President Hayes declares that any canal dug across the Isthmus of Panama must be controlled by the United States.

1887

The treaty of 1875 with Hawaii is amended to provide that the United States have the exclusive right to build a naval base at Pearl Harbor.

1889

The Tripartite Agreement (United States, Great Britain, Germany) on the Samoa Islands confirms the United States' title to its base in Pago Pago.

The First International American Conference (Pan-American Conference) is held in Washington; Secretary of State James Blaine presides.

Economy and Society

1878

January. The Noble Order of the Knights of Labor, which ceases to be a secret organization, is officially founded.

February. With the Bland-Allison Act, the federal government resumes the minting of silver.

December. The depression that began with the Panic of 1873 ends.

1879

January. Greenbacks are once again convertible into gold.

May. Anti-Chinese unrest occurs in California.

1880

Gold is discovered in Alaska.

The American branch of the Salvation Army is founded.

The American Red Cross is founded.

The Western Union Telegraph Company obtains a near total monopoly on telegraph service.

1882

January. John D. Rockefeller creates the Standard Oil Trust. It will serve as a model for the concentration of many businesses.

A New York law banning the making of cigars at home (in tenements) is declared unconstitutional by the Supreme Court.

May. The Chinese Exclusion Act bans Chinese immigration for ten years.

June–September. Steelworkers go out on strike.

August. A law prohibits the immigration of paupers, the insane and criminals.

1883

The Supreme Court declares the Civil Rights Act of 1875 unconstitutional.

1884–1885

The nation suffers another economic depression.

1885

The Contract Labor Law prohibits the hiring of foreign workers under contract. Congress passed the law under pressure from the Knights of Labor.

1885–1886

Trusts are formed in various industries: lead, steel, sugar, whiskey.

1886

February. An anti-Chinese riot occurs in Seattle, Washington. Federal troops are sent to restore order.

March–May. A general railroad strike organized by the Knights of Labor takes place.

May 1. In Chicago, a demonstration by the Knights of Labor demands the eight-hour workday. A strike begins at the McCormick Reaper Company; on May 3, police will fire on a crowd and kill six.

May 4. In Chicago, workers meet at Haymarket Square to protest against police brutality. Anarchists demonstrate alongside the Knights of Labor. A bomb kills seven policemen.

June–August. Several leaders of the Haymarket Square demonstration are sentenced, and the Knights of Labor are discredited; the real culprits of the bombing are never identified.

December. A new, more moderate trade union, the American Federation of Labor, is founded, with Samuel Gompers as president.

1887

The Interstate Commerce Act is signed into law, creating the Interstate Commerce Commission.

1888

Congress creates the Department of Labor.

1889

In Chicago, Jane Addams founds Hull House, one of the most successful settlement houses, which serve as centers of social welfare and activism in poor districts of large cities.

Kansas passes the nation's first antitrust law; other states will soon follow its example.

White settlers rush to the Indian lands in Oklahoma.

May 31. The Johnstown Flood claims more than 2,000 lives in Pennsylvania.

1890

The national census sets the population at 63 million. The Frontier is declared to be no longer a distinctive region, signaling an end to the open settlement of the continent.

January. The United Mine Workers, a labor union, is founded.

July. The Sherman Antitrust Act outlaws business contracts and monopolies that restrain free trade and commerce.

The Sherman Silver Purchase Act, which requires the Treasury Department to purchase a set amount of silver each month, supersedes the Bland-Allison Act of 1878.

September. The Sequoia and Yosemite National Parks are created in California.

October. The McKinley Tariff Act raises import duties to 49.5 percent in response to tariffs of other nations.

Technological Progress and Transportation

1878

George Eastman produces the first photographic plates.

1879

Thomas Edison perfects a durable filament for his incandescent lamp.

1880

Eastman perfects the roll of photographic film.

1881

The elevated subway system (the "El") is completed in New York.

Edison establishes the Edison Electric Illuminating Company, which provides light to an entire district of Manhattan.

1882–1883

Two new transcontinental railroads are completed, the Santa Fe and the Southern Pacific.

1883

The first telephone link between New York and Chicago is established.

The Brooklyn Bridge opens in New York. Begun in 1869 by John and Washington Roebling, it is the longest suspension bridge in the world (3,450 feet).

Another transcontinental railroad, the Northern Pacific, is completed.

Four time zones across the United States and Canada are established in order to facilitate railroad commerce.

1884

Ottmar Morgenthaler patents his Linotype.

1887

The first electric tramways are built in Richmond, Virginia.

1888

Nikola Tesla develops a motor using alternating current.

Eastman develops the Kodak camera, which uses his rolls of film.

1889

The first I beams made with Bessemer steel are produced.

Thomas Edison makes the first cinematographic film and the first projector for viewing it.

Isaac Singer makes the first electric sewing machine.

Civilization and Culture

1878

Joseph Pulitzer begins his career as a journalist.

1879

Henry George's *Progress and Poverty* is published.

1880

The Metropolitan Museum of Art opens in New York.

Henry Adams's *Democracy* is published.

1881

Mary Cassat exhibits her paintings in Paris with the French Impressionists.

Helen Hunt Jackson writes a courageous critique of U.S. policy toward the Indians in *A Century of Dishonor*.

In Alabama, Booker T. Washington founds his Tuskegee Normal and Industrial Institute to train young blacks.

1883

The nation's first vaudeville theater opens in Boston.

The first issue of the *Ladies Home Journal* is published.

William "Buffalo Bill" Cody begins his Wild West Show.

The sociologist William G. Sumner defends Social Darwinism.

1884

Mark Twain's *Huckleberry Finn* is published.

1884–1885

In Chicago, the Home Life Insurance Building is constructed by William Le Baron Jenney; it is one of the first skyscrapers with a metal frame.

1885

In Chicago, the architect Henry Richardson designs the Marshall Field warehouse, a magnificent example of commercial architecture.

The American Economic Association is founded; it supports the tempering of laissez-faire capitalism through government intervention.

Ragtime appears as a musical style in St. Louis, Missouri.

1886

The Statue of Liberty, sculpted by Frédéric-Auguste Bartholdi and donated by France, is dedicated in New York.

The magazine *Cosmopolitan* begins publication.

1888

Edward Bellamy's *Looking Backward, 2000–1887* is published.

The Boston Public Library is built in the Renaissance style by McKim, Mead & White.

1889

Dow Jones & Co. begins publishing the *Wall Street Journal.*

The Social Gospel movement, which supports social Christianity, is begun.

The United States participates in the Exposition Universelle in Paris, where Edison's phonograph and incandescent lamp are exhibited.

1890

Admiral Alfred Thayer Mahan publishes *The Influence of Sea Power Upon History, 1660–1783,* an influential study on the importance of sea power in international affairs.

The architect Louis Sullivan builds the Wainwright Building, a skyscraper, in St. Louis.

How the Other Half Lives, Jacob Riis's study on the New York slums, is published.

Chapter 12   1891–1901

From Populism to Imperialism

The last decade of the 19th century was marked by wide-ranging political and ideological debates. At the same time, a lengthy economic depression, together with violent social unrest, provided the backdrop for the birth of a resolutely imperialist foreign policy.

Industrial capitalism, seen as irreconcilable with American democratic values, became the target of protests orchestrated by anarchists, socialists, and above all the Populists, whose movement sprang from the dissatisfaction of western farmers. Lack of coordination between the cities and the countryside, however, led in 1896 to the electoral defeat of this protesting segment of America society. Still, a majority of Americans had come to recognize the necessity of reform. By the beginning of the 20th century, the Progressive Party was adopting some of the Populists' demands.

The imperialism of the 1890s has sometimes been viewed as a consequence of domestic problems. Americans might have been looking abroad for what they could no longer find at home: land, untapped markets, new and exciting adventures. However one explains it, imperialism, which led in 1898 to a war with Spain and to the acquisition of colonies (Puerto Rico and the Philippines), signaled a fundamental change in the international role of the United States. Public opinion, however, quickly came to view imperialism and colonialism as contrary to the fundamental American values of freedom and democracy. Despite this popular sentiment, the nation was unable to return to the isolationist ideal of Washington and Monroe. Indeed, America had opened itself to the outside world: Waves of non-Anglo-Saxon immigrants were pressing at its borders, and American products were finding new markets in Europe, Asia and Latin America.

The assassination of President McKinley in September 1901 had little impact on American policy. This tragic event did, however, bring onto the public stage an energetic young man full of ambitious schemes, Theodore Roosevelt.

Political Life and Monetary Issues

1891

The People's (Populist) Party is founded. Its program calls for the unlimited minting of silver, the nationalization of railroads, an income tax, the eight-hour workday, universal suffrage for the election of senators, and loans to farmers.

1892

November 8. Democrat Grover Cleveland is elected president for the second time; Adlai Stevenson is elected vice president. The Populists received 8.5 percent of the popular vote. Cleveland will take office as the 24th president on March 4, 1893.

1893

Colorado grants voting rights to women.

August. Worried about the financial crisis caused the dwindling of gold reserves, Cleveland asks Congress to repeal the Sherman Silver Purchase Act of 1890.

1895

In order for the Treasury Department to buy gold, Cleveland requests loans from the major banks. This earns him the hostility of the Populists and those Democrats who favor making both gold and silver the standard for U.S. currency (bimetallism).

1896

January. Utah becomes the 45th state in the Union and grants voting rights to women.

Cleveland launches a public loan.

June. William McKinley, a protectionist who favors gold as the standard for U.S. currency (monometallism), is chosen by the Republican Party as its candidate for the presidency.

July. The Democratic Party chooses as its presidential candidate William Jennings Bryan, who also receives the nomination of the Populist Party. Bryan favors the free minting of silver (bimetallism).

November 3. After a bitter campaign, McKinley is elected the 25th president with 7 million votes versus Bryan's 6.7 million. Garret Hobart is elected vice president. McKinley will take office on March 4, 1897.

1897

Alaskan gold production helps solve the monetary crisis.

1900

March. McKinley signs the Gold Standard Act, establishing monometallism. The gold reserves are replenished.

September. The first primary elections in America are held in Minnesota.

After being struck by a devastating hurricane, the city of Galveston, Texas, creates a new form of municipal government consisting of a five-member commission, each member having a particular area of expertise.

November. McKinley again defeats Bryan in a presidential election. Theodore Roosevelt, the Progressive Republican governor of the state of New York, is elected vice president. McKinley will be sworn in for his second term on March 4, 1901.

1901

September 6. McKinley is shot twice by the anarchist Leon Czolgosz during a visit to the Pan-American Exposition in Buffalo, New York.

September 14. McKinley dies of the wounds he suffered on September 6. Theodore Roosevelt becomes the 26th president.

Foreign Policy

1891

In Valparaiso, a crowd kills two American sailors, bringing the nation to the verge of war with Chile.

1893

January. In Hawaii, a revolution is fomented by American sugarcane planters. A treaty of annexation will be submitted to the Senate by President Benjamin Harrison on February 15, but President Cleveland will withdraw it on March 9.

1894

A treaty of commerce is concluded by the United States and Japan.

1895

February. Cubans begin a revolt against the Spanish colonial government. The rebellion is backed by many Americans.

December. After accusing Great Britain of violating the Monroe Doctrine, Cleveland announces that the United States will arbitrate a border dispute between Venezuela and British Guiana. War with Britain appears possible.

1896

In Athens, the United States participates in the first Olympic Games in modern history.

1897

Venezuela and Great Britain agree to submit their dispute over the border of British Guiana to arbitration.

Describing in detail the brutal Spanish repression of the revolt in Cuba, the American press calls for war.

1898

February 9. A letter ridiculing McKinley, written by the Spanish ambassador to Washington, is published.

February 15. The American battleship *Maine* explodes in the harbor of Havana: 260 officers and crewmen are killed. Responsibility for the explosion will never be determined.

April 20. Ignoring concessions offered by Spain, McKinley signs a joint congressional resolution recognizing the independence of Cuba and authorizing the use of the armed forces; a blockade of Cuban ports will be ordered on April 22.

April 24. Spain declares war on the United States.

April 25. The United States formally declares war on Spain. Assistant Secretary of the Navy Theodore Roosevelt will be commissioned a lieutenant colonel in a volunteer cavalry regiment, the "Rough Riders," and fight in Cuba.

May 1. Commodore George Dewey's ships defeat a Spanish squadron in Manila Bay in the Philippines; the city of Manila will be captured on August 13.

June 10. American troops land near Santiago, Cuba.

June 20. Americans capture the island of Guam in the Pacific.

July 1. In the Battle of San Juan Hill in Cuba, Roosevelt leads the Rough Riders to victory.

July 3. A Spanish naval squadron is destroyed in Santiago Bay.

July 7. After lengthy debate, Congress approves the annexation of Hawaii.

July 25. Americans troops occupy Puerto Rico.

July 26. Spain sues for peace.

December 10. The Treaty of Paris ends the Spanish-American War. Spain cedes Puerto Rico, Guam and the Philippines to the United States for $20 million; Spain also recognizes the independence of Cuba.

1899

February. In the Senate, the ratification of the peace treaty with Spain sparks stormy debates between imperialists and anti-imperialists.

March. In the Philippines, an insurrection against American rule begins; led by Emilio Aguinaldo, Filipino rebels are dissatisfied that their country has not been given independence.

May. The United States takes part in the First International Peace Conference at The Hague, in the Netherlands; the conference establishes the Permanent Court of Arbitration.

September. Faced with the ongoing division of China into spheres of influence by the European powers, Secretary of State John Hay informs other countries of the U.S. policy of upholding the principle of the "Open Door" (freedom of trade for all, and preservation of China's territorial integrity).

1899–1901

The Boxer Rebellion, a violent anti-foreign rebellion, occurs in China. The United States reaffirms its Open Door policy and sends troops to participate in an allied force to put down the rebellion.

1901

February. Cuba adopts a constitution modeled on that of the United States.

March. The Platt Amendment becomes law: Cuba cannot sign any treaty with another country without the consent of the United States; this restriction will be embodied in a treaty with the United States in 1903.

The rebel leader Aguinaldo is arrested, effectively ending the revolt in the Philippines.

Economy and Society

1891

March. Eleven Sicilian immigrants are lynched by an anti-Mafia mob in New Orleans.

April. Nebraska establishes the eight-hour workday.

July. Miners go on strike in Briceville, Tennessee. The strike is broken through the use of common criminals under the supervision of the army.

1892

Ellis Island, a reception center for immigrants, is opened in New York harbor.

The General Electric Company is created by the merger of the Edison and Thompson Companies.

July. Strikes take place across the nation. At the Carnegie steelworks in Homestead, Pennsylvania, Pinkerton agents are sent to protect strike-breakers. Violent clashes leave 20 dead.

November. The strike at the Carnegie steelworks ends after the intervention of the state militia. Although the workers did not gain anything, the image of the Carnegie company is tarnished.

1893

February. A financial panic begins, leading to numerous bankruptcies.

June. The stock market crashes. The depression spreads.

Eugene V. Debs founds the American Railway Union, a union of railroad employees.

1894

April. Strikes and riots occur in Pennsylvania and Ohio. An "army" of the unemployed, led by Jacob Coxey, marches on Washington and is brutally suppressed by the police.

May. Workers go on strike in Pullman City, Illinois, protesting against cuts in wages and excessive rents for housing owned by the Pullman company, which builds railway cars.

June. Debs calls all railroad employees out on a solidarity strike to help the Pullman workers; most of the nation's railways are affected.

July. A federal court enjoins the railway workers to end their strike; President Cleveland sends federal troops to Chicago to enforce the injunction.

August. The Pullman strike ends. Pullman yields nothing, but workers win public sympathy.

September. In New York, workers in the clothing industry go on strike against the "sweat shop" system.

Labor Day (the first Monday of September) becomes a national holiday.

December. Debs is sentenced to six months in jail for his role in the railroad strike. He will become a socialist.

1895

The Supreme Court rules that the Sherman Antitrust Act does not apply to intrastate manufacturing combinations; the act loses much of its efficacy.

May. The Sherman Antitrust Act is invoked against the American Railway Union, which is considered an "illegal association."

1896

May. In *Plessy v. Ferguson*, the Supreme Court upholds state laws mandating segregation in schools and public places by approving the principle of "separate but equal" facilities.

August 16. Gold is discovered in the Klondike region of Canada, near Alaska. More than 100,000 people will rush to the area in the following months.

1897

The economic depression that began in 1893 ends.

June. President McKinley signs the Dingley Tariff Act, which imposes the highest tariff in American history.

September. The police fires on striking miners in Pennsylvania. After organizing a successful strike, the miners' union will obtain the eight-hour workday, bimonthly wages and the right of assembly.

1900

The International Ladies' Garment Workers' Union is founded.

IMMIGRANT ARRIVALS, 1821–1940	
1821–1830	143,439
1831–1840	599,125
1841–1850	1,713,251
1851–1860	2,598,214
1861–1870	2,314,824
1871–1880	2,812,191
1881–1890	4,246,613
1891–1900	3,687,546
1901–1910	8,795,386
1911–1920	5,735,811
1921–1930	4,107,209
1931–1940	528,431

1901

Despite the Sherman Antitrust Act, the U.S. Steel Corporation is founded in New Jersey after buying out the Carnegie Steel Company. Capital stock is valued at $1.4 billion.

Technological Progress and Transportation

1891

Edison patents his motion picture camera.

1892

The Duryea brothers build the first American automobile in Springfield, Massachusetts.

1893

Edison's first movie projector and movie studio are built in West Orange, New Jersey.

Henry Ford builds the first internal combustion engine.

The Great Northern transcontinental railroad is completed.

1894

The first hydroelectric plant is built at Niagara Falls, New York.

GEOGRAPHICAL ORIGIN OF IMMIGRANTS, 1851–1920
(in percent, approximate)

	Northern and Western Europe	Central and Eastern Europe
1851–1860	93.6	0.1
1861–1870	87.8	0.5
1871–1880	73.6	4.5
1881–1890	72.0	11.9
1891–1900	44.5	32.8
1901–1910	21.7	44.5
1911–1920	17.4	33.4
	Southern Europe	Other
1851–1860	0.8	5.6
1861–1870	0.9	10.8
1871–1880	2.7	19.2
1881–1890	6.3	9.7
1891–1900	19.1	3.5
1901–1910	26.3	7.5
1911–1920	25.5	23.7

SOURCES: U.S. Bureau of the Census, *Statistical Abstract of the United States, 1982;* Stephan Thernstrom, ed., *Harvard Encyclopedia of American Ethnic Groups* (Cambridge: Belknap Press of Harvard University Press, 1980).

1895

Charles Duryea patents his gasoline-powered automobile.

1896

The first public showing of a movie takes place in New York.

Henry Ford builds the first automobile with a two-cylinder engine.

X-rays are used to treat cancer for the first time.

1900

The yellow fever virus, transmitted by mosquitoes, is discovered (numerous cases of yellow fever occurred among U.S. soldiers in Cuba during the Spanish-American War).

Civilization and Culture

1891

Carnegie Hall opens in New York.

In Chicago, construction of the Masonic Temple, the tallest skyscraper at the time (20 stories), is completed by Daniel Burnham.

Basketball is invented by James Naismith in Springfield, Massachusetts.

1892

The University of Chicago, founded by John D. Rockefeller, opens.

Antonin Dvorak is invited to lead the New York Conservatory. He will compose his New World Symphony in 1893.

1893

The Columbian Exposition opens in Chicago; the exposition is called the "White City" because of the beauty of its neoclassical architecture.

Frederick Jackson Turner's *Significance of the Frontier in American History* and Stephen Crane's realist novel *Maggie, A Girl of the Street* are published.

The Antisaloon League is founded.

1894

Henry Demarest Lloyd's criticism of contemporary society, *Wealth against Commonwealth*, is published.

William Dean Howells's utopian romance inspired by the Columbian Exposition, *A Traveler from Altruria*, is published.

1896

The comic-strip character *The Yellow Kid* lends his name to the sensationalistic "Yellow Journalism" associated primarily with William Randolph Hearst's *New York Journal*.

1898

In New York, Adler and Sullivan build the Bayard Building, with its notable facade.

1900

The United States participates in the Exposition Universelle in Paris.

Theodore Dreiser's *Sister Carrie* is published.

Albert P. Ryder paints *The Workers of the Sea*.

Chapter 13

1901–1914

The Era of Reform

European visitors to the New World around 1900 could see the gigantic buildings of the New York skyline as the manifestation of a "conquering genius to whom nothing seems impossible." Was not this powerful and wealthy America a hope and a model for the modern world?

Indeed, the economic crisis of 1893–1897 seemed almost forgotten. Yet while the country benefited from a widely shared enrichment, problems lingered. More numerous than ever before, immigrants from eastern and southern Europe crowded the industrial centers (13 million arrived from 1900 to 1914). Their languages, cultures and religions made their assimilation into Anglo-Saxon America difficult, notwithstanding the melting-pot image created by a Jewish author, Israel Zangwill, in 1908. In addition to the urban misery of the immigrants, most Southern blacks lived in abject poverty, and the Indians continued to suffer under debilitating conditions on their reservations.

Still, a new spirit of reform was growing. Progressivism, a movement of the educated middle class, sought to correct the abuses revealed by the muckrakers, those writers and journalists who specialized in exposing scandals. Progressive targets included the corruption and inefficiency of local governments, the confiscation of political power by party machines dominated by moneyed interests, the monopolies of the trusts, the destruction of the environment, and urban poverty. The Progressives implemented their reformist ideas first at the municipal level and in the field of social activism. They then began to penetrate the political parties to such an extent that the two greatest presidents of the period, the Republican Theodore Roosevelt and the Democrat Woodrow Wilson, both claimed to belong to their movement. Both men, however, had different approaches to the thorniest contemporary issue, controlling the excesses of laissez-faire capitalism. Roosevelt, recognizing that the concentration of businesses was unavoidable, thought the federal government should regulate the trusts. Wilson, on the other hand, wanted to destroy the trusts in order to return to the American people a "New Freedom" of enterprise. The intelligence and ambitions of both presidents contributed to the prestige of the executive branch, which had been diminished since Lincoln's death. Although Wilson remained president until March 1921, by the end of 1914 Americans had become preoccupied with the war in Europe; the reform movement quickly lost momentum and finally disappeared when the United States entered World War I in 1917.

Political and Institutional Life

1901

September 14. Upon William McKinley's death, Vice President Theodore Roosevelt becomes the 26th president.

1902

June. Oregon adopts several democratic reforms sought by Progressives, including the referendum by popular initiative and the right to recall representatives who have not fulfilled their mandate.

1903

Wisconsin holds the nation's first primary elections for president.

The Department of Commerce and Labor is created; a separate Department of Labor will again be created in 1913.

1904

November 8. Roosevelt is elected president; Charles Fairbanks is elected vice president.

1907

Oklahoma becomes the 46th state of the Union.

1908

November 3. Republican William Howard Taft is elected the 27th president; James Sherman is elected vice president. Taft will assume office on March 4, 1909.

1910

Roosevelt attempts a political comeback by criticizing Taft as being too conservative. He proposes a reform program that he labels "New Nationalism," which would reinforce the authority of the federal government in economic matters.

1911

Republican senator Robert La Follette founds the National Progressive League, which includes Progressive Republicans such as Roosevelt.

1912

New Mexico and Arizona become the 47th and 48th states of the Union.

June. A divided Republican Party nominates Taft as its candidate for the coming presidential election.

July. The Democratic Party nominates Woodrow Wilson, governor of New Jersey and former president of Princeton University, as its candidate for president.

August. Roosevelt decides to run for president as the candidate of the new Progressive ("Bull Moose") Party.

November 5. Benefiting from the divisions among Republicans, Wilson defeats Roosevelt and is elected the 28th president; Thomas Marshall is elected vice president. The socialist candidate, Eugene V. Debs, obtains 1 million popular votes.

1913

February. The 16th Amendment, providing for a federal income tax, is ratified by the states.

March 4. Wilson takes office.

March 15. Wilson holds the first formal presidential press conference.

April. Wilson appears in person to deliver a message to Congress, the first president to do so since John Adams.

May. The 17th Amendment, which provides for the popular election of senators, is adopted; hitherto, senators were chosen by state legislatures.

Foreign Policy

1901

September 1. Vice President Roosevelt declares that the United States must "speak softly and carry a big stick" with regard to Latin America.

November. The Hay-Pauncefote Treaty is signed with Great Britain. Superseding the Clayton-Bulwer Treaty of 1850, the new agreement grants the United States the right to build and fortify a canal across the Isthmus of Panama that will be open to the ships of all countries.

1902

January. In a treaty signed with Columbia, the United States is authorized to purchase a strip of land across the Isthmus of Panama for the construction of a canal. Columbia will refuse to ratify the treaty in August 1903.

July. A civilian government is installed in the Philippines.

1903

November. Following Columbia's refusal to sell the United States land on which to build a canal, the United States assists in a revolution of Panamanians who declare Panama independent of Columbia. On November 18, Panama and the United States sign a treaty giving the latter permanent sovereign rights to a 10-mile-wide Canal Zone in exchange for an initial payment of $10 million and $250,000 per year.

1904

December 6. Roosevelt announces his "Corollary" to the Monroe Doctrine: The United States retains the right to intervene in the affairs of Latin American nations in order to ensure order and security.

1905

Applying the Roosevelt Corollary, the United States seizes the customs houses of the Dominican Republic, which had declared its inability to repay debts to Germany, Great Britain and other nations. The Dominican government grants the United States the right to collect customs revenue to pay the foreign debts and thereby avert a possible intervention by European powers.

September. Roosevelt's mediation at the Portsmouth (New Hampshire) Peace Conference results in a treaty between Russia and Japan, which had been at war with one another since February 1904. The treaty succeeds in maintaining a balance between the ambitions of both powers, and it will earn Roosevelt the Nobel Peace Prize in December 1906.

1906

January. The United States participates in the Algeciras Conference, which settles a dispute between France and Germany over Morocco.

August. The United States intervenes in Cuba to restore order; U.S. troops will remain there until 1909 and the election of a new Cuban president.

November. Roosevelt visits Panama. This is the first official visit of an American president to a foreign country.

1907

March. U.S. Marines are sent to Honduras to protect American interests during a revolution there.

June. The United States participates in the Second Hague Peace Conference.

December. Roosevelt sends a fleet of 16 battleships (the Great White Fleet) on a world tour to demonstrate American naval power.

1907–1908

The Gentlemen's Agreement with Japan sharply curtails Japanese immigration to the United States.

1911

The United States sends troops to the border with Mexico, where it has been backing General Victoriano Huerta since the Revolution of 1910 against President Porfirio Díaz's dictatorship; Díaz is overthrown.

1912

U.S. Marines intervene once again in Cuba.

1914

April. Following the Tampico Incident, in which a U.S. naval shore party was briefly detained in the Mexican city on April 9, American forces shell and occupy Veracruz on April 21.

May–June. The mediation of the ABC Powers (Argentina, Brazil, Chile) succeeds in defusing the Veracruz Incident and avoiding a U.S.-Mexican war. The American troops will withdraw on November 25, but the resulting anti-American sentiment in Mexico will soon be exploited by Germany.

August. The United States proclaims its neutrality in World War I, which has just begun in Europe.

Economy and Society

1901

October. Roosevelt receives the black leader Booker T. Washington at the White House; the meeting causes indignation in the South.

1902

Coal miners led by John Mitchell, president of the United Mine Workers, go on strike for higher wages and an eight-hour workday. Roosevelt's arbitration, which brings an end to the strike, is an important personal success for him.

1903

The Elkins Act requires railroads to publish their rates and abide by them.

The Ford Motor Company is created in Detroit.

In Boston, the National Women's Trade Union League, a movement to defend the rights of women in the workplace, is founded.

1904

The Supreme Court rules that a huge trust, the Northern Securities Company, must be dissolved. Roosevelt earns his reputation as a "trust buster."

A lengthy strike occurs in the textile mills in Massachusetts; at issue are harsh working conditions, especially for children.

1905

June. In Chicago, the Industrial Workers of the World (I.W.W.), a revolutionary trade union, is founded.

1906

April 18–19. In San Francisco, the worst earthquake and fire in American history leave nearly 500 dead and 225,000 homeless.

May. The Hepburn Act permits the Interstate Commerce Commission to regulate railroad rates.

June. The Pure Food and Drug Act empowers the federal government to regulate food products.

September. A racial riot in Atlanta leaves 21 dead (18 are blacks).

October. San Francisco requires Asian children to attend segregated schools. A furious Roosevelt will force the city to rescind the law.

1907

October. A financial panic begins when the Knickerbocker Trust Company of New York fails; a depression will last until 1908.

1908

The General Motors Company is founded.

A law regulating child labor is passed in the District of Columbia.

In *Muller v. Oregon*, the Supreme Court rules that a law limiting the working hours of women is constitutional.

1909

April. The Payne-Aldrich Tariff maintains high import duties.

June. W. E. B. Du Bois founds with white liberals the National Association for the Advancement of Colored People (NAACP), which seeks racial equality through legal means.

September. Women workers in the clothing industry go on strike in New York.

1910

The Mann-Elkins Act increases the powers of the Interstate Commerce Commission.

1911

March 25. In New York, a fire at the Triangle Shirtwaist Company results in the deaths of 146 workers, mostly immigrant women. The fire attracts attention to "sweatshop" working conditions in the garment industry.

May 15. The Supreme Court orders the breakup of the Standard Oil Company and the reorganization of the American Tobacco Company, both of which are found to be in violation of the Sherman Antitrust Act.

1912

The I.W.W. organizes a strike in the textile mills of Lawrence, Massachusetts.

1913

Henry Ford adopts the mass-production assembly line.

October. The Underwood Tariff Act reduces import duties for the first time since the Civil War. The act also establishes an income tax.

December. The Owen-Glass Federal Reserve Act creates a central bank and 12 regional banks of which national banks must become members. The Federal Reserve System thus establishes control over the money supply and credit.

1914

The Federal Trade Commission is created to regulate interstate commerce.

The Clayton Antitrust Act strengthens the Sherman Antitrust Act of 1890. Trade unions no longer constitute a statutory offense under this law.

Science, Technology and Environment

1902

Arthur Little discovers rayon.

The first law on the environment is passed; it creates dams to irrigate arid lands in the West and sets aside 150 million acres for national forests.

1903

The first transpacific cable is installed, linking San Francisco to the Philippines.

The first automobile to cross the United States, a Packard, travels from San Francisco to New York in 52 days.

Wilber and Orville Wright make the first successful powered flight of a heavier-than-air machine at Kitty Hawk, North Carolina.

1904

The first subway opens in New York.

The first diesel engine is introduced at the St. Louis World's Fair.

1905

There are 77,988 automobiles in the United States.

1906

Construction of the Panama Canal begins.

Sixteen national monuments and approximately 50 national parks are created.

1908

The National Conservation Commission is created, with Gifford Pinchot as president.

Henry Ford introduces his "Model T."

1909

Robert Peary reaches the North Pole.

Bakelite is first produced.

1911

Construction of Roosevelt Dam in Arizona is completed.

General Motors equips its cars with a starter.

May 1. Following the sinking of the passenger liner *Titanic* (1,502 dead), the federal government requires steamships to carry sufficient lifeboats for all passengers.

1913

Construction of Keokuk Dam on the Mississippi River is completed.

1914

The Panama Canal is opened to ships.

Civilization and Culture

1901

Frank Norris describes the clashes between farmers and railroad companies in California in *The Octopus.*

Frank Lloyd Wright builds the Ward Willits house in Highland Park, near Chicago.

The McMillan Commission issues its report on the rebuilding and improvement of the federal capital in Washington, D.C.

1902

The Carnegie Institution, a philanthropic foundation supporting higher learning, is established.

In New York, the architect Daniel Burnham completes the Flatiron Building, a skyscraper.

The Child and the Curriculum, by the educator John Dewey, emphasizes problem-solving instead of rote learning.

The first junior college is founded in Illinois.

1903
The Great Train Robbery, the first motion picture to tell a story, is shown in theaters.

Henry James writes about Americans in Paris in *The Ambassadors*.

W. E. B. Du Bois's influential analysis of black life in America, *The Souls of Black Folk*, is published.

McClure's magazine begins publishing Ida Tarbell's investigative articles on the history of the Standard Oil Company.

1904
Lincoln Steffens depicts the corruption of city governments in *The Shame of the Cities*.

Jack London publishes *The Sea Wolf*.

In St. Louis, a World's Fair is held to celebrate the centennial of the Louisiana Purchase.

The American Academy of Arts and Letters is founded.

1905
The first World Series, the crowning event of the annual baseball season, is held.

The Federal Council of Churches of Christ in America, the first major interdenominational organization, is established.

1906
The Jungle, Upton Sinclair's description of the Chicago slaughterhouses, influences legislation on the quality of meat.

The Manhattan Opera House is opened by Oscar Hammerstein.

The Four Million, by the short-story writer O. Henry, is published.

1907
William James's *Pragmatism* is published.

The first volume of photographer Edward S. Curtis's *The North American Indian* is published.

The first "Ziegfeld Follies," featuring showgirls and comedy, appears on a New York stage.

1908
In New York, painters of the Ash-Can School exhibit their realist art.

The Singer Building, at 47 stories the tallest in New York, is completed.

1909
W. C. Handy writes *Memphis Blues*.

Leopold Stokowski is named the conductor of the Cincinnati Orchestra.

In Chicago, Frank Lloyd Wright completes the Robie House, the most famous example of the Prairie Style.

1910
Pennsylvania Station, built by McKim, Mead & White on the model of the thermal baths of Caracalla in Rome, opens in New York.

1911
Frederick W. Taylor's *Principles of Scientific Management* is published.

The novelist Edith Wharton publishes *Ethan Frome*, about life in rural New England.

Ragtime music reaches the peak of its popularity with Irving Berlin's "Alexander's Ragtime Band."

1912
In New York, the Woolworth Building (55 stories), built by Cass Gilbert, dwarfs the Singer Building.

The Autobiography of an Ex-Colored Man, a novel by the black civil rights leader James Weldon Johnson about a light-skinned black who passes himself as a white, is published.

1913
The Armory Show, a major art exhibition in New York, exposes the public to the trends of European modernism and the works of young American artists.

The Rockefeller Foundation is established.

O Pioneers! Willa Cather's novel about the passing of the American frontier, is published.

Robert Frost publishes his first poems.

1914
The New Republic, a liberal weekly journal of opinion, is founded.

The Congo and Other Poems is published by Vachel Lindsay.

Chapter 14   1914–1920

The United States and the First World War

When war broke out in Europe, many Americans had trouble under-standing a conflict so violent and generalized, and seemingly belong-ing to another era. European civilization, it was thought, had moved beyond fighting over borders or nationality issues. A dismayed Wilson offered his mediation to the belligerents but was ignored.

Although the United States proclaimed its neutrality in August 1914, the American people were too heterogeneous to hold a single opinion on the hostilities. Some were resolutely pacifist because of their religious or political beliefs, while others immediately sympathized with the Allies and wanted to help them. Wilson was sometimes accused of belonging to the latter party, despite his professions of neutrality. German-Americans naturally sympathized with Germany, and Irish immigrants were deeply anti-British.

How could the United States force the belligerents to respect its neutral-ity? As early as the beginning of 1915, the British blockade of German ports and Germany's submarine counterattack hurt American trade. Merchant ships and passenger liners were attacked by German submarines, causing numerous civilian casualties. In 1917, the situation worsened to the point where, on February 3, the United States broke diplomatic relations with Germany. In a dramatic speech on April 2, Wilson asked Congress to declare war to save democracy, in the hope of reestablishing international relations on a new basis. Three years later, however, Wilson's crusade ended in failure when the Senate refused to ratify the Treaty of Versailles, fearing that the League of Nations would impinge on U.S. sovereignty and force America to constantly intervene in world affairs.

Americans were deeply disappointed by the revanchist attitude of the Allies at the Paris Peace Conference. Moreover, the Russian Revolution, which had been welcomed at first, was now deeply disturbing to many who feared the influence of Communist and other radical ideologies in the United States. Americans were also worried about the powers that had accrued to the federal government during the war, especially in economic matters. The war had deeply influenced American society and its institutions. The election of 1920 brought a conservative Republican back to the White House, a sure sign that Americans yearned for a return to "normalcy."

Political and Institutional Life

1915

May 15. In *Guinn v. United States*, the Supreme Court rules unconstitutional the "grandfather clause" used by some Southern states to deny blacks the right to vote. Such clauses typically exempted men entitled to vote before 1867 (that is, whites), and their lineal descendants, from having to take literacy tests to obtain voting rights. Blacks, however, were compelled to take such tests in order to vote.

1916

November 7. Wilson is reelected president under the slogan "He Kept Us Out of War." Jeanette Rankin of Montana becomes the first woman elected to Congress (in some western states, women are enfranchised).

1917

March 2. Puerto Rico becomes a territory of the United States, and its inhabitants become American citizens.

April 2. Wilson appears before a special session of Congress and asks for a declaration of war on Germany.

November. The state of New York gives women the right to vote.

1918

November 5. Republicans win a majority in both the Senate and the House.

December. Wilson sails for France to attend the Paris Peace Conference, which will convene in January 1919.

1919

The states ratify the 18th Amendment, which prohibits the manufacture and sale of alcoholic beverages.

March. The Socialist Eugene V. Debs, accused of having publicly protested against the draft, is sentenced to 10 years in jail.

August. The Communist Party of America is founded in Chicago.

September. Wilson tours the United States in an effort to garner public support for the Treaty of Versailles.

October 2. After becoming ill on his speaking tour of the country, Wilson suffers a stroke in Washington, D.C. Partially paralyzed, he will be near death for a week.

November 19. The Senate refuses to ratify the Treaty of Versailles by a vote of 39 yeas and 55 nays.

1920

January. The Red Scare begins. Attorney General A. Mitchell Palmer orders a series of raids, seizing individuals suspected of harboring socialist, Communist, or anarchist sympathies. Many foreigners will be expelled.

March 19. The Senate refuses to ratify the Treaty of Versailles for the second time, by a vote of 49 yeas and 35 nays (short of the needed two-thirds majority).

April. The New York State Assembly expels six of its representatives for belonging to the Socialist Party.

May. In an atmosphere of anti-Communist hysteria, two Italian anarchists, Nicola Sacco and Bartolomeo Vanzetti, are arrested for theft and murder in Braintree, Massachusetts (they will be tried in 1921 and executed in 1927).

August. The 19th Amendment, giving the vote to women, is ratified.

September. In New York, the Morgan Bank is bombed, leaving 38 dead.

Women's Suffrage Before the 19th Amendment, 1920

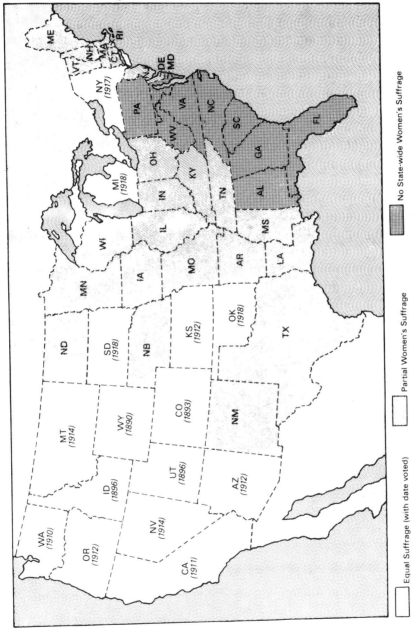

No State-wide Women's Suffrage

Partial Women's Suffrage

Equal Suffrage (with date voted)

November 2. The Republican Warren Harding is elected the 29th president; Calvin Coolidge is elected vice president. Although in jail, Debs, the Socialist Party's candidate, receives nearly 1 million votes.

December 10. Wilson is awarded the Nobel Peace Prize.

Diplomacy and the Road to War

1914

August 4. Wilson proclaims America's neutrality in the European war, advises Americans not to take sides and proposes to the belligerents that he mediate an end to the conflict.

November. Submarine warfare begins in the Atlantic.

1915

January. Wilson sends Colonel Edward House, a close aide, to Europe in an attempt at mediation.

February. German submarines begin attacking neutral vessels. On February 10, Wilson protests and declares that Germany will be held responsible for any loss of human life.

March. Great Britain declares a blockade of all German ports. Wilson protests, recalling the right of neutral countries to free trade.

May 7. The British passenger liner *Lusitania* is sunk by a German submarine off the coast of Ireland: 1,198 passengers and crew die, including 128 Americans. (The American tanker *Gulflight* had been torpedoed but not sunk on May 1, resulting in 3 deaths.)

May 13. William Jennings Bryan, the secretary of state, demands an apology and compensation from Germany for the sinking of the *Lusitania;* on May

28, Germany will reject the U.S. demand, claiming that the *Lusitania* was transporting troops and arms. (Although the liner carried no troops, it did have ammunition in its cargo.)

June 9. Wilson sends a second diplomatic note to Germany, asking that it pledge not to attack neutral vessels. Bryan, a pacifist, refused to sign the note and resigned the previous day.

July. A German spy network is discovered operating in the United States. American public opinion is indignant. Several American ships are sunk.

July 29. Marines land in Haiti, which is proclaimed an American protectorate; the island had been plagued by disorder, and several European nations had claims against it.

August. A conference of Latin American countries meets to discuss the political instability in Mexico.

October. American banks loan $500 million to France and Great Britain.

1916

March 9. The Mexican revolutionary Francisco "Pancho" Villa, who earlier had murdered 18 Americans in Mexico, conducts a cross-border raid on Columbus, New Mexico, killing 24 Americans.

March 15. Wilson sends a punitive expedition led by General John J. Pershing into Mexico in pursuit of Villa's forces.

March 24. Four Americans are injured when a French ship, the *Sussex*, is torpedoed in the English Channel. On April 18, Wilson will threaten to break diplomatic relations with Germany.

May. Marines land at Santo Domingo, in the Dominican Republic, to quell disorder; the Marines will not be withdrawn until 1924.

December. A new effort by Wilson to mediate the war in Europe ends in failure.

1917

January. The Senate ratifies a treaty with Denmark transferring the Virgin Islands to the United States for $25 million; the islands are strategically important for the defense of the Panama Canal.

January 22. In an address to Congress, Wilson calls for a "peace without victory" in the European war and the creation of a league of nations.

January 28. Having failed to capture Pancho Villa, Pershing's expedition is ordered withdrawn from Mexico.

January 31. Germany declares unrestricted submarine war against all shipping, whether neutral or belligerent.

February 3. The United States breaks diplomatic relations with Germany.

February 24. The British give to the United States the text of an intercepted telegram from Alfred Zimmermann, the German foreign minister, in which he encourages Mexico to declare war on the United States in the event that the latter declares war on Germany.

April 6. Congress, meeting in special session, declares war on Germany. Great Britain, France and Russia are America's principal allies.

December 7. The United States declares war on Austria-Hungary.

1918

January 8. In an address to Congress, Wilson unveils his Fourteen Points for peace, including the abolition of secret diplomacy, freedom of the seas, arms reductions and a "general association [league] of nations" to ensure the territorial integrity and political independence of all states.

October 6. Germany sues for peace on the basis of the Fourteen Points.

November 11. An armistice is signed in Compiègne, France.

1919

January–June. The Paris Peace Conference is held at Versailles. The Treaty of Versailles, formally ending the war, is signed on June 28; the treaty includes a covenant creating the League of Nations.

Military Preparations and War Chronology

1915

August. The first training camps for civilian volunteers are established.

1916

June. Wilson signs the Army Reorganization Act, which expands the army to 206,000 men and the National Guard to 425,000 men and includes a budget of $182 million.

1917

February 26. Wilson asks Congress for the authority to arm merchant ships.

April. The United States enters the war on the 6th. Wilson signs the Liberty Loan Act, which authorizes the selling of treasury bonds to the public, on the 24th.

May 18. Wilson signs the Selective Service Act, which authorizes the registration and classification of all men between the ages 21 and 30.

June 15. The Espionage Act provides for up to 20 years imprisonment for those convicted of aiding the enemy, obstructing recruitment or refusing military service.

June 24. The first U.S. troops of the American Expeditionary Force under General Pershing arrive in France.

July. The War Industry Board is created to take charge of war production.

November. The 42nd "Rainbow" Division, representing all the states of the Union, arrives in France.

December 26. Management of the railroads is taken over by the federal government.

1918

April. After a major German offensive, French general Ferdinand Foch, the supreme commander of the Western Front, and Pershing ask Wilson for reinforcements.

May 16. The Sedition Act provides severe penalties for any expression hostile to the war, the flag or the Constitution.

June 4. At Château-Thierry, the American 2nd Division stops the German advance on Paris.

June 6–25. American troops stop the Germans at Belleau Wood.

July. Additional American troops (300,000) arrive in France.

July 15. In the Second Battle of the Marne, near Reims, the American 3rd Division halts a German advance.

July 18–August 6. An Allied offensive on the Aisne and Marne Rivers drives back the German army; the battle turns the tide of the war in favor of the Allies.

August. Ten thousand American soldiers join an Allied intervention in Russia, which has withdrawn from the war following the Bolshevik Revolution. American troops will not leave Russia until April 1920.

September 12–16. Pershing's First Army repels German forces at St.-Mihiel.

September 26–November 11. Nearly 1 million American troops are engaged in the Meuse-Argonne offensive.

November 11. The armistice ending the fighting is signed.

Economy and Society

1915

November. The Ku Klux Klan is reorganized in Atlanta, Georgia.

December. Steelworkers in Youngstown, Ohio, go on strike and are granted the eight-hour day.

1916

Margaret Sanger founds the first birth-control clinic in the nation in Brooklyn, New York.

July. The Federal Farm Loan Act establishes a system of guaranteed loans to farmers.

September. Wilson signs an act establishing the eight-hour workday on interstate railroads, and an act on child labor that the Supreme Court will declare unconstitutional in 1918.

1917

February. An immigration bill imposing a literacy test becomes law over Wilson's veto.

August. Suffragettes are arrested in front of the White House.

1918

October. A great influenza epidemic begins; it will claim hundreds of thousands of American lives.

1919

A wave of strikes will sweep through the mining, transportation and steel industries from September to January of the next year.

European Immigration to the United States, 1820–1920

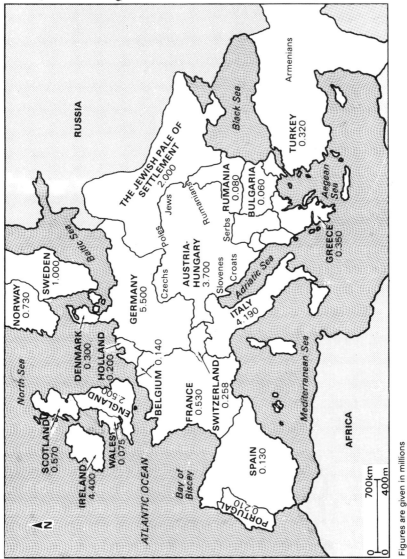

May–June. Bombings and bomb scares occur across the country.

September. A strike by Boston police officers is crushed by Calvin Coolidge, the governor of Massachusetts.

November. In Centralia, Washington, a riot against the radical Industrial Workers of the World union takes place.

1920

The National League of Women Voters is established.

The nation's population is set at 105,711,000; for the first time, the urban population exceeds that of rural areas.

February. Railroads again become private companies (the federal government had taken control of them in December 1917 as a war measure).

June. Merchant marine ships built by the government during the war are sold to the private sector.

An economic depression begins.

Science, Technology and Environment

1915

The Rocky Mountain National Park is created.

Henry Ford builds his millionth car.

Coast-to-coast telephone service is inaugurated with a call from New York to San Francisco.

A radio communications link with Japan is established.

A World's Fair is held in San Francisco.

1916

The National Park Service, an agency of the Department of the Interior, is established.

There are 3.5 million cars in the United States.

1919

The Grand Canyon National Park is created.

1920

The railroad network reaches its maximum length of 253,000 miles.

November 2. The radio station KDKA in Pittsburgh becomes the first to broadcast the results of the presidential election.

Civilization and Culture

1915

Max Weber paints *Chinese Restaurant.*

Spoon River Anthology, by poet Edgar Lee Masters, is published.

D. W. Griffith's movie *Birth of a Nation* presents a complacent picture of the Ku Klux Klan during Reconstruction. Liberals protest.

1916

Carl Sandburg's *Chicago Poems,* and *Sea Garden,* by the poet H. D. (Hilda Doolittle), are published.

The first Norman Rockwell illustration appears in the *Saturday Evening Post.*

The Dixieland Jazz Band begins performing in Chicago, then in New York.

Building regulations in New York are modified: skyscrapers can be of any height as long as their upper floors occupy only a certain proportion of the surface area on the ground (terraced towers).

1917

Hamlin Garland's realist novel about the Midwest, *A Son of the Middle Border,* is published.

The Committee on Public Information is created and made responsible for censorship and propaganda during the war.

The Pulitzer Prizes in journalism and letters are established to encourage "public service, public morals, American literature and . . . education."

1918

The Education of Henry Adams, the author's autobiography, and Booth

Tarkington's novel *The Magnificent Ambersons* are published.

The "Lost Generation" of disillusioned American writers and intellectuals in the post–World War I years rebels against prewar values and turns to cynicism and hedonism. Members include Gertrude Stein, Ernest Hemingway and F. Scott Fitzgerald.

1919

H. L. Mencken's *The American Language*, on the use of English in America, and Sherwood Anderson's novel *Winesburg, Ohio* are published.

The Harlem Renaissance (1919–1930), a flourishing of literary activity in the black district of Harlem in New York, begins. Notable participants include W. E. B. Du Bois, James Weldon Johnson and Langston Hughes.

1920

Sinclair Lewis's *Main Street* and F. Scott Fitzgerald's *This Side of Paradise* are published.

Eugene O'Neill receives the Pulitzer Prize for his play *Beyond the Horizon.*

Musical comedies begin appearing on Broadway.

Chapter 15   1921–1929

Prosperity and Conservatism

The 1920s were a decade full of contradictions. It was the Age of Jazz, the Charleston and the cigarette, of liberated women with short hair and short dresses, of the radio and the automobile, of illuminated billboards, movie stars, boxing champions and the feats of aviators. In contrast, politics, dominated by the Republicans, was largely conservative. The federal government intervened as little as possible in economic life, overlooking the quickening pace of financial concentration as well as the anti-union activities of business leaders. In foreign affairs, the country continued to refuse to bear the burdens of world responsibility. The United States did, however, take part in several international conferences and agreed to accept reduced repayments on its World War I loans to European countries with deeply weakened economies.

The prosperity of the period came only after a postwar depression. Ever taller skyscrapers mushroomed in urban business districts. Industrial products like the automobile and the radio contributed to the unprecedented growth. Although per capita income rose, large disparities in salaries remained, and some sectors of the economy faced hardship. Agriculture had to deal with foreign competition, while the textile and coal industries were weighted down by aging equipment. Despite the appearance of prosperity, 60 percent of Americans had a yearly income below the poverty level of $2,000, according to official statistics.

Nor was modernization a source of joy for everyone. Some Americans were apprehensive of the changes taking place about them and sought refuge in a narrow conservatism mixed with xenophobia and racism. Prohibition, once a Progressive demand, was found to be unenforceable, contributing only to smuggling and gangsterism. To "protect" American "values," a renewed Ku Klux Klan turned once again to violence. An ideological debate between fundamentalist Protestants who took the Bible literally, and modernists who accepted the scientific method, came to a head in 1925 when a Tennessee primary-school teacher was put on trial for having taught the theory of evolution. And for the first time in its history, the United States began closing its door to immigration by dramatically reducing the number of refugees admitted from eastern and southern Europe.

The "Roaring Twenties," full of violent contrasts, ended abruptly with the Crash of Wall Street in 1929.

Political and Institutional Life

1921

March 4. The Republican Warren Harding takes the oath of office as president.

June. The Bureau of the Budget is created within the Treasury Department.

December 23. Harding pardons the socialist Eugene V. Debs, who was sentenced to 10 years in prison in 1919 for violating the Sedition Act.

1922

April and December. Interior Secretary Albert Fall secretly leases Teapot Dome and Elk Hill naval oil reserves. (Fall will be found guilty of corruption in 1929.)

1923

March. The Senate begins an inquiry into alleged corruption in the Veterans' Bureau. A close relation of Harding commits suicide.

May. The state of New York refuses to enforce prohibition.

August 2. Harding, surrounded by rumors of scandal in his administration, dies of apoplexy in San Francisco.

August 3. Vice President Calvin Coolidge becomes the 30th president.

September. The governor of Kansas establishes martial law to put an end to the terrorism of the Ku Klux Klan.

October. The Teapot Dome scandal is revealed after a lengthy inquiry. Members of the Harding cabinet received kickbacks in exchange for leasing a federally owned Wyoming oil field, which was supposed to be set aside for the navy, to a private oil company.

1924

June. Several members of the Harding administration are found guilty of corruption.

November 4. Coolidge is elected president, defeating the Democratic candidate John Davis and the Progressive candidate Robert La Follette. Charles Dawes is elected vice president.

Two women are elected governor: Miriam Ferguson in Texas and Nellie Ross in Wyoming.

1925

August. The Ku Klux Klan stages a demonstration in Washington.

1926

The Tenure of Office Act (1867) is declared unconstitutional: the Supreme Court rules that the president has the right to dismiss the members of his cabinet without the consent of the Senate.

1927

The anarchists Sacco and Vanzetti, convicted of murder in 1921, are executed.

1928

November 6. The Republican Herbert Hoover is elected the 31st president in a landslide victory over the Democrat Alfred E. Smith, a Catholic and antiprohibitionist. Charles Curtis is elected vice president.

1929

March 4. Hoover takes office.

Foreign Policy

1921

August. Separate peace treaties are signed with Germany and the countries formed from the defunct Austro-Hungarian empire.

November. An international conference on disarmament convenes in Washington. Agreements are reached with Great Britain, Italy, France and Japan on limiting major warships and on the prerogatives of the various powers in the Pacific (the United States agrees not to further fortify the Philippines and Guam, and Britain agrees not to build additional fortifications in Hong Kong). The agreements will be signed on February 6, 1922.

1922

February. Congress establishes the Commission for the Repayment of War Debts.

December. The Second Central American Conference is held in Washington.

1924

A treaty with the Dominican Republic leads to the withdrawal of U.S. troops, which were sent there in 1916.

September. The Dawes Plan for the payment of German war reparations to the European Allies is adopted.

1926

April. France and the United States sign an agreement cancelling 60 percent of the former's war debt.

May. The U.S. Marines are sent to Nicaragua to safeguard American interests during a revolt there.

1928

January. Coolidge chairs a Pan-American Conference in Havana. Latin American delegates condemn American intervention in the internal affairs of other countries.

August 27. In Paris, the United States and 14 other countries sign the Kellogg-Briand Pact outlawing war.

1929

January. The Senate ratifies the Kellogg-Briand Pact. Frank Kellogg, the secretary of state, will receive the Nobel Peace Prize for his work in drafting the pact.

June. The Young Plan reduces German war reparations.

October. British prime minister Ramsay MacDonald visits Washington to discuss an agreement establishing naval parity between the two countries.

Economy and Society

1921

January. Having founded a "bloc" of representatives in Congress, farmers demand that the federal government extend the War Finance Corporation, which provided assistance during the war.

May. Higher tariffs are imposed on agricultural imports.

The first immigration quota law is enacted. To control the flow of immigrants, the number of annual entries from each country is limited to 3 percent of its nationals living in the United States in 1910; an absolute ceiling of 375,000 admissions per year is imposed.

July. A serious economic crisis begins, leading to numerous bankruptcies, wage cuts and unemployment.

September. A national conference on unemployment is chaired by Secretary of Commerce Herbert Hoover.

1922

The economy recovers, ushering in the "Era of Prosperity."

1923

Under pressure from President Harding, the U.S. Steel Company institutes the eight-hour workday.

1924

A second immigration quota law limits the annual entries from each country to 2 percent of the number of its nationals living in the United States as of 1890. The law limits primarily immigration from eastern and southern Europe; neither Canadians nor Mexicans are affected, but Japanese immigration is barred.

Following the death of Samuel Gompers, William Green becomes president of the American Federation of Labor.

1925

A real estate boom begins in Florida; it will end in 1926.

July 10–21. The "Scopes Monkey Trial": John Scopes is put on trial in Dayton, Tennessee, for teaching the theory of evolution, which the state had outlawed. Defended by attorney Clarence Darrow, Scopes is convicted and fined $100.

1926

The income tax is reduced.

Ford Motor Company adopts the 40-hour workweek.

1927

Coolidge vetoes the McNary-Haugen Bill, which is aimed at helping farmers through the purchase of their surplus production.

1929

February 14. In the St. Valentine's Day Massacre in Chicago, six gangsters are murdered by a rival gang. Al Capone is implicated.

June. The Federal Farm Board is created to grant farmers loans and purchase their surpluses.

October 29. The stock market crashes on "Black Tuesday," ushering in the Great Depression.

Science, Technology and Transportation

1922

A baseball game is broadcast on radio for the first time.

The Technicolor process for cinematography is invented.

1923

December 6. Calvin Coolidge makes the first presidential speech broadcasted on radio.

1924

Ford announces the production of its 10-millionth car.

The German dirigible Z.R.3 arrives in New Jersey.

1926

May 9. Admiral Richard Byrd and Floyd Bennet make the first airplane flight over the North Pole.

TYPICAL HOUSEHOLD EXPENSES, 1900 AND 1928			
1900		**1928**	
Two bicycles	$ 70	Car	$ 700
Wringer and washboard	5	Radio	75
Brushes and brooms	5	Phonograph	50
Mechanical sewing machine	25	Vacuum cleaner	50
		Washing machine	150
		Electric sewing machine	60
		Other electrical appliance	25
		Telephone service	25
Total	$105		$1135

SOURCE: Paul A. Carter, *Another Part of the Twenties* (Columbia University Press, 1977).

1927

The Federal Radio Commission is created to regulate the growing number of radio stations.

The first television broadcast is made in New York.

Two Harvard physicians perfect the "iron lung" for artificial respiration.

In New York, the Holland Tunnel, the first road tunnel under the Hudson River, opens.

May 20–21. Charles Lindbergh completes the first nonstop airplane flight across the Atlantic, from New York to Paris, in 33.5 hours in the *Spirit of St. Louis.* He receives a hero's welcome.

1928

Amelia Earhart becomes the first woman to fly an airplane across the Atlantic.

Richard Byrd explores the South Pole.

Candidates in the presidential election use radio for the first time.

In New York's Times Square, the first animated illuminated billboard appears.

Civilization and Culture

1921

Edith Wharton receives the Pulitzer Prize for *The Age of Innocence.*

James Joyce's *Ulysses,* published in Paris, is banned in the United States.

Films: *The Playhouse,* featuring silent-film comedian Buster Keaton; *The Sheik* with matinee idol Rudolph Valentino.

1922

Louis Armstrong joins King Oliver's jazz orchestra in Chicago.

An international architectural competition is held to determine who will build the offices of the *Chicago Tribune.* The winning design is a tower in the neogothic style.

Sinclair Lewis's novel *Babbitt* describes the life of a businessman from small-town America.

T. S. Eliot's widely influential poem *The Waste Land* is published, as is Edward Arlington Robinson's *Collected Poems.*

The Lincoln Memorial is dedicated in Washington.

1923

The groundbreaking modern dancer Isadora Duncan makes her controversial tour.

Time, the first news magazine, begins publication.

The Harp Weaver and Other Poems, by Edna St. Vincent Millay, and *Tamar and Other Poems*, by Robinson Jeffers, are published.

Georgia O'Keefe paints *Dark Corn*.

Maxwell Anderson's drama *What Price Glory?* is performed.

1924

The first performance of *Rhapsody in Blue* takes place in New York; composer George Gershwin is at the piano.

1925

Theodore Dreiser publishes *An American Tragedy*. John Dos Passos publishes *Manhattan Transfer*. F. Scott Fitzgerald's *The Great Gatsby* is a success. The poet Ezra Pound publishes *A Draft of XVI Contos*.

The New Yorker, a cultural magazine, begins publication.

Aaron Copland completes *Symphony for Organ and Orchestra*.

Charlie Chaplin stars in *The Gold Rush*.

Edward Hopper paints "House by the Railroad."

The photographer Man Ray: "Clock Wheels."

1926

Hemingway's novel *The Sun Also Rises* is published. Langston Hughes's collection of poems *The Weary Blues* appears.

Dorothy Parker, famous in New York literary circles for her biting wit, publishes *Enough Rope*, a collection of wry, polished poems.

The Love Nest, by short-story writer Ring Lardner.

1927

Al Jolson appears in the first talking picture (movie with sound), *The Jazz Singer*; Cecil B. DeMille's silent film *Ben Hur*.

Gutzon Borglum begins sculpting the faces of four presidents (Washington, Jefferson, Lincoln and Roosevelt) on Mount Rushmore, South Dakota.

The Academy of Motion Picture Arts and Sciences, which presents the annual Oscar awards, is founded.

The "Grand Ole Opry," a country music radio show, begins broadcasting from Nashville, Tennessee.

Charles A. and Mary R. Beard publish *The Rise of American Civilization*.

Thornton Wilder's novel *The Bridge of San Luis Rey* is published.

1928

The Ash-Can School of modernist and realist painting reaches its peak of popularity; John Sloane's work is representative.

Walt Disney's "Steamboat Willie" is his first cartoon featuring the character of Mickey Mouse.

George Gershwin's *An American in Paris*.

Ernest Hemingway publishes *A Farewell to Arms*.

Good Morning, America, by the poet Carl Sandburg.

1929

The sociologists Robert and Helen Lynd publish *Middletown*, study of American society.

The Museum of Modern Art is founded in New York.

Thomas Wolfe's novel *Look Homeward, Angel*.

Chapter 16   1929–1932

The Great Depression

A major landmark in American history, the Great Depression began with the stock market crash of October 1929 and did not end until December 1941, when the United States entered World War II.

In 1929, President Herbert Hoover was still predicting a "new era" for the nation. Consequently, the stock market crash and the resulting depression caught Americans by surprise. Nobody seemed to believe a depression would last very long, since America had always quickly recovered from such economic crises in the past. Signs of economic malaise thus went largely unnoticed. The stock market continued an unbelievable climb until the beginning of October, and many Americans found speculation in stock a quick and easy road to wealth. Nor were banks and businesses immune to the lure of the stock market: Profits were large, the value of stocks continued to rise, and stocks could always be sold at the first sign of a faltering market.

When on October 24 and again on October 29, millions of certificates of stock were suddenly thrown into the market, many found no buyers. Brokers were ruined, and banks were forced to close their doors. The crisis spread quickly. Unable to sell their products, businesses cut hours and wages and fired employees. Within a few months the crisis had enveloped the entire country. The number of unemployed was alarming. Farmers, already facing economic problems before the crisis began, now found themselves unable to pay their debts, and they were soon evicted from their land. In the cities, the hardest hit were unskilled workers, women and blacks. Trade unions rapidly lost their members. As poverty spread, charitable organizations were overwhelmed with the task of feeding the hungry. Makeshift shelters appeared overnight in "Hoovertowns," and the homeless fought the cold by wrapping themselves in old newspapers, or "Hoover blankets."

In 1932, with the depression seemingly at its nadir, the American people voted Hoover out of office. Many held the president personally responsible for their suffering because he was unable to solve the crisis and seemed not to grasp its seriousness. The presidential election of 1932 pitted two styles or philosophies of governance against one another. Hoover, a competent man lacking in communication skills, remained committed to liberalism and resisted pushing the federal government further down the road of economic interventionism. Franklin D. Roosevelt, the Democratic candidate, was full of energy and promised government assistance, but his economic recovery program was vague. Although Americans chose the vigorous, positive Roosevelt, the election by itself did not solve the crisis, which worsened during the winter of 1932–1933.

Political and Institutional Life

1929
December 2. In a message to Congress, Hoover states that confidence in the economy has been restored and that business will soon pick up.

1930
July. The Veterans' Administration is created to coordinate assistance to war veterans.

November. In the congressional elections, the Democrats win a majority in the House of Representatives, and the Republicans lose eight seats from their majority in the Senate.

1931
January. The report of the Wickersham Commission on Prohibition recommends a revision to, rather than a repeal of, the 18th Amendment.

February. Congress debates the payment of bonuses to war veterans before their due date.

1932
March. Congress approves the 20th Amendment, which sets January 20 rather than March 4 as the date when the president will take office; the amendment is sent to the states for ratification.

July. The Democratic Party's convention is held in Chicago. Franklin D. Roosevelt, nominated for president, flies into Chicago and in his acceptance speech proposes a "New Deal" for America.

November 8. Roosevelt is elected the 32nd president in a landslide; John Nance Garner is elected vice president. The Democrats win control of both houses of Congress.

Foreign Policy

1929
December. Henry Stimson, the secretary of state, asks China and the Soviet Union to settle their dispute over Manchuria through negotiation rather than war.

1930
January–April. An international naval conference is held in London. The United States, Great Britain and Japan agree on naval arms limitations; France and Italy refuse to adhere to all provisions of the agreement.

1931
June 20. Hoover proposes a moratorium on both Allied war debts and German reparations, in order to stabilize the international financial situation.

October. Following Japan's invasion of Manchuria, the League of Nations invites the United States to send a delegation to discuss the violation of the Kellogg-Briand Pact.

1932
January. Stimson warns Japan that the United States will not recognize its annexation of Manchuria.

February. The United States sends a delegation to the World Disarmament Conference in Geneva, which will end in failure in 1934. Hoover proposes the abolition of offensive weapons and a one-third reduction of land armaments.

June. At the Lausanne Conference, European nations decide to cancel virtually all of Germany's war reparations in an effort to persuade the United States to forgive its Allies' war debts; the Hoover administration will refuse to do so.

Economy and Society

1929

October 24. The collapse of the stock market begins. Nearly 13 million shares are sold, and stock prices plummet, on Wall Street's "Black Thursday." Several financiers step in and try to shore up stock prices.

October 29. "Black Tuesday": 16 million shares are sold on the most disastrous day in the history of the stock market.

November 13. Losses since the beginning of the stock market crisis are estimated at $30 billion; many speculators are ruined, and a few commit suicide.

November 21. Meeting with industry leaders and representatives of labor unions at the White House, Hoover asks that they not make the economic crisis worse by layoffs or strikes.

1930

January. Four million are unemployed. Hoover asks Congress to finance a public works program.

March. Congress approves a law on public works and budgets $230 million for its implementation.

April. Congress approves a credit of $300 million to permit the states to build roads.

June. The Smoot-Hawley Tariff raises import duties; some economists protest, considering it a threat to international trade.

September. The immigration of foreign workers is banned.

October. Hoover appoints a committee to help the unemployed; it is charged with coordinating all state and municipal programs.

December. Congress approves $116 million in new credits for public works.

1931

January. Hoover's committee on the unemployed reports that nearly 5 million are out of work. The crisis worsens.

March. Hoover vetoes a congressional resolution that would have privatized a government hydroelectric plant at Muscle Shoals, Alabama.

In Scottsboro, Alabama, nine young blacks are arrested, charged with the rape of a white woman, and found guilty. The convictions will be overturned by the Supreme Court in 1935.

July. Farmers riot in Iowa and Kansas.

August. Miners go on strike over wage cuts in Harlan County, Kentucky.

September–October. A new series of bank failures occurs after Great Britain gives up the gold standard; many fear that the United States will do likewise.

October. The gangster Al Capone is arrested and sentenced to 11 years in jail for tax evasion.

December. The Hunger March takes place in Washington.

1932

January. Hoover signs into law a bill creating the Reconstruction Finance

Corporation, a federal organ that will make emergency loans to banks, savings and loans, and insurance companies in order to stimulate industrial investment and create jobs. The RFC will not have as great an impact as was hoped.

February. Under the Glass-Steagall Act, the Federal Reserve is allowed to relax its credit requirements for banks and put some gold into circulation.

March. The Norris-La Guardia Act prohibits federal injunctions against strikers under certain circumstances.

Charles Lindbergh's infant son is kidnapped in New Jersey; he will be found dead in May after a ransom of $50,000 had been paid.

May. Thousands of World War I veterans begin arriving in Washington to demand the payment in cash of their bonus certificates. The Senate in June will reject the cash payment of the bonuses. The "bonus army" veterans (17,000) will camp out in the city; many will leave after the government offers to pay their way home, but approximately 2,000 will remain with their families to pressure Congress.

July. Following a vain attempt by the Washington police to evict the bonus army veterans (four deaths), Hoover calls on General Douglas MacArthur to employ the U.S. Army to expel them forcibly. The whole affair is disastrous for Hoover's image.

Hoover approves an increase in funding for the Reconstruction Finance Corporation.

Congress passes the Federal Home Loan Bank Act, which is aimed at reviving the construction industry.

August. Milk farmers go on strike in the Midwest.

December. Thirteen million are unemployed.

Science and Technology

1930

In New Jersey, Thomas Edison operates the first electric train.

The Coolidge Dam is dedicated in Arizona.

The Adler Planetarium opens in Chicago.

The Nobel Prize in medicine is awarded for the first time to an Ameri-

DETERIORATION OF THE ECONOMY, 1929–1932				
Measure	1929	1930	1931	1932
GNP (millions of $)	104.0	91.0	76.0	59.0
Unemployment (millions)	1.6	4.3	8.0	12.1
Investment (billions of $)	16.2	10.3	5.5	0.9
Index of industrial production	100.0	83.0	67.0	52.0
Agricultural income (billions of $)	11.3	9.1	6.4	4.8

SOURCE: André Kaspi, *Les Américains* (Paris: Le Seuil, 1986), vol. 1.

can, Karl Landstein, who discovered the blood groups.

1931

Wiley Post and Harold Gatty make the first airplane flight around the world (8 days, 15 hours and 51 minutes).

In New York, the George Washington Bridge spanning the Hudson River is completed; the Empire State Building, the tallest in the world, opens.

Harold Urey, a researcher at Columbia University, discovers heavy water, an indispensable element in atomic fission.

The Nation of Islam, better known as the Black Muslims, is founded. The organization preaches black supremacy and separation.

1932

Neutrons are discovered by James Chadwick.

Vitamin C is discovered.

Civilization and Culture

1930

William Faulkner publishes *As I Lay Dying*.

Dashiell Hammett's novel *The Maltese Falcon*, and *The Bridge*, by the poet Hart Crane, are published.

Sinclair Lewis becomes the first American to receive the Nobel Prize for literature with *Babbit*.

Grant Wood paints *American Gothic*.

CBS makes the first radio broadcast of a concert; it is given by the New York Philharmonic, with Arturo Toscanini conducting.

1931

Pearl Buck's novel *The Good Earth* wins a Pulitzer Prize.

1932

Moral Man and Immoral Society, by theologian Reinhold Niebuhr, is published, as is the poet Archibald MacLeish's *Conquistador*.

Franklin D. Roosevelt and the New Deal, Act I

With the election of the governor of New York Franklin D. Roosevelt as president, 12 years of Republican domination in the White House came to an end. Roosevelt won the 1932 election by a large margin, polling 57 percent of the electorate, or 22.8 million votes, against 15.8 million for Herbert Hoover (in the electoral college, Roosevelt received 472 votes to his opponent's 59). Faced with the worst economic crisis in its history, America wanted change, but it also wanted traditional solutions. Indeed, voters cast only 884,000 ballots for the Socialist Norman Thomas, and 103,000 for the Communist William Foster. During his electoral campaign, Roosevelt promised "a new deal for the American people."

By 1933, states and municipalities were running out of money, and the time for individual charity had passed. Considering the vast dimensions of the crisis, only the federal government had enough resources to intervene efficiently. Roosevelt knew he had to act quickly. Within days of taking office, he asked for and received broad executive powers and took an unprecedented series of measures to revive the economy, create jobs and help the neediest.

The New Deal was not a coherent program. Rather, it was a set of ad hoc and pragmatic responses intended to address the most urgent problems, correct the most serious deficiencies and inject some energy into a distressed economy. On the international scene, the United States developed a "good neighbor" policy with respect to the other American nations, especially those in Latin America. The London Economic Conference was a failure partly because of disagreement over monetary policy: the United States wanted to revive its international trade by allowing the value of the dollar to float, whereas its European partners wanted to give priority to stabilizing the exchange rates of their currencies.

Political and Institutional Life

1933

February 6. The 20th Amendment to the Constitution is ratified by the states.

Beginning in 1937, the president-elect will take office on January 20th, and if he should die before taking office, the vice president-elect will become president.

February 15. Giusseppe Zangara attempts to assassinate the president-elect in Miami. Roosevelt is uninjured, but the mayor of Chicago is killed, and Zangara will be executed on March 20.

March 4. Roosevelt takes office.

March 9. The 73rd Congress convenes and passes the Emergency Banking Relief Act.

March 12. Roosevelt broadcasts his first "fireside chat," which is devoted to the economy.

December 5. The 21st Amendment to the Constitution, repealing the 18th Amendment and bringing an end to Prohibition, is declared ratified.

Foreign Policy

1933

June 12–July 27. The London Economic Conference meets; the participating nations fail to agree on stabilizing the value of their currencies.

October. At the Rio de Janeiro Conference of American States, the United States signs a nonaggression treaty that will be ratified by the Senate on June 15, 1934.

November 7. Maxim Litvinov, the Russian commissar of foreign affairs, meets with Roosevelt at the White House to prepare for the establishment of diplomatic relations between the United States and the Soviet Union (relations will be established on November 16).

December. The Seventh Pan-American Conference meets in Montevideo, Uruguay. The United States signs a treaty proclaiming that "No state has the right to intervene in the internal or external affairs of another."

Economy and Society

1933

January 1. Fifteen million Americans, or 25 percent of the working-age population, is unemployed. The marriage rate is 40 percent below that in the 1920s. Life expectancy is 59 years, 10 more than in 1900.

March 5. Roosevelt orders a "bank holiday": banks will close March 6–9.

March 20. An economy act cuts the wages of federal employees and the pensions of veterans, and reorganizes the federal administration.

March 31. Congress creates the Civilian Conservation Corps (CCC) to relieve unemployment among young jobless males.

April 19. The dollar is taken off the gold standard, and its value overseas begins to fall immediately.

May 12. The Federal Emergency Relief Act creates an administration for distributing assistance to the states in order to help the neediest (the initial budget is $500 million).

May 13. The Agricultural Adjustment Act creates the Agricultural Adjustment Administration, charged with helping farmers curtail their surplus production.

Mid-May. The gold value of the dollar is 85 cents on the international currency market.

May 18. Federal legislation establishes the Tennessee Valley Authority, which will construct dams and power stations to develop the region.

May 27. The Federal Securities Act regulates stock exchanges. Any issue of

ECONOMIC INDICATORS, 1933

	Industrial Output[a]	Employment[a]	Wages[a]	Wholesale Prices[b]
March	56	58.8	37.1	60.2
April	65	59.9	38.8	60.4
May	77	62.6	42.7	62.7
June	93	66.9	47.2	65.0
July	101	71.5	50.8	68.9
August	91	76.4	56.8	69.5
September	83	80.0	59.1	70.8
October	65	79.6	59.4	71.2

SOURCE: Arthur S. Link and William B. Catton, *American Epoch*, Vol. 1, *1900–1945*, 5th ed. (New York: Alfred A. Knopf, 1980).
[a]Monthly average for 1923–1925 = 100.
[b]Average for 1926 = 100.

shares or bonds must be registered with the Federal Trade Commission.

June 6. The National Employment System Act creates a national employment administration that will cooperate with the states.

June 13. The Home Owners Refinancing Act creates the Home Owners Loan Corporation (HOLC), which will refinance mortgage debts.

June 16. After 100 days of debate, the 73rd Congress adopts a series of laws:

The National Industrial Recovery Act (NIRA) creates the Public Works Administration (PWA) and the National Recovery Administration (NRA), two essential components of the New Deal program to boost the economy.

The Farm Credit Act facilitates low-interest loans to farmers.

A banking act establishes the Federal Bank Deposit Insurance Corporation (FDIC), a federal insurance fund for bank deposits under $5000.

June 21. The American Federation of Labor (AFL) announces that hirings have increased: 1.5 million of its members have found new jobs.

August 5. The National Labor Board, part of the NRA, is established. Led by Senator Robert F. Wagner, the board is responsible for protecting union rights and deciding disputes between unions and employers.

September. At the start of the new school year, 2,000 schools and several universities remain closed, 200,000 teachers are unemployed and approximately 2.3 million children do not attend school.

October 20. The American Federation of Labor launches a boycott of German-made goods to protest against the policy of the new Nazi regime toward trade unions.

The five-day workweek becomes official.

October 25. Roosevelt permits gold to be purchased at $31.36 an ounce instead of the previous price of $29.80; the dollar is devalued.

November 8. The Civil Works Administration (CWA) is created to fund employment on public works projects.

Headed by Harry Hopkins, and with an initial budget of $400 million, the CWA has as its primary aim the creation of 4 million new jobs.

Science and Technology

1933

Edwin Armstrong develops the frequency modulation (FM) radio. Philo T. Farnsworth perfects a television receiver.

Thomas Hunt Morgan discovers the role of chromosomes in heredity. He receives the Nobel Prize for physiology and medicine.

July 23. The aviator Wiley Post lands in New York after completing the first solo flight around the world, in 7 days and 19 hours. His average speed was 125 miles per hour, and he stopped 10 times to refuel.

National Industrial Recovery Act (NIRA)

This law was one of the cornerstones of the early New Deal. Passed on June 16, 1933, it allocated funds to establish two government programs, the National Recovery Administration (NRA) and the Public Works Administration (PWA).

The NRA sought to stimulate commerce by encouraging the collaboration of government, business and labor. Employers in various industries met in working groups that, with the participation of government, created regulatory codes dealing with fair competition. In addition to setting profit margins, a minimum wage and the length of the workday, participants pledged to allow trade unions to function in their industries. Although membership in these groups was not compulsory, participants were permitted to display an emblem—a blue eagle—which permitted the public to identify NRA members. Within a few months, the most important firms had joined the NRA, which also quickly won the support of trade unions: more than 500 businesses had adopted its codes, and approximately 2.5 million workers were enjoying improved working conditions. But just as quickly, the bureaucracy of the NRA expanded to the point of paralysis. Moreover, the codes turned out to be too complex to enforce quickly and easily, and they too often favored big business. Trade unions were soon disappointed: the minimum wage was set too low, and the codes glossed over the issue of relations between employers and employees, allowing the former to organize in-house unions under their control. By the end of 1933, the program was already under intense criticism, and in May 1935 the Supreme Court declared the NRA unconstitutional.

The PWA, headed by Secretary of the Interior Harold Ickes, directed public works programs. Major projects overseen by the organization included the Grand Coulee Dam in the state of Washington, the Triborough Bridge in New York City, and the building of public schools. The success of the PWA was real but limited, in that it failed to put to work as many unemployed as had been hoped.

Civilian Conservation Corps (CCC)

Conceived by Roosevelt, the CCC was established by federal legislation passed on March 31, 1933. The CCC had two aims: to provide employment and to protect and maintain natural resources. Work camps for some 300,000 young people between the ages of 18 and 25 were built in wilderness areas. In addition to being paid $30 a month, workers were housed, fed and dressed, and received free medical care. As volunteers, they could elect to serve six months to two years. By the time the program was terminated in 1942, 2.5 million young adults had participated in projects ranging from reforestation, clearing land and controlling soil erosion to fighting fires and floods and building roads, hiking trails, national parks and camp sites.

October 17. Fleeing ahead of the wave of anti-Semitism engulfing Hitler's Germany, Albert Einstein and his wife take refuge in the United States.

Civilization and Culture

1933

Erskine Caldwell publishes *God's Little Acre.*

The leading film comedienne Mae West stars in *I'm No Angel.*

Fred Astaire and Ginger Rogers first appear together in the film *Flying Down to Rio.*

Gertrude Stein publishes her autobiography *The Autobiography of Alice B. Toklas,* which is written as if it were by her secretary and companion, Alice B. Toklas.

Calderberry Bush, an early mobile (moving sculpture) by Alexander Calder.

December 6. Judge John Woolsey lifts the ban on James Joyce's *Ulysses.*

The New Deal, Act II

In 1933, the New Deal consisted of emergency measures aimed at shoring up the nation's economy. The next phase, which began in early 1934, would be characterized by greater attention to social justice.

The measures taken in 1933 had already begun producing results. In 1934, there were 4 million more jobs than in the preceding year, and fewer business failures. The purchasing power of industrial workers increased by 25 percent, and the prices of agricultural products were notably higher. The year 1935 was marked by trade union battles, and the New Deal came under attack from both the right and the left. On May 27, 1935, "Black Monday," the Supreme Court declared the National Industrial Recovery Act of 1933 unconstitutional, providing one more argument for the right, which accused the New Deal of being un-American. Still, the passage of the Social Security Act marked an important milestone, as the federal government for the first time assumed major social responsibilities toward workers and needy individuals. The year 1936 ended with Roosevelt's triumph in the presidential election: he carried every state except Maine and Vermont over his Republican rival, Alfred Landon. Roosevelt polled 27.7 million popular votes, 5 million more than he received in 1932, and garnered an overwhelming 523 out of a possible 531 votes in the electoral college.

Overseas, the situation in Europe grew more worrisome. But despite the fears caused by the rise of nazism and fascism, the United States remained firmly isolationist. This position was strengthened in 1934 when a Senate committee led by Gerald Nye began a two-year inquiry into the causes of America's entry into World War I. The committee's report, which concluded that inadequate safeguards of U.S. neutrality had allowed the nation to be drawn into the conflict, helped bring passage of strict neutrality laws in the mid- and late 1930s. Meanwhile, in the Far East, Japanese expansionism sparked a conflict that would continue to spread after Japan left the League of Nations in 1936.

Political and Institutional Life

1935
May 27. The Supreme Court rules unconstitutional the National Industrial

Recovery Act of 1933 (including the Public Works Administration and the National Recovery Administration). This marks the beginning of Roosevelt's conflict with the Supreme Court.

1936

November 3. Roosevelt is reelected president, defeating the Republican Alfred Landon; John Garner is reelected vice president.

Foreign Policy

1934

March 31. Roosevelt signs the Tydings-McDuffie Act, which provides for the independence of the Philippines after a 10-year transition period.

May 29. A treaty with Cuba relieves the island nation of the restrictions on its sovereignty imposed by the Platt Amendment of 1901.

June 12. The Reciprocal Trade Agreements Act allows the president to negotiate international trade agreements without the approval of the Senate.

December 29. Japan announces that it will no longer be bound by the Washington Naval Treaty of 1922 and the London Naval Treaty of 1930 as of December 1936.

1935

August 31. The Neutrality Act bans the shipment of ammunition or arms to a country in a state of war and warns Americans not to travel on ships belonging to a belligerent. Congress also approves an arms embargo that will remain in force until March 1, 1936.

October 5. Roosevelt proclaims that Italy and Ethiopia are in a state of war.

December. The second London Naval Conference convenes. The conference opposes Japan's bid to develop a navy equal to that of Great Britain or the United States. Japan walks out of the conference.

1936

February 29. The second Neutrality Act extends the first Neutrality Act to May 1, 1937, and adds to it a ban on loans or credits to belligerents.

March 25. The second London Naval Conference ends with a treaty between the United States, Great Britain and France limiting their own naval strength.

August 7. The United States declares that it will not invervene in the Spanish Civil War.

Economy and Society

1934

January 30. The Gold Reserve Act grants the president the power to set the value of the dollar with respect to gold. The gold heretofore held by the federal reserve banks will be transferred to the Treasury. Henceforth, the federal government will control the value of the dollar.

January 31. Roosevelt sets the value of the dollar at 59.06 cents and the value of gold at $35 an ounce.

The Farm Mortgage Refinancing Act creates a government agency to extend low-interest loans to farmers unable to repay their bank loans.

February 2. Roosevelt creates the Import-Export Bank, which will encourage international trade.

February 15. The Civil Works Emergency Relief Act authorizes $950 million for emergency relief and public works. It allocates funds to new public works programs and for projects managed by the Federal Emergency Relief Administration.

February 23. The Crop Loan Act authorizes loans for crop planting and harvesting.

March 15. To demonstrate his confidence in the economy, Henry Ford raises the minimum wage to $5 a day for 47,000 of his 70,000 employees.

April 7. The Jones-Connally Act on farmers' relief expands the list of agricultural products subject to control by the Agricultural Adjustment Administration.

April 28. The Home Owners Loan Act complements the Home Owners Refinancing Act of 1933. The law is aimed at reviving the home building industry.

May 10–11. Dust storms strike the states of Texas, Oklahoma, Arkansas, Kansas and Colorado, expanding the "dust bowl" of poor farmland. Great numbers of farmers will give up their farms and move westward, especially to California.

June 6. The Securities Exchange Act creates the Securities and Exchange Commission (SEC), which will regulate all stock market operations. Its head will be Joseph P. Kennedy.

June 12. The Farm Mortgage Foreclosure Act sets up loans for farmers threatened with foreclosure.

June 18. The Wheeler-Howard Act reorganizes Indian reservations and orders restitution to various tribes for lands that were sold.

June 19. The Communications Act creates the Federal Communications Commission (FCC), which is charged with regulating national and international radio, telegraph and telephone communications.

The Silver Purchase Act authorizes the president to increase the silver hold-

ECONOMIC INDICATORS, 1934–1936			
	1934	**1935**	**1936**
Gross National Product			
Index	76	83	95
Per capita	73	80	91
Employment			
Working-age population			
employed (in millions)	40.9	42.3	44.4
Index	86.0	89.0	93.0
Unemployed (in millions)	11.3	10.6	9.0
Unemployed (in percent)	21.6	20.0	16.8
Industrial Production			
Index of output	71.0	82.0	95.0

SOURCE: Jim Potter, *The American Economy Between the World Wars* (New York: John Wiley & Sons, 1974), cited in André Kaspi, *Les Américains* (Paris: Le Seuil, 1986), vol. 1.

ings of the Treasury until their value reaches a third of the value of the gold reserve. The president is also authorized to nationalize silver mines.

June 28. The Frazier-Lemke Act (Federal Farm Bankruptcy Act) imposes a moratorium on confiscations in rural areas.

The National Housing Act creates the Federal Housing Administration (FHA) to help finance home repairs or additions and to encourage construction.

July 16. Twelve thousand members of the International Longshoremen's Association go on strike and call for a nationwide general strike. This marks the beginning of a period of social unrest.

August 9. Roosevelt nationalizes silver and sets its value at 50.01 cents an ounce.

1935

April 8. The Emergency Relief Appropriation Act establishes the Works Progress Administration, which will employ the jobless in building highways, parks, public buildings and airports. Ultimately, more than 8.5 million people will be employed on such projects, at a cost of $11 billion.

May 11. Roosevelt establishes the Rural Electrification Administration, which is charged with financing the electrification of rural areas.

July 5. The Wagner-Connery Act (National Labor Relations Act) creates a strengthened National Labor Relations Board (NLRB) to replace the ineffective National Labor Board of 1933. The act upholds the right of workers to form unions and bargain collectively with employers.

August 14. The Social Security Act establishes a system of compensation and benefits for retired people over 65

years of age and for the unemployed and the handicapped.

November 9. John L. Lewis, the president of the United Mine Workers, which is a part of the American Federation of Labor (AFL), becomes the leader of a new trade union, the Committee for Industrial Organization (CIO).

1936

December 30. The United Auto Workers (UAW) begins a wildcat strike at a Michigan factory of General Motors. The strike will last until February 11, 1937.

Science and Technology

1934

January 11. The aviator Amelia Earhart becomes the first woman to fly solo from Honolulu to the mainland, landing in Oakland, California, 16 hours later.

May 23. Wallace Carothers, a chemist, discovers a highly resistant synthetic fiber that he names "polymer 66"; it will later be called "nylon."

1935

The first portable device for the hearing-impaired weighs more than two pounds.

The DC-3, the first commercial airplane for the transportation of passengers, is equipped with a heated and insulated cockpit. It can travel across the United States without stopovers in 15 hours.

1936

Construction of the Hoover Dam is completed; the tallest dam in the United States, it is on the Colorado River at Boulder City, Nevada, and creates Lake Mead.

The pilot Howard Hughes sets a time record flying across the United States.

The first experimental flight of a helicopter takes place.

Florescent lighting is invented.

An artificial heart is developed.

Civilization and Culture

1934

Shirley Temple makes her film debut.

The Catholic Legion of Decency institutes censorship and a moral code for motion pictures.

Alcatraz Island, in San Francisco Bay, is converted into a maximum-security prison. The bank robbers Bonnie Parker and Clyde Barrows are shot and killed in Louisiana.

The Daring Young Man on the Flying Trapeze, short stories by William Saroyan. Lillian Hellman's first play, *The Children's Hour*. Robert E.

Sherwood's drama *The Petrified Forest*. Virgil Thompson's opera *Four Saints in Three Acts*.

The School of American Ballet is founded in New York by the Russian-born choreographer George Balanchine.

1935

John Steinbeck's first commercial success, *Tortilla Flat*. *Waiting for Lefty*, a play by the poet Clifford Odets.

The Federal Writers' Project (1935–1939), a New Deal program to provide work for unemployed writers, editors and journalists, is created.

Premiere of George Gershwin's *Porgy and Bess*, the first opera purely American in its inspiration. The film *A Night at the Opera*, starring the Marx brothers.

The sculptor Louise Nevelson has her first exhibit at the Brooklyn Museum.

May 1. 300 volunteers leave for Alaska to raise cattle and develop the territory.

Works Progress Administration (WPA)

This employment program was established by the Emergency Relief Appropriation Act, passed on April 8, 1935. Headed by Harry Hopkins, the WPA operated from May 6, 1935, to December 4, 1942. On the whole, it focused on relatively small public works projects, leaving the larger ones to the PWA (Public Works Administration). The WPA was also active in artistic fields, funding shows, concerts and exhibits to help artists in need. It also hired women and blacks. A branch was started for young people: the NYA (National Youth Administration) provided part-time jobs for students. In 1939, the WPA became the Works Projects Administration. Accused of using the unemployed for useless tasks, and criticized for its bloated administration, the WPA was terminated in 1942, when an economic upturn had already begun and hiring had picked up because of World War II. Actually, the failure of the WPA can be traced not to the excessive spending denounced by its critics but to its inadequate scope. It never provided more than 3 million jobs at any one time, whereas 10 million were necessary.

1936

Margaret Mitchell's *Gone with the Wind* and Djuna Barnes's novel *Nightwood* are published.

Jesse Owens wins four gold medals at the summer Olympic Games in Berlin.

Life magazine begins publication.

November 12. Eugene O'Neill is awarded the Nobel Prize for literature.

Chapter 19

The New Deal in Decline

The years 1937 and 1938 saw a slow economic recovery end with a worsening of the depression, prompting new government efforts to combat the downturn. Although the economy began to improve again by the end of 1938, the New Deal was no longer arousing enthusiasm: within the two main political parties, conservative forces were arraying themselves to resist its expansion. Roosevelt took several steps to readjust the political balance of power in his own favor. For example, he began replacing the "nine old men" on the Supreme Court, as they retired or died, with liberals more in agreement with his aims. But in the midterm elections of November 1938, the Democrats were distinctly in retreat before the Republicans.

The international situation grew more perilous. The Spanish Civil War continued; Germany rearmed and invaded Austria; Italy left the League of Nations, which had condemned the Italian invasion of Ethiopia; and Japan was waging an undeclared war against China. All of these events served to revive the old quarrel between the supporters of a strict isolationism and those who wanted the United States to take a stand or even intervene in a limited fashion overseas.

Political and Institutional Life

1937

January 20. Roosevelt begins his second term as president by declaring "I see one-third of a nation ill-housed, ill-clad, ill-nourished."

February 5. Roosevelt proposes to Congress legislation that would reorganize the Supreme Court by increasing the number of justices from 9 to as many as 15. He is immediately accused of trying to "pack" the Court with his supporters, and of subverting the Constitution to strengthen the executive's power. Congress will reject the legislation in July.

March 1. The Supreme Court Retirement Act permits the retirement with full salary of justices who have served 10 years on the Court at age 70.

August 12. Roosevelt nominates Hugo Black, a liberal, to the Supreme Court, replacing Justice Willis Van Devanter, who resigned. This nomination, confirmed by the Senate in August, will tip the balance on the Court in favor of the New Deal, but a scandal will ensue after it is revealed that Black was once a member of the Ku Klux Klan.

1938

May 26. The House Committee to Investigate Un-American Activities (HUAC) is created to inquire into Nazi, fascist, Communist and other radical groups.

Foreign Policy

1937

January 6. Congress bans the shipment of arms or ammunition to either side in the Spanish Civil War.

March 1. The Reciprocal Trade Agreements Act extends to 1940 the period within which the president can negotiate trade agreements under the 1934 law.

May 1. The third Neutrality Act extends the restrictions of the first two Neutrality Acts of 1935 and 1936 but also introduces the "cash and carry" clause. For the next two years, arms (but not ammunition) may be sold to belligerents if the latter pay cash and carry (ship) their purchases themselves.

September 14. A presidential order prohibits U.S. government-owned ships from delivering arms to China or Japan.

December 12. The American gunboat *Panay* is sunk by Japanese warplanes on the Yangtze River in China. On December 14, Japan will officially apologize and pledge to pay reparations.

1938

January 3. In his annual State of the Union message to Congress, the president declares that the nation must take steps to strengthen its military defenses.

January 28. The president recommends to Congress a major increase in the defense budget.

March 31. Herbert Hoover warns against any intervention in Europe that could lead to war.

May 17. The Naval Expansion Act authorizes a 10-year naval construction program.

September 26. The president sends messages to Great Britain, France, Germany and Czechoslovakia requesting that they find a peaceful solution to the crisis over Czechoslovakia's Sudetenland, which will be surrendered to Hitler in the Munich Agreement of September 29. An opinion poll will show that a majority of Americans support the Munich Agreement.

November 14. The American ambassador to Germany is recalled to Washington to brief the president on the treatment of Jews in Nazi Germany. In response, the German ambassador to Washington will be recalled to Germany on November 18.

December 6. Former British foreign secretary Anthony Eden, during a visit to the United States, warns in a radio broadcast that all democracies share the same values and are therefore threatened by the same dangers.

Economy and Society

1937

January–February. A series of wildcat strikes occur in automobile factories. Some General Motors factories are forced to close. General Motors, followed by Chrysler, recognizes the unionization of its labor force by the United Automobile Workers. Ford decides to continue fighting the union.

March 1. John L. Lewis, the head of the Committee for Industrial Organization (CIO), and the president of the U.S.

Steel Company jointly announce that the firm officially recognizes the unionization of its labor force by the United Steel Workers. This marks a major victory for the trade unions.

March 29. The Supreme Court lets stand the principle of a minimum wage for women.

April 12. The Supreme Court rules in favor of the National Labor Relations Act.

May 24. The Supreme Court rules in favor of the Social Security Act. This ruling, together with the one on April 12, brings an end to the conflict that had been brewing between the president and the Court.

May 30. A metalworkers' strike in Chicago results in a riot that leaves 10 dead and many wounded.

August. A sudden and serious fall of the stock market reveals the depth of the recession.

September 1. The National Housing Act (Wagner-Steagall Act) creates the U.S. Housing Authority, a national agency that will grant loans to cities and states that wish to build low-income housing.

1938

February 16. The second Agricultural Adjustment Act supersedes the first, which was passed in 1933 and declared unconstitutional in 1936. The new act creates the Federal Crop Insurance Corporation to insure wheat crops.

March. The stock market continues its fall, having lost 50 points since the previous August. The depression continues.

June 21. The Emergency Relief Appropriation Act addresses the economic recession of the preceding 10 months.

June 25. The Fair Labor Standards Act sets the minimum hourly wage at 40 cents and the maximum length of the workweek at 44 hours. Labor by children under 16 years of age is prohibited.

INDUSTRIAL INDEXES, 1937–1938			
	Employment Index	Wages Index	Output Index
1937			
October	110.3	104.9	102
November	104.2	93.3	88
December	97.7	84.6	84
1938			
January	91.0	75.4	80
February	91.6	77.7	79
March	91.2	77.8	79

SOURCE: Arthur S. Link and William B. Catton, *American Epoch*, Vol. 1, *1900–1945*, 5th ed. (New York: Alfred A. Knopf, 1980).

Science and Technology

1937

Howard Hughes sets a new aviation record, flying from Los Angeles to Newark, New Jersey, in 7 hours and 28 minutes.

May 6. The German dirigible *Hindenburg* explodes and burns while landing in Lakehurst, New Jersey.

May 27. The Golden Gate Bridge is dedicated in San Francisco.

July 2. The aviator Amelia Earhart disappears over the Pacific during her solo flight around the world.

1938

A toothbrush is the first commercial product made of nylon to appear on the market.

The Xerox machine is invented.

July 14. Howard Hughes sets a new aviation record by flying around the world in 3 days, 19 hours and 14 minutes.

Civilization and Culture

1937

John Steinbeck's *Of Mice and Men. The Man with the Blue Guitar*, by the poet Wallace Stevens.

The first full-length animated movie produced by Walt Disney, *Snow White and the Seven Dwarfs*, is released. William A. Wellman's film *A Star Is Born*.

June 22. Joe Louis becomes the world heavyweight boxing champion, a title he will retain until his retirement in 1949.

1938

Richard Wright's *Uncle Tom's Children*. Thornton Wilder's Pulitzer Prize-winning play *Our Town*. The Nobel Prize for literature is awarded to Pearl Buck.

October 30. "War of the Worlds, a Martian Invasion," a radio program by Orson Welles, sparks panic among its listeners.

The Shadow of War
and the End of Neutrality

From 1939 to 1941, the domestic situation in the United States was closely linked to international events. Germany expanded its aggression in Europe and Japan was preparing to wage war in the Pacific. Germany and the USSR signed a nonaggression pact in Moscow on August 23, 1939, and on September 1 Germany invaded Poland, triggering World War II. Two days later, Poland's allies Great Britain and France declared war on Germany. Italy sided with Germany the following year.

Roosevelt understood very early on that America's entry into the war was unavoidable, and he pressured Congress to abandon neutrality. The United States gradually allied itself with the countries fighting fascism. During these two years, American participation in the alliance evolved step by step until the country found itself at the brink of war.

Because of the seriousness of the international situation, Roosevelt decided to run for a third term in the presidential election of 1940. The Republican candidate, Wendell Willkie, was actually a former Democrat. He was not well known, but his energy and enthusiasm made him a formidable rival. Still, Roosevelt was reelected with 27.3 million popular votes and 449 ballots in the electoral college, over Willkie's 22.3 million votes and 82 electors.

Political and
Institutional Life

1939

April 3. The Administrative Reorganization Act authorizes the president to streamline the executive branch.

August 2. The Hatch Act prohibits employees of the federal government from actively participating in political campaigns.

1940

June 20. Roosevelt appoints prominent Republicans to two key governmental positions, Henry L. Stimson as secretary of war and Frank Knox as secretary of the navy.

November 5. Roosevelt defeats the Republican Wendell Willkie and is reelected president; Henry Wallace is elected vice president.

1941

January 20. Roosevelt begins his third term as president. Henry Wallace is sworn in as vice president.

The Coming War

1939

January 4. In his State of the Union Address, Roosevelt dwells on the critical international situation and calls on all democracies to prepare for every eventuality.

January 5. In the $9 billion budget he submits to Congress, the president asks for $1.3 billion for national defense.

April 1. With the Spanish Civil War over, Washington recognizes Francisco Franco's government.

April 14. Roosevelt asks Hitler and Mussolini to guarantee the peace in Europe and the Middle East for 25 years in exchange for American cooperation on a world disarmament conference and international trade agreements.

July 18. Roosevelt and Secretary of State Cordell Hull ask Congress to revise the Neutrality Acts.

July 26. The United States abrogates the treaty of commerce signed with Japan in 1911. Although the United States is still technically neutral, it wishes to make its sympathies clear.

September 3. Following the outbreak of war in Europe, the British passenger ship *Athenia* is sunk by a German submarine off the Hebrides Islands west of Scotland. Thirty American passengers are killed. The president reaffirms American neutrality.

September 4. Secretary of State Hull asks Americans to keep their European trips to a minimum.

September 5. Roosevelt issues an official proclamation of neutrality and prohibits the export of arms and ammunition to the belligerents in Europe.

September 8. The president proclaims a limited state of emergency, which grants him powers to act quickly when needed.

September 21. In an address to Congress, the president asks for the repeal of the clause banning arms sales in the Neutrality Act of 1937.

October 18. The president declares that American territorial waters and harbors are closed to the submarines of all nations taking part in the war.

October 20. The secretary of state declares that the United States does not recognize the partition of Poland by Germany and the USSR, and that it will maintain diplomatic relations with the exiled Polish government.

November 4. The fourth Neutrality Act repeals all existing restrictions on the sale of arms to belligerents except the "cash and carry" clause.

November 30. The United States announces its support for Finland, which has been invaded by the USSR.

1940

April 29. The president asks Musssolini to try to restore order in Europe. Mussolini does not respond.

May 15. British prime minister Winston Churchill sends his first telegram to Roosevelt requesting assistance in the war.

May 16. The president asks Congress for an additional $1.2 billion for national defense, in particular for the development of the Army Air Forces.

May 25. The Office for Emergency Management (OEM) is created to prepare for and deal with war emergencies.

June 3. The United States agrees to sell military equipment and surplus stocks of ammunition to Great Britain.

June 10. In a speech at the University of Virginia, the president uses the term "non-belligerence" rather than "neutrality" and declares that the United States will materially support the Allies without entering the war. The speech is well received by the public.

June 11. Roosevelt signs appropriation bills totaling $1.3 billion for the army and the navy.

June 29. The Smith Act (Alien Registration Act) requires all aliens to register with the government and be fingerprinted. The act also makes it illegal to advocate the violent overthrow of the government.

July 10. The president asks Congress for an additional $4.8 billion for national defense.

July 20. Congress allocates $4 billion for a two-ocean navy.

August 18. An agreement is reached with Canada for the development of a common defense plan.

September 3. Fifty destroyers are sent to Great Britain in exchange for British air and naval bases in the Western Hemisphere.

September 16. The Selective Training and Service Act establishes the first peacetime draft.

October 16. All men between the ages of 21 and 36 register for military service.

October 29. The first draft numbers are selected.

1941

January 6. In his State of the Union Address, the President enunciates the "Four Freedoms": freedom of speech, freedom of religion, freedom from fear and freedom from want. The address will serve as an ideological reference during the war years.

January 29. American and British military planners begin meeting secretly in Washington to select a strategy to pursue in the event that the United States enters the war (the ABC-1 Plan).

March 11. The Lend-Lease Act permits the United States to lend weapons and war matériel to nations "whose defense the President deems vital to the defense of the United States."

April. In an agreement with Denmark, the United States agrees to defend Greenland in exchange for the right to establish military bases there.

April–May. American convoys cross the North Atlantic.

April 11. Roosevelt announces an extension of the American security zone in the Atlantic.

April 21–27. American, British and Dutch military commanders meet in Singapore to adopt a common strategy against Japan in the event of war.

May 21. A German submarine sinks the American merchant ship *Robin Moor* within the American security zone.

May 27. Roosevelt declares a state of emergency.

June 14. Roosevelt freezes German and Italian assets in the United States.

June 16. Roosevelt orders the closing of all German and Italian consulates in the United States. Germany and Italy reciprocate by ordering the closing of U.S. consulates in Axis-occupied territory.

June 24. The United States promises aid to the USSR, which was invaded by Germany on June 22.

July 7. American marines land in Iceland.

July 26. Japanese assets in the United States are frozen. The army of the Philippines, a dependent territory of the United States, is placed under the command of General Douglas MacArthur, who becomes commander in chief of American forces in the Far East.

August 14. Churchill and Roosevelt meet on warships off Argentia, Newfoundland, and adopt the Atlantic Charter. It defines the main goals of both governments: the right of people to self-determination, unhindered access to raw materials, the rejection of all territorial expansion, and respect for freedom. In the following weeks, the charter will be endorsed by 15 other nations.

September 11. After a German submarine attacks an American warship, the president orders U.S. planes and warships in the Atlantic security zone to "shoot-on-sight."

October 17. Eleven Americans are killed when the destroyer *Kearny* is damaged by German submarines off the coast of Iceland.

October 30. The destroyer *Reuben James* is sunk by a German submarine off of Iceland. More than one hundred Americans die.

December 7. Japanese forces launch a surprise attack on the U.S. naval base at Pearl Harbor in Hawaii, resulting in heavy material and human losses to the U.S. Pacific Fleet. The Japanese also attack U.S. bases in the Philippines, Guam and Wake Island, and the British bases in Hong Kong and Malaysia.

December 8. Calling December 7 "a date which will live in infamy," Roosevelt asks Congress for a declaration of war against Japan. Congress declares war in 33 minutes.

December 10. The Japanese invade the Philippines.

December 11. Germany and Italy declare war on the United States, which recognizes the state of war.

December 15. The third Defense Appropriation Act allocates $10 billion for the war.

December 22. The amended Selective Service Act makes all men between the ages of 20 and 44 eligible for the draft.

Roosevelt and Churchill meet in Washington.

The Japanese capture Wake Island.

December 25. The Japanese capture the British colony of Hong Kong.

Economy and Society

1939

February 27. The wildcat strike (one begun in violation of a contract) is ruled illegal by the Supreme Court.

July 1. The Federal Works Agency (FWA) is created. It consolidates five existing administrations, the Public Building Administration, the Public Roads Administration, the Public Works Administration, the Works Progress Administration (renamed Works Projects Administration) and the U.S. Housing Authority. The FWA will permit reductions in staff.

1940

A census sets the population at 131,669,275, and life expectancy at 64 years.

July 2. The Export Control Act authorizes the president to limit or halt the export of any product deemed vital for national defense.

November 18. Making good on his pledge, John L. Lewis resigns as president of the Committee for Industrial Organization (CIO) and joins the Republican Party after Roosevelt's victory in the presidential election.

December 20. The Office of Production Management (OPM) is created to coordinate and facilitate the production of ammunition and military equipment.

1941

January. OPM makes its first requisitions of materials and machinery.

January 22. A wave of strikes begins in the defense industry.

February 26. Metalworkers go on strike.

April 11. The Office of Price Administration (OPA) is created within OPM to regulate prices. The agency has the power to restrict consumption in the event of inflation.

Ford Motor Company signs its first contract with a trade union after a nine-day strike that mobilized 85,000 workers and resulted in 150 deaths.

April 14. The steel industry raises wages by 10 cents an hour.

April 17. The automobile industry agrees to cut its production by 20 percent.

May 16. General Motors raises wages by 10 cents an hour.

June 25. The Fair Employment Practice Committee is created to ensure fair working conditions and to protect workers in the defense industry against any discrimination based on color of skin, race or religion.

July 24. The American Federation of Labor (AFL) signs an agreement with OPM, pledging not to hold strikes among construction workers as long as a state of emergency exists.

September 20. The Revenue Act imposes the largest tax increase in the nation's history. Taxes on individual incomes and business profits are increased to help finance defense expenditures.

December 15. The AFL signs an agreement with OPM not to hold strikes among workers in defense industry.

December 27. The OPA announces a requisition of all rubber; the quantity available for public consumption will be reduced by 80 percent.

Science and Technology

1939

Researchers succeed in splitting atoms of uranium, thorium and protactinium by bombarding them with neutrons.

Clara Adams becomes the first woman aviator to fly around the world.

The first helicopter is built by Igor Sikorsky.

Color television is successfully demonstrated.

June 28. The first regularly scheduled commercial airliner crosses the Atlantic.

August 2. Albert Einstein, alarmed by the recent advances of German physicists, writes to Roosevelt, asking him to authorize research and development of an atomic bomb. Referring to the fission of uranium, Einstein notes: "This new phenomenon would also lead to the construction of bombs, and it is conceivable . . . that extremely powerful bombs of a new type may thus be constructed."

October 25. Nylon hose is sold for the first time.

1940

Karl Pabst designs the jeep.

1941

The federal government's Manhattan Project begins researching ways to build an atomic bomb.

Some metals are rationed, bringing about an increase in the use of plastic.

Albert Einstein becomes an American citizen.

June 28. The Office of Scientific Research and Development is created to coordinate scientific and technological research linked to defense, in particular, the research on radars and sonars, and the first work on the atomic bomb.

Civilization and Culture

1939

John Steinbeck's *The Grapes of Wrath.* Mystery writer Raymond Chandler's *The Big Sleep*, featuring the tough sleuth Philip Marlowe.

In New York, the first complete performance of Charles Ives's *Concord Sonata.*

Hitler's *Mein Kampf* is published in English.

Victor Fleming's movies *Gone With the Wind* and *The Wizard of Oz*, John Ford's *Stagecoach*, and *You Can't Cheat an Honest Man*, with the comedian W. C. Fields, are released.

Hardball, by the painter Ben Shahn.

The Unknown American Painters Exhibition at the Museum of Modern Art brings the elderly "primitive" painter "Grandma Moses" (Anna R. Moses) to national attention.

April 30. The World's Fair opens at Flushing Meadows in New York City.

June 7–12. King George VI and Queen Elizabeth become the first British sovereigns to visit the United States.

1940

Ernest Hemingway's *For Whom the Bell Tolls.* Carson McCuller's novel *The Heart Is a Lonely Hunter*, about a deaf-mute in a southern town.

Release of Charlie Chaplin's movie *The Dictator* and Walt Disney's movie *Fantasia.* Bugs Bunny makes his movie debut.

Samuel Barber completes his *Violin Concerto.*

Bebop jazz, with such practitioners as Charlie Parker and Dizzy Gillespie, achieves popularity.

Approximately 30 million households own a radio set.

1941

James Agee publishes his study of Alabama sharecroppers, *Let Us Now Praise Famous Men.*

Release of Orson Welles's movie *Citizen Kane*, and John Huston's movie *The Maltese Falcon.*

The Federal Communications Commission permits the broadcasting of television programs. One million TV sets are sold.

Chapter 21   1942–1945

The Second World War

The United States was a country at war, and its most immediate task was the conversion of a civilian economy into a wartime economy. This was achieved quickly and easily, thanks to the creation of several governmental agencies. The most important of these, the War Production Board (WPB), managed and regulated the production of all war matériel and equipment. Its aim was clearly defined by the slogan the "Victory Program," and the scope of its activity grew very quickly. In 1941, 15 percent of the nation's industrial production went to the military, compared with 33 percent in 1942. The economic revival that was already getting under way became spectacular after 1942. Unemployment disappeared almost entirely because of mobilization and the jobs it opened. The defense industry also hired a great number of women. Faced with a sudden and sizable economic expansion, the government resorted to anti-inflationary measures, but the cost of living continued to rise. And as consumer goods became increasingly scarce, a widespread network of illegal trafficking sprang up.

A presidential election was held in 1944, and Roosevelt remained the Democratic Party's candidate. In light of the president's poor health, his entourage wanted someone on the ticket better able than Henry Wallace to rally the American people should the president die in office. Harry S. Truman, a senator from Missouri, was eventually chosen as Roosevelt's running mate, and the president was reelected for an unprecedented fourth term. Roosevelt polled 25.6 million popular votes against 22 million for his Republican rival Thomas E. Dewey, and 432 votes in the electoral college against Dewey's 99.

In the theaters of operation, the fighting intensified in both the Atlantic and the Pacific. The Allies took the offensive first in North Africa, then in Italy. The landing in Normandy in June 1944 was a decisive factor in their final victory. Once Germany's defeat became certain, the Allied leaders met in Yalta to prepare the peace and begin laying the foundation for a reorganized Europe.

Roosevelt's death at the age of 63 marked the end of an era. But even though America had emerged from the Great Depression, the war had yet to be concluded. Faced with continued Japanese resistance in the Pacific, Truman decided to drop the first two atomic bombs on the Japanese cities of Hiroshima and Nagasaki. Within days, Japan surrendered and World War II was over.

Political and Institutional Life

1942

January 16. The War Production Board is established to manage the production of war materials and equipment.

May 14. For the first time ever, women are enlisted into noncombat military service with the creation of the Women's Army Auxiliary Corps, later renamed Women's Army Corps (WAC).

June 13. The Office of War Information and the Office of Strategic Services are created; the latter is charged with collecting intelligence on other countries.

November 13. The Selective Service Act of 1940 is amended, lowering the draft age to 18. According to one estimate, 10 million men will soon be in the armed forces.

1943

May 27. The Office of War Mobilization is created to coordinate the war effort.

1944

November 7. Roosevelt is reelected president, defeating Thomas Dewey; Harry Truman is elected vice president.

1945

January 20. Roosevelt begins his fourth term as president.

April 12. Roosevelt dies of a cerebral hemorrhage in Warm Springs, Georgia. Truman takes the oath of office at the White House, becoming the 33rd president.

Foreign Policy

1942

January 1. Representatives of 26 countries, including the United States, sign the United Nations Declaration pledging their cooperation in the defeat of the Axis.

January 15–28. At a Pan-American conference in Rio de Janeiro, the foreign ministers of 21 American states agree to break all relations with the Axis nations.

June 19. Meeting in Washington, Roosevelt and Churchill discuss the possibility of invading Nazi-occupied North Africa.

August 12–15. In Moscow, Churchill, Roosevelt's emissary W. Averell Harriman and Stalin meet to elaborate a common strategy.

November 7. The USSR becomes eligible for Lend-Lease assistance.

1943

January 14–24. Churchill, Roosevelt and Free French leaders Henri Giraud and Charles de Gaulle hold a conference at Casablanca, in North Africa. The Allies insist on the "unconditional surrender" of the Axis and agree on strategic plans. General Dwight D. Eisenhower is put in charge of Allied operations in North Africa.

May 12–25. The Trident Conference is held in Washington. Roosevelt, Churchill and their military staffs set

May 1, 1944, as the target date for the invasion of France.

May 19. In an address before Congress, Churchill predicts the certain defeat of Germany and Japan.

August 17–24. At the Quebec Conference, Roosevelt and Churchill agree to intensify the war against Japan and to recognize de Gaulle's French Committee on National Liberation as the representative of all Free French forces.

October 19–30. At the Moscow Conference, the U.S., British and Soviet foreign ministers agree on the establishment of an international organization to ensure the postwar peace.

November 5. The Senate approves the future creation of the United Nations.

November 22–26. At the Cairo Conference, Roosevelt, Churchill and Chinese general Chiang Kai-shek discuss the war in the Pacific.

November 28–December 1. At the Teheran Conference, Roosevelt, Churchill and Soviet leader Joseph Stalin discuss the planned invasion of Western Europe. Stalin agrees to enter the war against Japan at a future date.

1944

July 6. De Gaulle confers with Roosevelt in Washington.

August 21–October 7. A conference is held at Dumbarton Oaks, an estate in Washington, D.C. Representatives of Britain, Russia, China and the United States agree on the framework for what will become the United Nations after the war is over.

September 11–16. At a conference in Quebec, Roosevelt and Churchill discuss the postwar occupation of Germany and the war against Japan.

1945

February 4–11. Meeting in the Crimean city of Yalta, Roosevelt, Churchill and Stalin agree to facilitate free elections in the liberated countries of Eastern Europe.

April–June. The San Francisco conference establishes the United Nations. The new organization's charter, signed on June 26, will be approved by the Senate on July 28.

June 5. Following Germany's surrender, the Big Four (the United States, Great Britain, France and the Soviet Union) discuss the occupation of Germany and the partition of Berlin.

July 17–August 2. At the Potsdam Conference, the leaders of the United States, Britain and the USSR issue an ultimatum to Japan, demanding its unconditional surrender and threatening it with total destruction. President Truman informs Stalin that the United States possesses an atomic bomb. Differences appear among the Allies.

War Chronology: The Atlantic, Africa and Europe

1942

January 26. American troops land in Northern Ireland.

February 6. The United States and Great Britain decide to place their joint armies under a single commander.

June 11. General Dwight D. Eisenhower is appointed commander of the European Theater of Operations.

July 4. The first Anglo-American bomber raids take place on the European continent.

August 17. The first American strategic bomber raid occurs at Rouen.

September 10–14. German U-boats (submarines) in the North Atlantic sink 12 freighters and 1 destroyer en route to Great Britain.

November 7–8. Under Eisenhower's command, 400,000 Allied soldiers begin the invasion of North Africa.

1943

January 27. American bombers attack German submarine works at Wilhelmshaven.

February 14–25. In North Africa, the Allies are defeated by German field marshal Erwin Rommel at Kasserine Pass (Tunisia). On the 25th, American troops retake their lost positions and stop Rommel's advance.

May 7. In Tunisia, American forces capture Bizerte and British forces take Tunis, marking the end of the North African campaign.

May 10. German and Italian forces in North Africa surrender after having lost 500,000 men, dead or captured.

July 10. The Allies, led by Eisenhower, land in Sicily.

July 19. American bombers attack Rome.

August 17. With the capture of Messina, the Allies retake Sicily. The Allies lose 25,000 men, the Germans and the Italians 167,000, during the five-week campaign.

September 3. The Allies cross the Strait of Messina to begin their invasion of Italy.

September 8. Following the overthrow of Mussolini, the Italian government surrenders unconditionally to the Allies. German troops in Italy continue resisting the Allied invasion.

September 9. Allied troops enter Salerno.

September 19. The Allies capture the island of Sardinia. On Corsica, French troops battle the German and Italian forces that control the island.

October 1. Naples is taken by the U.S. Fifth Army under General Mark Clark.

October 13. Italy declares war on Germany.

December 24. Eisenhower is appointed supreme commander of the Allied Expeditionary Forces that will invade France in 1944.

1944

January 22. In Italy, the Allies make an amphibious landing at Anzio and occupy Nettuno, south of Rome.

February 20–27. Heavy air raids are mounted against German industrial centers.

March 6. American bombers make their first raid on Berlin.

March 8. The second American air raid on Berlin will be followed by daily raids on German cities.

March 15. The Allies bomb Monte Cassino, the key to German defenses in central Italy, without success.

May 18. The Germans retreat from Monte Cassino. The Germans' Gustav Line across central Italy is penetrated.

June 4. The American Fifth Army enters Rome, which was abandoned by the Germans.

June 5. The Allies continue pursuing German forces north of Rome.

June 6. D Day: In Operation Overlord, the Allies conduct a successful landing on the beaches of Normandy.

June 10. U.S. forces, having established themselves on Omaha Beach and Utah Beach, begin moving forward from the coast of Normandy.

June 27. U.S. forces capture Cherbourg.

July 18. American troops take Saint-Lô.

July 25. In Operation Cobra, under the command of General Omar Bradley, the U.S. First Army begins advancing from Saint-Lô to cut off German units in Brittany.

August 9. Eisenhower moves the Supreme Headquarters Allied Expeditionary Forces (SHAEF) from Great Britain to France.

August 15. In Operation Anvil, the Allies land in southern France and meet weak German resistance. The Allies move north.

August 25. Paris is liberated by U.S. and Free French forces.

August 28. The Germans surrender Toulon and Marseille.

September 12. American troops enter Germany.

September 17–27. In Operation Market Garden, the Allies attempt an airborne assault on German forces in Holland. The operation fails.

October 21. After a week of fighting, the Allies take Aachen in Germany.

December 16–30. In the Battle of the Bulge, in the Ardennes forest, the Germans are initially successful in pushing back the Allies.

1945

January 2. The Battle of the Bulge ends when the Germans fail to capture Bastogne. An Allied counteroffensive will begin the following day.

January 12. Soviet troops begin their final offensive against Germany.

February 1. American bombers carry out a raid on Berlin.

February 13–14. U.S. and British bombers attack Dresden.

March 7. The U.S. 9th Armored Division crosses the Rhine River at Remagen.

April 25. American troops meet Soviet soldiers advancing from the east at Torgau, on the Elbe River.

May 7. Eisenhower accepts the surrender of the German army at his headquarters in Reims, France.

May 8. V-E Day (Victory in Europe): Germany signs an unconditional surrender in Berlin.

War Chronology: The Pacific

1942

January 2. Manila falls to the Japanese. American forces in the Philippines retreat to the Bataan Peninsula. General Douglas MacArthur establishes his headquarters on Corregidor Island.

February 15. In a major setback to the Allies, the British garrison at Singapore surrenders as Japanses troops sweep across Southeast Asia.

February 23. An oil refinery near Santa Barbara, California, is shelled by a Japanese submarine. This is one of the very few military actions in the war that will actually take place in the continental United States.

February 27–March 1. Allied forces are defeated by the Japancsc navy in the Sea of Java.

March 11. MacArthur leaves the Philippines for Australia, where the general will take command of Allied forces in the Southwest Pacific.

April 9. After resisting for three months, 75,000 American and Filipino soldiers surrender to the Japanese on the Bataan Peninsula. The captured soldiers will be led on foot to a prison camp 90 miles away, and several thousand will die en route (Bataan "Death March").

April 18. Led by Lieutenant Colonel James H. Doolittle, 16 bombers of the Army Air Forces are launched from the aircraft carrier *Hornet* and conduct the first American air raid over Tokyo and other Japanese cities.

May 7–8. In the Battle of the Coral Sea, off the coast of New Guinea, American naval forces inflict sizable losses on the Japanese fleet, which is forced to retreat.

May 7. General Jonathan Wainwright, who succeeded MacArthur on Corregidor, surrenders the island to the Japanese.

June 4–6. American naval forces are victorious in the Battle of Midway. Japan loses its naval superiority, marking a turning point in the war in the Pacific.

June 6–7. The Japanese invade two islands in the Aleutian Archipelago off of Alaska.

June 21. A Japanese submarine fires on the coast of Oregon. No damage is done.

August 7. An American counterattack begins in the Solomon Islands. In the first amphibious operation in the Pacific, U.S. troops land on Guadalcanal and Tulagi.

October 23–27. The Japanese launch an offensive on Guadalcanal. U.S. Marines halt the Japanese advance in bloody fighting.

In the Battle of the Santa Cruz Islands, the American navy suffers a defeat.

November 12–15. The naval Battle of Guadalcanal ends with a decisive American victory.

1943

February 7. American operations in the Solomon Islands succeed in forcing Japanese troops to abandon Guadalcanal.

March 2–4. American and Australian fighter-bombers are successful against Japanese ships in the Bismarck Sea off of New Guinea.

May 11–29. American forces recapture the Aleutian island of Attu, seized by the Japanese the previous year.

August 17–21. Japanese troops suffer heavy losses in Wewak, New Guinea.

November. American naval and ground forces launch a new offensive in the Central Pacific.

1944

January 31–February 21. American troops invade the Marshall Islands.

February 3. In the first direct attack on Japanese territory, the American navy bombards the Kuril Islands, north of Japan's main islands.

April 22. Allied forces land in Dutch New Guinea.

June. The Mariana Islands are invaded by American forces.

June 19–21. The Battle of the Philippine Sea results in an important Japanese defeat.

July 9. American troops capture the island of Saipan after 25 days of fighting.

August 10. American troops retake the island of Guam after 20 days of fighting.

October 20. American troops begin landing on the island of Leyte, in the Philippines. MacArthur redeems his promise "I shall return."

October 23–26. The Battle of Leyte Gulf ends in a defeat for the Japanese navy.

November 24. American forces begin an intensive air bombardment of Tokyo.

1945

February 7. General MacArthur recaptures Manila.

February 19–March 16. American forces are victorious in the Battle of Iwo

Jima, one of the most ferocious of the war.

April 1–June 22. U.S. troops invade Okinawa, the main island of the Ryukus, only 360 miles south of Japan. The Japanese defenders mount a fanatical resistance. In the bloodiest U.S. engagement in the Pacific, American forces finally seize the island.

May 11. The aircraft carrier *Bunker Hill* is attacked by Japanese kamikaze (suicide) planes off Okinawa; 373 Americans are killed.

July 15. MacArthur takes back the Philippines.

August 6. The American bomber *Enola Gay* drops an atomic bomb on the Japanese city of Hiroshima.

August 9. Another atomic bomb is dropped on the city of Nagasaki.

August 14. Japan surrenders.

August 15. V-J Day (Victory over Japan): The war in the Pacific ends. The formal Japanese surrender will take place in Tokyo Bay aboard the battleship *Missouri* on September 2.

Economy and Society

1942

The federal government forcibly moves more than 100,000 Japanese-Americans living on the West Coast to detention centers for the duration of the war.

January 1. The Office of Production Management (OPM) bans the sale of new cars and trucks to civilians.

March 17. The presidents of the AFL and the CIO pledge not to hold strikes for the duration of the war.

May 5. Sugar is rationed.

May 15. Gasoline is rationed in 17 states.

May 18. Retail prices are controlled.

July 22. A system of coupons is instituted to ration gasoline.

September 10. The Baruch-Compton-Connant commission reports that a shortage of rubber is imminent.

September 11. The United States signs an agreement with Mexico to buy all of the latter's rubber production during the next four years. The synthetic rubber industry is asked to accelerate its research and development effort.

November 29. Coffee is rationed.

December 1. Gasoline is rationed in all states.

December 4. The Works Projects Administration (WPA) is disbanded.

1943

February 7. Leather shoes are rationed.

February 9. A minimum workweek of 48 hours is instituted in factories producing military equipment.

March 1. Canned goods are rationed.

COST OF WORLD WAR II TO THE UNITED STATES
(estimates in millions of dollars)

Cost of the War	Veterans' Pensions	Interest on Loans	Long-term Cost
260,000	65,231	200,000	625,200

SOURCE: U.S. Bureau of the Census, *Statistical Abstract of the United States, 1984.*

April 1. Meat, butter and cheese are rationed.

June 20–22. A racial disturbance occurs in Detroit when whites pro- test against the hiring of blacks: 35 die and more than 500 are wounded, mostly blacks. During the summer, more racial disturbances will take place in Mobile, Los Angeles, Harlem and Texas.

December 17. The laws excluding Chinese immigrants are repealed.

1944

May 3. Meat rationing is ended.

June 22. Roosevelt signs the Servicemen's Readjustment Act (GI Bill of Rights), which provides education and unemployment assistance, as well as low-interest loans, to veterans returning to civilian life.

July 1–22. At the Bretton Woods Conference in New Hampshire, 44 nations sign an agreement establishing the International Monetary Fund (IMF) and the International Bank for Reconstruction and Development (IBRD or World Bank).

August 14. The production of certain consumer goods, restricted at the start of the war, resumes.

November 18. Economic indicators show that the cost of living has increased by 30 percent since 1943.

1945

The gross national product (GNP) has increased by two-thirds since 1939.

April 30. The sugar ration is doubled.

May 25. The production of military airplanes is reduced by 30 percent.

Science and Technology

1942

Glenn T. Seaborg extracts plutonium from uranium (Plutonium Project).

Henry Kaiser and Howard Hughes design an eight-engine airplane capable of carrying 700 passengers.

Napalm is invented.

Bazookas are first produced.

Radar is used for the first time.

October 1. The XP-59, the first American jet airplane, is flight-tested.

December 2. The first nuclear chain reaction is achieved at the University of Chicago by Leo Szilard and Enrico Fermi (Project Argonne).

1943

J. Robert Oppenheimer establishes a laboratory in Los Alamos, New Mexico, to develop the atomic bomb (Manhattan Project).

Selman Waksman discovers streptomycin, which is used for the treatment of tuberculosis. He coins the term "antibiotic."

Penicillin is mass-produced.

1945

July 16. The first atomic bomb is tested at Alamogordo, New Mexico.

Civilization and Culture

1942

The journalist William L. White publishes *They Were Expendable*, about the patrol boat squadron that transported General Douglas MacArthur from the Japanese-controlled Philippines to Australia.

Yalta Conference

From February 4 to 11, 1945, Roosevelt, Churchill and Stalin meet at Yalta (in the Crimea) to discuss the future of Europe, Asia and the United Nations.

Germany. The principle of partitioning the country is adopted. The decision to occupy the country according to zones is maintained, and a French zone is added. The question of war reparations is raised, but no decision is reached on their amount.

Eastern Europe. In Poland, the Soviet-backed Lublin government will be reorganized to include democrats exiled abroad. Elections will take place to create a permanent government. In the other countries, provisional governments will be established until free elections can bring about permanent governments.

Asia. The USSR will declare war on Japan as soon as the hostilities in Europe come to an end. The USSR recognizes Chinese sovereignty in Manchuria and will sign a treaty with the government of Chiang Kai-shek. Japan will return to the USSR the territories captured in 1905.

United Nations. The decisions made at Dumbarton Oaks are upheld. A conference is planned in San Francisco to draft a charter.

Release of Michael Curtiz's movie *Casablanca*, with Humphrey Bogart and Ingrid Bergman.

1943

The 1940 Republican presidential candidate and internationalist Wendell L. Willkie publishes *One World.*

Richard Rodgers and Oscar Hammerstein's musical comedy *Oklahoma!* opens on Broadway.

The painter Jackson Pollock has his first major exhibit.

The Pentagon is built to house the Navy and War Departments.

1944

The Glass Menagerie by the dramatist Tennessee Williams.

Dangling Man, by Saul Bellow. War correspondent Ernie Pyle's *Brave Men.*

George Cukor's film *Gaslight.*

Because of rationing, paperback books are produced for the first time.

December 24. The band leader Glenn Miller is presumed dead when his military flight from England to Paris vanishes.

Chapter 22   1945–1947

The Organization of the Postwar World

The United States emerged from World War II a wealthy and united country. Both public and private sectors worked to quickly reconvert the economy into a peacetime one capable of satisfying the long-pent-up demand of consumers. Indeed, the demand for consumer goods was so strong that the government soon took measures to diminish it in the hope of avoiding inflation. Suddenly, after a long silence the demands of workers also rang out, and 1946 was marked by a wave of strikes: A total of 4.6 million workers walked the picket lines at some point during the year. The reaction came in 1947, when a law was passed restricting union activities.

Because events overseas had played such an important role in recent American history, the nation could no longer afford to isolate itself again from the rest of the world, whether politically, diplomatically or economically. The Allied powers occupied Germany, where a court at Nuremberg convicted 19 Nazi leaders of war crimes. The United States needed strong allies; with the Marshall Plan it helped finance the reconstruction of Europe. The USSR, denouncing the plan as a manifestation of economic imperialism, refused to take part in it and also prevented its satellite countries in Eastern Europe from participating. It soon became clear to Western leaders that Joseph Stalin, the Soviet leader, had no intention of honoring the commitments made in the international conferences at the end of the war, and that his expansionist ambitions threatened the restoration of democracy in several countries. Already in 1946, Winston Churchill could speak of an "Iron Curtain" descending on Europe. Two blocs quickly formed, and the Cold War began.

The United States adopted a strategy aimed at "containing" Soviet expansionism. The strategy was conceived by George Kennan, a diplomat well acquainted with the USSR, in an anonymous article published in the journal *Foreign Affairs* in July 1947. Kennan's analysis of the USSR and of East-West relations would guide American policy for decades. One early manifestation of the strategy of containment was the Truman Doctrine, which committed the United States to helping countries threatened by communism.

Political and Institutional Life

1946

January 22. President Truman establishes the Central Intelligence Group, the forerunner of the Central Intelligence Agency (CIA).

August 1. The McMahon Act establishes the Atomic Energy Commission, which places nuclear energy development under the supervision of a five-member civilian panel headed by David E. Lilienthal. Both the army and the navy are authorized to make atomic bombs. Any distribution of nuclear materials or information is prohibited.

November 5. In the congressional elections, Republicans win majorities in both houses: 51 seats in the Senate and 245 seats in the House of Representatives.

1947

January 8. George C. Marshall, the former chief of staff of the army, is appointed secretary of state.

March 22. The president institutes a loyalty program. All federal employees and applicants for government jobs will be investigated. The fear of communism grows.

July 26. The National Security Act creates the National Security Council (NSC), the CIA and the U.S. Air Force. The act also unifies the three armed services under the Department of Defense. James V. Forrestal, the secretary of the navy, is appointed the first secretary of defense.

October 18. The House Un-American Activities Committee (HUAC) begins an investigation of Communist influence in the movie industry.

Foreign Policy

1945

August 17. The Allies that defeated Germany and Japan in World War II divide Korea at the 38th parallel. American troops occupy the southern sector, while Soviet troops occupy the northern sector.

August 21. The Lend-Lease program is terminated.

August 29. General Douglas MacArthur is named commander in chief of Allied forces in Japan.

August 30. The Allied occupation of Japan begins.

September 2. Representatives of Japan formally surrender on the battleship *Missouri* in Tokyo Bay.

November 20. General Dwight D. Eisenhower replaces General Marshall as chief of staff of the army.

December 15. Marshall is named a special ambassador to China, with authority to mediate between the Chinese nationalists and the Chinese Communists.

1946

January 10. The first meeting of the General Assembly of the United Nations takes place in London. Secretary of State James F. Byrnes heads the American delegation.

February. After protests from the State Department and a personal message from Truman to Stalin, the USSR withdraws its troops from the territory they were occupying in northern Iran.

March 5. In a speech delivered in Fulton, Missouri, former British prime minister Winston Churchill warns that an "Iron Curtain" is descending on Europe, dividing the continent into two blocs.

June 14. Bernard Baruch, the U.S. delegate to the United Nations Commission on Atomic Energy, proposes placing atomic energy under international control. The USSR will veto the proposal.

July 1. The United States begins conducting atomic tests on Bikini in the Marshall Islands.

July 4. Truman proclaims the independence of the Republic of the Philippines.

October 1. Under Secretary of State Dean Acheson declares that the United States "will remain in Korea until the reunification of the country."

October 23. The second session of the United Nations General Assembly convenes in New York. The UN accepts John D. Rockefeller's gift of $8.5 million to purchase land in New York for its permanent headquarters.

November 4–December 12. Peace treaties are concluded with the minor former Axis powers in Europe.

December 31. The president officially proclaims an end to the hostilities of World War II.

1947

March 12. The president asks Congress to appropriate $400 million to help Greece and Turkey rebuild their economies and resist Communist subjugation. The program will become known as the Truman Doctrine. Congress will approve the president's request on May 15.

April 12. The United Nations places the United States in charge of the administration of the islands in the Pacific formerly controlled by the Japanese.

May 31. The president allocates $350 million to help countries destroyed by the war.

June 5. In a speech at Harvard University, Secretary of State George Mar-shall proposes his plan to help the countries of Europe rebuild their economies.

June 14. Peace treaties with Italy, Romania, Bulgaria and Hungary are signed by the president, who criticizes the latter three countries for having failed to establish representative governments.

July 12–September 22. An international conference is held in Paris to study the European requests for economic assistance under the Marshall Plan.

September 2. At the Pan-American Conference meeting in Brazil, the Treaty of Rio de Janeiro, a mutual defense pact, is signed by 19 nations.

September 17. The United States issues an appeal to the UN concerning Korea's independence, which was promised at the Cairo Conference in 1943. The United States requests that free elections take place in Korea as soon as possible.

October 9. Truman declares his support for a proposal of the United Nations to create two independent states in Palestine, one Jewish and one Arab. The UN resolution will be adopted on November 29.

November 25–December 15. In London, the Council of Foreign Ministers (United States, Great Britain, France and the Soviet Union) fails to agree on the political and economic reunification of Germany.

December 19. The president asks Congress to authorize the first installment of funds (totaling $17 billion) to finance the reconstruction of Western Europe under the Marshall Plan.

Economy and Society

1945

August 18. The president orders a relaxation of wage controls and a return to the production of consumer goods and free-market competition. Labor unions may resume their normal activity.

August 20. The War Production Board lifts controls on the production of 210 consumer goods.

October 30. The rationing of shoes is terminated.

November 21. The automobile workers' union declares a strike at all General Motors factories. The strike will last until March 13, 1946.

November 23. The rationing of meat and butter is terminated.

December 20. The rationing of tires is terminated.

December 31. The War Labor Board is disbanded and replaced by the National Wage Stabilization Board.

1946

January 9. Approximately 7,700 telephone operators of the Western Electric Company begin a strike that will last until April 7, 1947.

January 15. Radio technicians go on strike.

January 20. The metalworkers' union calls a strike that brings production to a virtual halt. Steel mills are forced to close.

January 25. John L. Lewis is elected vice president of the AFL, bringing an end to its dispute with Lewis's CIO.

February 20. The Employment Act creates the president's Council of Economic Advisors, which will prepare an annual economic report.

February 21. The Office of Economic Stabilization is created to oversee the reconversion of the economy.

April 1–May 30. Approximately 400,000 coal miners go on strike, demanding a raise and a social security plan. Their demands are granted.

May 23. Railroad workers go on strike. The next day, the president will threaten to call out troops to keep the railways open. The strike will end on May 25.

June 3. The Supreme Court rules that bus companies must provide seats for all passengers regardless of their race or skin color.

October 16. Controls on the price of meat are terminated.

November 9. Price controls are lifted on most necessities except rice, sugar and rents.

1947

Thanks to the 1944 GI Bill, 1 million veterans of World War II are enrolled in universities (out of a total of 2.5 million college students).

June 11. The rationing of sugar is terminated.

June 23. The Labor-Management Relations Act (Taft-Hartley Act) becomes law over the president's veto. The act imposes new restrictions on union activities.

Science and Technology

1945

The Constellation, a commercial airplane, sets a new aviation record by flying between Paris and New York in 12 hours and 57 minutes.

1946

Willard Frank Libby develops carbon 14 as a method for dating archaeological and geological materials.

February 15. ENIAC, the first electronic computer, is built; it weighs 50 tons.

In Tennessee, construction begins on the first atomic power plant.

Taft-Hartley Act (Labor-Management Relations Act)

Proposed by Republican senator Robert Taft of Ohio and Republican representative Fred Hartley of New Jersey, this law came into force on June 23, 1947, despite a presidential veto and after lengthy debate.

Henceforth, no strike can begin without warning, and a "cooling off" period of 60 days is mandated before a strike can begin. Should the president declare a strike to pose a threat to national security, he can stop it by injunction. Moreover, managerial staffs, civil servants whatever their rank, domestic employees and agricultural workers are forbidden to go on strike or to form unions. The closed shop, whereby trade unions can control hiring, is eliminated. Once hired, employees must join the union in their firm (union shop) if required under their contract and if the state does not forbid it. Several union practices are illegal, including solidarity strikes, secondary boycotts, refusals to negotiate a collective agreement, excessive dues, strikes against the government. Lastly, "all the officials [of a union] must attest that they are not Communists, that they are not sympathizers, nor members or sympathizers of groups promoting or teaching the overthrow of government by force, violence or other illegal means." If this clause is not respected, the union loses legal recognition as well as the protection of the National Labor Relations Board.

Nicknamed the "slave-labor law" by trade unionists, the Taft-Hartley Act aroused indignation among liberals.

June 17. The inaugural flight of the first commercial airplane to travel around the world begins; it will return to New York on June 30.

October 5. Truman becomes the first president to use television to address the nation; he speaks on the problem of hunger in the world.

October 14. In a flight over California, air force captain Charles Yeager becomes the first pilot to break the sound barrier.

Civilization and Culture

1945

The historian Arthur Schlesinger, Jr. publishes *The Age of Jackson.*

Humorist Bill Mauldin's drawings on army life, *Up Front.*

1946

John Hersey's *Hiroshima*, on the atomic bombing of the city.

The poets Robert Lowell and James Merrill publish *Lord Weary's Castle* and *The Black Iwan*, respectively.

Robert Penn Warren's novel *All the King's Men*, based on the life of the populist Louisiana politician Huey Long.

Frank Capra's film *It's a Wonderful Life*; William Wyler's *The Best Years of Our Lives.*

The Dymaxion House, a mass-producible circular dwelling, by the architect Buckminster Fuller.

1947

Senate hearings on alleged Communist subversion in the movie industry lead to the blacklisting (denial of work) of the

Hollywood Ten and other screenwriters and filmmakers.

The English translation of *The Diary of Anne Frank* is published.

James Michener's novel *Tales of the South Pacific*.

Margaret Truman, daughter of the president, makes her singing debut with the Detroit Symphony Orchestra.

The French artist Jean Dubuffet has his first major exhibit in New York.

Jackie Robinson signs with the Brooklyn Dodgers to become the first black to play major league baseball.

December 3. Premiere in New York of Tennessee Williams's play *A Streetcar Named Desire*, which will receive a Pulitzer Prize in 1948.

Chapter 23   1948–1952

The Cold War Takes Hold

Fear of domestic and international communism continued to dominate the nation's politics.

Harry Truman was elected president in 1948 with 24.2 million popular votes against 21.9 million for Thomas Dewey, and 303 electoral college votes against Dewey's 189. Safeguarding the country from any Communist influence soon became an obsession. The House Un-American Activities Committee (HUAC) intensified its investigations, and Senator Joseph McCarthy launched a full-blown witch-hunt to uncover Communists in government and various professions.

On the international scene, the situation became more unstable. Tensions heightened in Europe as the Soviets imposed a blockade on Berlin and Communist regimes came to power in the countries of Eastern Europe. In Asia, the Cold War turned into a "hot" war in Korean. The United States strengthened western defenses by creating the North Atlantic Treaty Organization (NATO) and establishing air bases around the USSR, which exploded its own atomic bomb in 1949.

The presidential election of 1952 enabled the Republican Party to return to power after a 20-year hiatus. Dwight D. Eisenhower, the charismatic military hero, was elected with 33.9 million votes over Adlai Stevenson's 27.3 million. Americans trusted Eisenhower's knowledge of internation issues, and his campaign themes were clear. Blaming the Truman administration for the Korean War, which it was unable to win or bring to an end, Eisenhower pledged to go personally to Korea and find a quick solution.

Political and Institutional Life

1948

May 19. A law sponsored by Senator Karl Mundt and Representative Richard Nixon requires members of the Communist Party to register with the government.

May 24. A new law on the draft requires all men 18 to 25 years of age to register. The number to be drafted is set at 837,000 for the army, 667,000 for the navy and the marines, and 502,000 for the air force.

July 20. Twelve leaders of the Communist Party of America are convicted of having promoted the overthrow of the government.

August 3. Whittaker Chambers, a former member of the Communist Party, accuses Alger Hiss, a senior official in the State Department from 1936 to 1945, of having been a Communist and of having passed secret documents to the USSR. Hiss denies the charges.

November 2. Truman is elected president; Alben Barkley is elected vice president.

December 6. Nixon, a member of HUAC, accuses the government of having hidden the truth in the Hiss scandal.

December 15. A federal grand jury indicts Alger Hiss for perjury.

1949

January 20. Harry Truman takes the presidential oath of office.

October 14. Eleven Communists are found guilty of conspiring against the government under the Smith Act of 1940.

December 9. Representative J. Parnell Thomas, the chairman of HUAC, is jailed for corruption.

1950

February 9. Senator Joseph McCarthy, in a speech to a women's club in Wheeling, West Virginia, claims to have in his possession the names of 205 Communists employed by the State Department.

February 20. McCarthy claims to possess a second list of Communists employed by the government.

March 7. Valentin Gubichev, an official in the Soviet consulate, is expelled for conspiracy and espionage.

May 8. The Supreme Court rules that the provision of the Taft-Hartley Act requiring union leaders to attest that they are not Communists is permissible under the Constitution.

September 23. The McCarran Act becomes law over Truman's veto. The act requires members of the Communist Party to register with the government. It also permits the internment of Communists during a state of emergency and creates an office for the control of subversive activities.

November 1. In Washington, two Puerto Rican nationalists fail in their attempt to assassinate President Truman.

November 17. Alger Hiss, convicted of perjury, is sentenced to five years in prison.

1951

February 27. The 22nd Amendment to the Constitution is adopted: No person can be elected president more than two times. If a vice president serves as president during more than two years of a previous president's term, he can be elected president only once.

March 21. George Marshall, now the secretary of defense, reports that the size of the armed forces has doubled to 2.9 million men since the outbreak of the Korean War.

April 5. Julius and Ethel Rosenberg are sentenced to death for espionage on behalf of the USSR.

June 19. The draft law is extended to July 1, 1955. The draft age is raised to 18½ years, military service is set at 2 years, and the draft is made compulsory for every male.

1952

March 3. The Supreme Court rules that members of groups advocating the violent overthrow of the government may be barred from teaching in public schools.

March 18. Connecticut Senator William Benton accuses McCarthy of using Nazi tactics in his investigations.

June 27. The Immigration and Nationality Act of 1952 (McCarran-Walter Act) becomes law over Truman's veto. The act establishes a system of quotas to determine the number of immigrants from each foreign nation.

September 23. Republican vice-presidential candidate Richard Nixon, in a televised address subsequently known as the "Checkers Speech" after his reference to the family dog Checkers, denies having profited personally from a fund established for his use by political supporters.

October 23. In New York, eight teachers are fired because of their activities as members of the Communist Party.

November 4. Dwight D. Eisenhower is elected the 34th president; Richard Nixon is elected vice president.

Foreign Policy

1948

April 3. A foreign aid act authorizes military assistance to Greece and Turkey to stem the spread of communism; military and economic aid to nationalist China; and a contribution to the United Nations Children's Fund.

June 24. The Soviet Union imposes a blockade on the Western sectors of Berlin.

June 26. Truman orders the air force to begin airlifting food and other necessities into West Berlin.

October 24. Before a Senate committee, Bernard Baruch speaks of a thaw in the Cold War.

1949

January 20. In his Inaugural Address, Truman outlines a four-point program of technological and economic aid to other countries. The "Point Four" program will provide technological assistance to underdeveloped nations.

April 4. The North Atlantic Treaty, a mutual security pact, is signed by the United States, Canada, Great Britain, France, Belgium, the Netherlands, Luxembourg, Iceland, Norway, Denmark, Portugal and Italy.

May 12. The Berlin Blockade ends.

June 29. American troops are withdrawn from Korea, except for 500 military advisors.

September 21. The Mutual Defense Assistance Act funds American participation in the North Atlantic Treaty Organization (NATO).

September 23. Truman announces that the USSR has conducted its first atomic test and possesses the atomic bomb.

October 1. The United States refuses to recognize the Communist government of Mao Tse-tung on the mainland of China.

October 24. The permanent headquarters of the United Nations is dedicated in New York.

December 8. The Chinese nationalist leader Chiang Kai-shek flees to the island of Taiwan (Formosa); the United States will recognize his government as that of China.

1950

January 12. Secretary of State Dean Acheson omits Korea from the U.S. defensive perimeter in the Pacific.

January 31. The president authorizes the development of the hydrogen bomb.

June 5. The Foreign Economic Aid Act establishes an aid program for underdeveloped countries.

September 8. Following the start of the Korean War, the Defense Production Act authorizes the president to control wages and prices.

December 19. General Eisenhower is named supreme commander of NATO forces.

The United States recognizes the new state of Vietnam.

1951

April 2. Eisenhower establishes NATO headquarters in France.

August 30. The United States signs a trade agreement with the Philippines.

September 1. The ANZUS Treaty, a mutual defense agreement, is signed by the United States, Australia and New Zealand.

September 8. A peace treaty is signed with Japan in San Francisco. Full Japanese sovereignty is restored. In a separate mutual-security pact, the United States retains its military bases in Japan.

October 10. The Mutual Security Act authorizes $7 billion in foreign aid. The Mutual Security Agency is created.

December 13. Veteran foreign service officer and China expert John Service is dismissed by the State Department as a possible security risk, even though previous charges that he provided confidential documents to a left-wing magazine had been dropped for lack of evidence.

1952

January 5. Winston Churchill, reelected prime minister of Great Britain in 1951, meets in Washington with Truman to strengthen the links between Great Britain and the United States and define a common policy for the Western alliance.

January 8. The United States pledges not to use atomic weapons based in England without the prior consent of the British.

May 26. The United States, Great Britain and France sign a peace treaty with West Germany.

July 25. Puerto Rico becomes a U.S. commonwealth.

August 2. The military occupation of the Federal Republic of Germany (West Germany) is terminated. Allied troops will remain in West Germany as NATO forces.

November 1. The United States detonates the first thermonuclear device, the forerunner of the hydrogen bomb, at Eniwetok atoll in the Marshall Islands.

Korean War Chronology

1950

June 25. North Korean troops cross the 38th parallel and invade South Korea.

June 26. Truman orders U.S. Air Force and Navy units to assist South Korean troops in repulsing the North Korean attack.

June 27. The UN Security Council authorizes member states to intervene militarily in Korea "to restore international peace and security in the area." The United States will provide the bulk of the assistance to South Korea.

June 30. The president sends American ground troops to South Korea and orders the navy to blockade the Korean coast.

July 8. General Douglas MacArthur is appointed commander of UN forces in Korea.

August 4. The army recalls 62,000 reservists to active duty for 21 months.

August 6–September 15. Driven southward by the Communist invasion, South Korean and U.S. troops cling to a defensive perimeter around the city of Pusan on the southern coast of South Korea.

September 15. In a daring amphibious operation, UN forces under MacArthur land far behind North Korean lines at the western South Korean port city of Inchon and sweep inland, halting the North Korean offensive.

September 26. UN forces recapture Seoul, the South Korean capital.

September 29. UN troops, spearheaded by American forces, reach the 38th parallel.

October 7. UN forces cross the 38th parallel into North Korea.

October 11. Communist China issues a protest against the entry of UN forces into North Korea and threatens to intervene in the war.

October 15. Truman and MacArthur meet on Wake Island to define a strategy for the war.

October 20. Pyongyang, the capital of North Korea, is captured by UN forces.

November 6. Chinese Communist troops infiltrate into North Korea.

November 20. American units reach the Yalu River on the border with Chinese Manchuria.

November 26. UN troops are forced to retreat before a surprise Communist Chinese offensive.

December 5. The Communists retake Pyongyang.

December 8. Truman announces an embargo on exports to Communist China.

December 16. The president declares a national emergency.

December 29. MacArthur requests authority to attack Communist China by air and naval bombardment.

1951

January 4. Seoul is evacuated by UN forces in the face of the Communist offensive.

March 14. UN forces reoccupy Seoul.

April 11. MacArthur is dismissed by the president from his dual command of UN forces and U.S. forces in the Far East. General Matthew Ridgway is appointed to replace MacArthur.

July 10. Truce negotiations begin at Kaesong, on the 38th parallel; participants include representatives of the UN, the United States, North and South Korea and Communist China.

1952

January 24. UN negotiators declare that the peace talks in Korea are stalled.

December 2–4. Fulfilling a campaign pledge, president-elect Eisenhower visits South Korea.

Economy and Society

1948

March 8. The Supreme Court rules that religious education in public schools violates the 1st Amendment.

March 15–April 12. Approximately 200,000 miners go on strike; they succeed in obtaining a better retirement plan.

May 3. The Supreme Court rules that racially restrictive covenants violate the equal protection clause of the 14th Amendment.

May 25. General Motors and the automobile workers' union agree to link wages to the cost of living.

July 26. An executive order signed by President Truman prohibits discrimination in the armed forces and in federal employment.

1949

January 20. In his Inaugural Address, Truman outlines his Fair Deal program: agricultural price supports, an extension of social programs, more low-income housing at affordable prices and more civil rights legislation.

February 25. General Motors announces a reduction in the price of its cars, the first since World War II.

July 15. The Housing Act authorizes funds to build affordable housing.

October 1–November 11. 500,000 steelworkers go on strike, asking for a retirement plan.

October 26. Legislation raises the minimum wage from 50 to 75 cents an hour, beginning in January 1950.

October 31. Walter Reuther, president of the automobile workers' union, wants to expel Communists from the CIO.

1950

The population of the United States is set at 150,697,361. Illiteracy is at its lowest level ever, 3.2 percent (1 percent less than in 1940, and 16.8 percent less than in 1870).

May 28. A special Senate committee headed by Tennessee senator Estes Kefauver begins an investigation into organized crime in America. The hearings, which will continue into 1951 when they become the first ever televised, draw nationwide attention.

August 25. Truman places the railroads under the army's control in order to prevent a railway workers strike.

August 28. A new Social Security Act extends coverage to an additional 10 million workers.

September 8. The Defense Production Act authorizes the president to allocate resources and control wages and prices.

1951

January 1. Congress authorizes the president to freeze prices.

1952

April 8. Truman nationalizes the steel mills to avert a general strike.

June 2. The Supreme Court rules unconstitutional Truman's seizure of the steel mills. More than 600,000 steelworkers immediately go on strike. On July 24, an agreement at the White House will bring an end to the strike.

July 16. A new GI Bill of Rights gives Korean War veterans the same benefits as those provided to veterans of World War II.

November 25. George Meany becomes president of the AFL.

December 4. Walter Reuther becomes head of the CIO.

Science and Technology

1948

Peter Goldmark develops the long-playing (LP) phonograph record.

The transistor is invented by William Shockley, Walter Brattain and John Bardeen.

June 3. The world's largest reflector telescope is inaugurated at Mount Palomar Observatory in California.

1949

Binac, an automatic binary computer built by John Mauch and J. Prosper Eckert, computes 12,000 times faster than the human brain.

The Atomic Energy Commission builds the first fast-breeder reactor.

March 2. A B-50 bomber makes the first non-stop flight around the world, refueling in flight four times.

1950

The first kidney transplant is performed by Dr. Richard Lowler.

1951

A team of researchers led by Edward Teller achieves the first thermonuclear reaction.

June 14. UNIVAC becomes the first electronic digital computer to be marketed.

June 25. The first color television broadcast lasts four hours. Color TV sets are not yet on the market.

September 4. In the first transcontinental TV broadcast, 94 stations relay Truman's speech given in Washington to the participants at the San Francisco Conference for the signing of the peace treaty with Japan.

November 10. The first direct transcontinental telephone call is made from New Jersey to California.

December 20. In Idaho, researchers succeed for the first time in producing electricity from nuclear energy.

1952

The United States detonates the first thermonuclear explosion.

Dr. Jonas Salk of Pittsburgh University tests his new vaccine against poliomyelitis.

May 8. The Department of Defense announces a program to build an atomic artillery piece.

June 14. President Truman christens the *Nautilus*, the first nuclear-powered submarine, at Groton, Connecticut.

Civilization and Culture

1948

The Age of Anxiety, by the poet W. H. Auden. Norman Mailer's novel *The Naked and the Dead*.

Kiss Me Kate, a musical by Cole Porter.

Painter Andrew Wyeth's *Christina's World*.

Virgil Thomson's *Suite for Orchestra*. Miles Davis introduces Cool jazz.

1949

Carol Reed's film *The Third Man*.

Radio Free Europe begins broadcasting news bulletins to listeners behind the Iron Curtain.

Arthur Miller's play *Death of a Salesman*, and *Guys and Dolls*, a musical by Frank Loesser, open on Broadway.

The abstract expressionist Robert Motherwell's *At Five in the Afternoon*.

José Limón's modern dance piece *The Moor's Pavane*.

1950

William Inge's play *Come Back, Little Sheba*.

The National Book Awards are established.

The New York School of abstract expressionist painters in the 1950s influences art worldwide. Members include Willem de Kooning, Jackson Pollock,

Mark Rothko and Robert Motherwell. Jackson Pollock's *Mural in Indian Red Ground* represents his new method of "action painting," which involves dripping and splashing paint on the canvas. Mark Rothko's *Tundra*.

From Here to Eternity, by James Jones. J. D. Salinger's *The Catcher in the Rye*. Herman Wouk's *The Caine Mutiny*.

Rock and roll music will become popular in the 1950s; early legends include Fats Domino, Chuck Berry, Bo Diddley and Bill Haley.

October 11. The Federal Communications Commission permits CBS (Columbia Broadcasting Company) to broadcast color TV programs.

November 10. William Faulkner is awarded the Nobel Prize for literature.

November 29. The National Council of the Churches of Christ in the U.S.A. is established, bringing together 30 Protestant and Eastern Orthodox denominations.

1951

Release of Vincente Minelli's movie *An American in Paris*.

The King and I, a musical by Richard Rodgers and Oscar Hammerstein, opens on Broadway.

Willem de Kooning's painting *Woman*.

1952

Ernest Hemingway's *The Old Man and the Sea*; John Steinbeck's *East of Eden*; Ralph Ellison's *Invisible Man*; Bernard Malamud's *The Natural*.

Films: John Ford's *The Quiet Man*; *Singing in the Rain*, with Gene Kelly and Stanley Donen; Fred Zinnemann's *High Noon*.

Composer John Cage's *Silence*.

American Bandstand premieres on television.

Chapter 24   1953–1960

Ike: The Quiet Man

D wight D. Eisenhower's arrival in the White House did not bring dramatic changes in the nation's domestic and foreign policies. Perhaps the first significant event of his presidency was the signing of an armistice halting the Korean War. In a country that was by and large prosperous despite threats of inflation and recession, the main problems were racial and ideological. The black population was becoming conscious of its political strength and began to organize itself to demand its civil rights. But Supreme Court rulings and subsequent attempts by the federal government to end racial segregation met with fierce resistance, especially in the South. By the end of Eisenhower's first term, in 1956, Senator Joseph McCarthy's excesses belonged to the past, and the country had begun to develop solutions to its racial problems. Eisenhower was reelected president by a very large margin, 35.6 million popular votes and 457 electoral votes against Adlai Stevenson's 26.0 million votes and 73 electors.

The period was marked by major advances in the area of national defense, achieved through a close collaboration between private industry and the military, and through the application of scientific discoveries to weapons. As the Cold War deepened, the United States adopted the tougher policy of "massive retaliation" toward the Soviet Union. After an attempt at a détente, the mutual hostility intensified in 1960 following the U-2 incident, in which a U.S. spy plane was shot down over Soviet territory. Both sides had meanwhile engaged in a nuclear arms race and a competition in space. The USSR took the lead in the latter by launching *Sputnik*, the first space satellite, on October 4, 1957. The spread of communism in the Far East emerged as another worrisome issue at the international level, especially following the French withdrawal from Indochina in 1954. Eisenhower feared Communist expansion in the Southeast Asian countries, which he compared to a row of dominoes, where the fall of one country would cause the fall, one by one, of all the others.

In the presidential election of 1960, a young Democratic senator from Massachusetts, John F. Kennedy, won with 34.2 million, votes over Vice President Richard M. Nixon's 34.1 million the slimmest majority since 1888. A novelty of this election was a series of four televised debates, which probably tipped the scales in favor of the Democratic candidate.

Political and Institutional Life

1953

January 20. Eisenhower takes office, with Richard Nixon as vice president.

January 21. In New York, a federal grand jury indicts 13 Communist leaders of conspiring against the government.

February 13. Senator Joseph McCarthy declares that Eisenhower's foreign policy is being "sabotaged" by the radio station Voice of America.

April 1. The Department of Health, Education and Welfare (HEW) is created.

April 20. The Communist Party is ordered to register with the Justice Department as an organization controlled and directed by the USSR.

April 27. Eisenhower issues an executive order implementing a new security program for executive-branch employees.

June 14. Speaking at Dartmouth College in Hanover, New Hampshire, Eisenhower warns against "the book burners" and indirectly criticizes McCarthyism.

June 19. Julius and Ethel Rosenberg, convicted in 1951 of espionage on behalf of the USSR, become the first Americans to be executed for treason in peacetime.

September 30. Eisenhower appoints Earl Warren chief justice of the Supreme Court.

December 9. General Electric announces that it will fire all employees affiliated with the Communist Party.

1954

April 12. Nuclear physicist J. Robert *Oppenheimer*, the war time head of the Los Alamos atomic bomb project, has his security clearance suspended by the Eisenhower administration. Oppenheimer is judged a potential security risk based on his past associations with Communists, despite his unequivocal obnunciation of Communist ideology.

April 22-June 17. Senate hearings are held on McCarthy's accusations that the army harbors Communists. The senator's image is irreparably damaged during the Televised hearings.

May 24. The Supreme Court rules that membership in the Communist Party is a justifiable cause for the deportation of aliens.

June 2. McCarthy alleges that the Central Intelligence Agency (CIA) is a victim of Communist infiltration.

July 30. A Senate committee censures McCarthy.

August 24. Communist Control Act removes all privileges and immunities of the Communist Party and makes it subject to penalties under the Internal Security Act.

September 3. An act of Congress makes espionage and sabotage, punishable by death even in peacetime.

September 30. Since May 28, 1953, 3,002 civil servants suspected of being security risks have been fired.

November 2. In congressional elections, the Democrats recapture majorities in the Senate and the House of Representatives.

December 2. McCarthy is officially condemned by his peers in the Senate, marking the end of McCarthyism.

1955

January 14. The Senate unanimously approves the continuation of investigations of Communist infiltration among civil servants.

January 19. Eisenhower holds the first televised presidential press conference.

September 24. Eisenhower suffers a heart attack in Denver, Colorado.

1956

November 6. Eisenhower is reelected president, defeating the Democratic candidate, Adlai Stevenson. In congressional races, the Democrats keep their majorities in the Senate and the House of Representatives.

1957

January 20. Eisenhower begins his second term.

February 9–12. A convention of the Communist Party of America, meeting in New York, affirms its independence from Soviet control. Any member accused of conspiracy against the government will be expelled.

July 16. Secretary of Defense Charles Wilson announces that the armed forces will be reduced by 100,000 men by January 1, 1958.

1958

July 29. Eisenhower signs the National Aeronautics and Space Act, creating the National Aeronautics and Space Administration (NASA) to coordinate the manned and unmanned exploration of outer space.

November 4. The Democratic Party scores a major victory in the mid-term congressional elections.

1959

January 3. Alaska becomes the 49th state of the Union.

April 15. Suffering from cancer, Secretary of State John Foster Dulles resigns. He will be succeeded by Christian Herter.

August 21. Hawaii becomes the 50th state of the Union.

1960

November 8. Senator John F. Kennedy, the Democratic candidate, is elected the 35th president, defeating Vice President Nixon in a campaign that featured the first televised presidential debates. Senator Lyndon B. Johnson is elected vice president.

Foreign Policy

1953

March 26. Eisenhower holds talks with French prime minister René Mayer. The United States will help France in its war in Indochina. The pledge will be confirmed on April 7, 1954.

July 27. An armistice between United Nations and Communist forces is signed at Panmunjom, in Korea. American losses in the Korean War total 54,246 dead and 103,284 wounded.

August 12. The Soviet Union detonates its first thermonuclear device, the forerunner of a hydrogen bomb.

September 26. The United States agrees to help Spain militarily and economically, in exchange for air and naval bases on Spanish territory.

December 4. Eisenhower and the prime ministers of Great Britain and France hold a "Big Three" summit conference in Bermuda.

December 8. Eisenhower proposes his "Atoms for Peace" program in an address to the UN General Assembly. The program calls for the creation of an international pool of nuclear material that will be devoted to the peaceful uses of atomic energy.

1954

January 7. In his State of the Union message to Congress, Eisenhower proposes to cut military spending.

January 12. John Foster Dulles unveils the new policy of "massive retaliation" vis-à-vis the USSR.

January 23. The Berlin Conference on the future of Germany is attended by the foreign ministers of the United States, Great Britain, France and the USSR.

February 25. The Bricker amendment to the Constitution is rejected by the Senate. Opposed by Eisenhower, the amendment would have limited the treaty-making powers of the president.

February 28. The United States tests its first hydrogen bomb.

March 1. A Pan-American conference meets in Caracas, Venezuela. Discussion revolves around the Communist threat to the members of the Organization of American States (OAS).

A U.S. thermonuclear bomb test on the island of Bikini, in the Pacific, contaminates the crew of the Japanese fishing boat *Lucky Dragon* with radiation.

May 7. In Indochina, a French army is defeated by Communist forces at Dien Bien Phu. Eisenhower had decided against direct U.S. military intervention to save the French garrison.

May–June. The CIA orchestrates a coup in Guatemala.

July 21. The Geneva Accords divide Vietnam into the Communist North and non-Communist South at the 19th parallel. The United States declines to sign the agreement with Communist China, which it does not recognize, but will back the emergence of an independent South Vietnam.

August 19. A CIA-sponsored coup overthrows the leftist Iranian government of Mohammed Mossadegh and returns Shah Reza Pahlavi to the throne.

September 8. In Manila, the United States, Great Britain, France, Australia, New Zealand, Pakistan, the Philippines and Thailand sign a mutual defense treaty creating the Southeast Asia Treaty Organization (SEATO).

December 2. A mutual defense treaty is signed with Taiwan.

1955

January 1. The United States begins a program of aid to Cambodia, Laos and Vietnam.

January 28. Congress authorizes the president to use armed force to defend Taiwan from attack by Communist China.

March 10. Eisenhower declares that in the event of war, the United States is prepared to use nuclear weapons.

May 15. The United States, Great Britain, France and the Soviet Union sign the Austrian State Treaty formally ending World War II for the central European nation and restoring its 1938 borders. Occupying forces will be withdrawn.

July 18–23. Eisenhower attends the Geneva Summit, the first postwar conference of the leaders of the United States, Great Britain, France and the Soviet Union, the victorious powers in World War II. The conferees discuss the reunification of Germany, security in Europe and disarmament. Eisenhower proposes his "Open Skies" plan, whereby the United States and the Soviet Union would fly reconnaissance planes over each other's country to guard against surprise attack. Despite the rejection of the plan by Nikita Khrushchev, the head of the Soviet Communist Party, the meeting fosters a

"Spirit of Geneva" hinting at an East-West détente.

August 8. An international conference is held in Geneva on the peaceful uses of atomic energy.

November 22. The Soviet Union tests its first hydrogen bomb.

December 17. The United States pledges a $56 million loan to Egypt for the construction of the Aswan Dam.

1956

March 7. Eisenhower refuses to ship arms to Israel, despite the fact that Egypt is receiving military assistance from the USSR.

July 4. The U-2, an American spy plane, makes its first flight over the Soviet Union.

July 19. John Foster Dulles cancels the offer of a loan to Egypt made on Dec. 17, 1955.

July 22. Eisenhower and the leaders of 18 other American nations sign the Panama Declaration, which calls for economic cooperation among their countries.

July 26. The Suez Canal is nationalized by Egyptian president Gamal Abdel Nasser.

October 26. The charter of the International Atomic Energy Agency is signed in New York by representatives of 70 countries. The agency is a result of Eisenhower's Atoms for Peace proposal of December 8, 1953.

October–November. In the Suez Crisis, Eisenhower stops the British-French-Israeli invasion of Egypt that was launched in response to Nasser's nationalization of the Suez Canal. The crisis coincides with the Soviet invasion of Hungary to suppress a popular revolt.

1957

January 5. In a speech to Congress, the president pledges that the United States will assist any nation in the Middle East threatened by communism (Eisenhower Doctrine).

January 14. John Foster Dulles informs the Senate that the threat of communism in the Middle East has reached critical proportions.

February 8. The United States agrees to continue its military aid to Saudi Arabia in exchange for a lease on the air base at Dharan.

May 11. In Washington, Eisenhower holds talks with Ngo Dinh Diem, the president of South Vietnam.

May 26–28. Eisenhower and German chancellor Konrad Adenauer discuss disarmament and German reunification.

June 7. An agreement with Poland provides loans for the development of Polish agriculture and mineral resources.

August 26. The Soviet Union announces it has successfully tested the world's first intercontinental ballistic missile (ICBM).

October 4. The Soviet Union launches *Sputnik I*, the world's first space satellite, into orbit around the earth.

December 16–19. Eisenhower attends a NATO heads-of-government meeting in Paris after suffering a mild stroke on November 25.

1958

January 27. An agreement is signed with the USSR on exchanges in the fields of education, culture, sports and technology.

May 12. The United States and Canada establish the North American Air Defense Command (NORAD) to defend the continent against nuclear attack.

May 13. Visiting South America, Vice President Nixon becomes the target of violently hostile demonstrations in Caracas.

May 14. The U.S. Sixth Fleet doubles its strength in the Mediterranean Sea. The United States sends arms to Lebanon as a demonstration of support for its independence.

July 15. Following a coup against the pro-Western government of Iraq, Eisenhower orders the marines of the Sixth Fleet into Lebanon at the request of the Lebanese government.

August 21. The marines begin leaving Lebanon. Their withdrawal will be completed on October 25.

August 22. Eisenhower offers a moratorium on U.S. testing of nuclear weapons provided the USSR reciprocates. He also calls for negotiations on a treaty to ban nuclear testing. Soviet premier Khrushchev will agree to negotiations on August 29.

October 31. The United States, Great Britain and the USSR begin negotiations on a treaty that would ban the testing of nuclear weapons.

1959

March 5. The United States signs bilateral defense pacts with Iran, Pakistan and Turkey.

July 9. Communists kill two American soldiers in Bien Hoa, South Vietnam.

July 23–August 2. Vice President Nixon visits the USSR. An impromptu televised debate between Nixon and Khrushchev takes place in Moscow on July 24, in the demonstration kitchen of a U.S. exhibit on American life ("Kitchen Debate").

August 27. The United States announces that military aid to Laos will be increased.

September 13. An unmanned Soviet space rocket reaches the Moon.

September 15–27. Khrushchev visits the United States. He meets with Eisenhower at Camp David, Maryland, and they agree to settle international questions by peaceful means.

November 21. An agreement on scientific, cultural and athletic exchanges is reached with the USSR.

1960

January 19. A new mutual defense treaty is signed with Japan.

May 1. A U-2 spy plane is shot down over the USSR, near the city of Sverdlovsk (Ekaterinburg).

May 7. Khrushchev announces that the pilot of the U-2 spy plane has been captured. After having previously stated officially that the plane had been lost on a weather reconnaissance flight, the United States admits that the U-2 was on a spying mission.

May 11. At a press conference, Eisenhower admits that the United States has been sending reconnaissance aircraft over Soviet territory for the last four years.

May 16. In Paris, a summit meeting of the United States, Great Britain, France and the Soviet Union breaks up after one session over the U-2 incident. Khrushchev rescinds his invitation to Eisenhower to visit the USSR.

June 12–26. Eisenhower visits Asia (the Philippines, Taiwan, Korea), Hawaii and Alaska.

July 6. Faced with Fidel Castro's increasingly hostile Cuban government, Eisenhower cancels 95 percent of Cuba's sugar exports to the United States.

August 19. In Moscow, the pilot of the U-2 plane, Francis Gary Powers, is convicted of espionage and sentenced to 10 years in jail. He will be freed on February 10, 1962.

October 20. An embargo is placed on exports to Cuba.

Economy and Society

1953

February 6. Wage controls are lifted.

March 17. Price controls are lifted.

August 7. The Refugee Relief Act allows 214,000 refugees to enter the United States.

October 1. Eisenhower invokes the Taft-Hartley Act to prevent a longshoremen's strike.

1954

March 3. New York longshoremen begin a strike that will last until April 2.

May 17. In a landmark case concerning racial segregation, the Supreme Court rules in *Brown v. Board of Education of Topeka* that providing "separate but equal" school facilities for whites and blacks is unconstitutional.

August 2. The Housing Act provides funds for building 35,000 new public housing units.

August 30. The Atomic Energy Act permits private corporations to build nuclear reactors to produce energy. The law also authorizes the exchange of information on nuclear weapons with European allies.

September 1. The Social Security Act is amended to provide coverage to an additional 7 million people, mostly farmers and agricultural workers.

December 31. On the New York Stock Exchange, stock prices reach their highest level since 1929.

1955

The rapid increase in population since World War II results in a shortage of 140,000 teachers and 300,000 classrooms.

May 31. The Supreme Court rules that school desegregation must be achieved "with all deliberate speed."

August 2. Congress approves funding for 45,000 new public housing units, to be completed by July 31, 1956.

Legislation increases the minimum wage to $1 an hour, effective March 1, 1956.

September 26. The New York Stock Exchange suffers its heaviest loss ever in a single day, $44 billion, after Eisenhower's heart attack on September 24.

August 28. Emmett Till, a black youth from Chicago, is murdered by two white men in Mississippi. Although Till's killers will be freed by a jury, the trial will attract national media attention to the plight of blacks in the South.

November 25. The Interstate Commerce Commission bans all forms of segregation on trains and buses traveling between states.

December 1. In Montgomery, Alabama, Rosa Parks, a black seamstress, is arrested for refusing to give up her seat on a bus to a white passenger. Her act will spark a boycott of the city's buses by blacks led by Reverend Martin Luther King, Jr.

December 5. The AFL and the CIO merge into a single trade union, the AFL-CIO, headed by George Meany, the former president of the AFL.

1956

February 6. Autherine Lucy becomes the first black student to attend the University of Alabama. She will be expelled after three days of violent protest against her admission.

March 20. A strike lasting 156 days, the longest in 20 years, ends at the Westinghouse Electric Corporation.

May 2. The Methodist Church calls for an end to all forms of segregation within the Church.

May 28. A law aimed at reducing agricultural surpluses and supporting prices provides aid to farmers who decide to leave their land fallow.

August 1. Legislation provides financing for 70,000 new public housing units.

1957

July 12. The Housing Act makes mortgage loans easier to obtain and opens low-income housing to the elderly.

August 29. The Civil Rights Act becomes the first federal law since 1875 to protect the rights of blacks. It establishes procedures for safeguarding blacks' right to vote and creates the Civil Rights Commission and the Civil Rights Division within the Department of Justice.

September 4. In Little Rock, Arkansas, the state's National Guard troops, on orders of Governor Orval Faubus, prevent black students from entering Central High School. The governor's effort to prevent the desegregation of Little Rock's schools is in violation of a federal court order.

September 14. Eisenhower meets with Governor Faubus in an effort to resolve the controversy in Little Rock.

September 20. Obeying a federal court order, Faubus withdraws his National Guard troops from Central High School.

September 23. After mob violence, Little Rock police remove black pupils from Central High School.

September 25. Eisenhower orders 1,000 federal troops into Little Rock to enable nine black students to attend classes. The president also places the Arkansas National Guard under federal control.

October 16. Great Britain's Queen Elizabeth and Prince Philip visit Jamestown, Virginia, to commemorate the 350th anniversary of the first British settlement in the New World.

1958

April 1. An emergency law on housing encourages construction in order to stimulate the economy.

June 29. In Birmingham, Alabama, a bomb explodes near a Baptist church whose minister is a civil rights leader.

September 2. Prompted by the Soviet launch of *Sputnik*, the National Defense Education Act provides funding for educational programs, with an emphasis on mathematics and science.

September 4. The Supreme Court intervenes in cases involving Columbus, Georgia, where violations of blacks' voting rights.

September 12. The Supreme Court refuses to grant a delay for the desegregation of Central High School in Little Rock.

September 29. The Supreme Court unanimously bans all "dilatory plans" for the desegregation of schools.

September 30. In Little Rock, Governor Faubus closes four high schools to avoid desegregation.

1959

June 26. The St. Lawrence Seaway, a joint American-Canadian project, is opened to shipping.

July 15. A steelworkers' strike begins: 28 companies producing 95 percent of the nation's steel are affected.

The strike, which will last until January 4, 1960, will be the longest in this industry's history.

August 12. High schools in Little Rock are reopened in compliance with federal desegregation policy. Approximately 250 segregationist demonstrators are kept away by police.

September 14. The Labor Management Reporting and Disclosure Act seeks to prevent racketeering in labor unions.

October 9. In an effort to end the steelworkers' strike, Eisenhower invokes the Taft-Hartley Act and orders an investigation of the facts behind the strike.

October 21. The steelworkers receive a federal court injunction ordering them back to work. The Supreme Court will uphold the injunction, obtained under the Taft-Hartley Act, on November 7.

1960

A census sets the population at 179,323,175.

The proportion of women working outside the home has increased from 25 percent in 1940 to 34 percent.

The states of Nevada, Florida, Alaska, Arizona and California enjoy the fastest population growth.

February 1. Four black college students in Greensboro, North Carolina, refuse to leave a Woolworth department store lunch counter after being refused service; this marks the beginning of a wave of sit-ins.

April 9. According to the review *Southern School News*, since the Supreme Court's 1954 *Brown* ruling, barely 6 percent of public schools in southern states have complied with the order to desegregate.

May 6. A new civil rights act strengthens the voting-rights provisions of the 1957 act and sets new criminal penalties for violent obstruction of federal court orders.

November 16. In order to slow the flight of gold to other countries and thereby reduce the trade deficit, Eisenhower asks Americans to reduce to a minimum their expenditures abroad.

November 17. Racial violence in New Orleans results in 200 arrests.

Science and Technology

1953

May 25. The first atomic artillery shell is tested in Nevada.

December 16. A new speed record for manned flight is set by Major Charles Yeager of the air force.

1954

The Boeing 707, a passenger airliner, undergoes its first test flights.

January 21. The first American nuclear-powered submarine, the *Nautilus*, is launched.

1956

Plastic tubes are used for the first time to replace blood vessels in heart surgery.

The first non-stop transcontinental flight of a helicopter is completed in 37 hours.

September 24. The first telephone cable under the Atlantic is completed; it stretches 2,235 miles, from Scotland to Newfoundland.

1957

Major John Glenn of the air force sets a new aviation speed record by flying across the country in 3 hours and 23 minutes.

January 18. Three B-52 jet bombers of the air force complete a non-stop flight around the world at an average speed of approximately 500 miles per hour.

September 19. Underground nuclear weapons tests begin in Nevada.

December 15. The air force successfully tests its first intercontinental ballistic missile (ICBM), the Atlas.

1958

The first stereo records are produced.

January 1. The army launches the first U.S. satellite, *Explorer I.*

April 28. Nuclear weapons tests take place in the Marshall Islands.

June 27. A new aviation speed record is set on a flight from New York to London (5 hours and 27 minutes).

August 5. The submarine *Nautilus* makes the first underwater crossing of the North Pole.

December 10. The Boeing 707 makes its first commercial flight.

1959

February 28. *Discoverer I*, a military satellite equipped with scientific measuring instruments, is launched into orbit.

August 7. *Explorer IV*, the first satellite built and launched by NASA, goes into orbit.

October 10. Commercial airline flights around the world begin.

1960

The "pill," the first oral contraceptive, is marketed.

The Light Amplification by Stimulated Emission of Radiation, or LASER, is invented by Theodore Maiman.

At the Mount Palomar Observatory, Quasars (Quasi-Stellar Objects) are discovered.

August 18. *Discoverer XIV*, the nation's first photoreconnaissance satellite, is launched into orbit.

Civilization and Culture

1953

James Baldwin's *Go Tell It on the Mountain* is published. *The Waking*, by poet Theodore Roethke.

Choreographer Merce Cunningham's *Suite by Chance.*

The first issue of *Playboy* magazine is published.

Maureen Connolly, at 19 years of age, becomes the first woman to win the Grand Slam of tennis by winning all four major tournaments in one year.

George Steven's film *Shane.*

January 22. In New York, the dramatist Arthur Miller's *The Witches of Salem* premieres.

September 16. *The Robe*, the first movie filmed in Cinemascope, is released.

1954

Sixty percent of American households own a TV set.

Elia Kazan's film *On the Waterfront*, starring Marlon Brando.

Roy Harris's *Symphony Fantasy.*

An annual jazz festival begins in Newport, Rhode Island.

April 1. President Eisenhower establishes the U.S. Air Force Academy, which will be located in Colorado Springs, Colorado.

October 28. The Nobel Prize for literature is awarded to Ernest Hemingway.

1955

Vladimir Nobokov publishes *Lolita.*

Films: Elia Kazan's *East of Eden*, with James Dean; Nicholas Ray's *Rebel Without a Cause*, starring James Dean; Richard Brooks's *Young Fury*, and his *The*

Blackboard Jungle, starring Sidney Poitier.

The White House Conference on Education endorses greater federal funding for public education.

In New York, Marian Anderson becomes the first black to sing at the Metropolitan Opera.

May 23. The ordination of women as ministers is approved by the Presbyterian Church.

June 17. The Disneyland amusement park opens in Anaheim, California.

1956

The Floating Opera, by John Barth. Allen Ginsberg's *Howl and Other Poems*. The poet John Berryman's *Homage to Mistress Bradstreet*. Grace Metalious's novel about life in a small New England town, *Peyton Place*, is a best-seller.

The Beat Generation of writers and other young artists who rebel against established society and pursue a bohemian lifestyle, including drugs, appears. Prominent members include the poets Allen Ginsberg and Lawrence Ferlinghetti and the novelist Jack Kerouac.

Release of Cecil B. DeMille's movie *The Ten Commandments*.

Elvis Presley's first hit record, "*Heartbreak Hotel.*"

June 29. The playwright Arthur Miller marries the actress Marilyn Monroe.

1957

Release of David Lean's movie *The Bridge over the River Kwai*. Sidney Lumet's film *Twelve Angry Men*.

The evangelist Reverend Dr. Billy Graham conducts a 16-week campaign in New York City.

John Cheever's *The Wapshot Chronicle*. *On the Road*, by Jack Kerouac. Senator John F. Kennedy's book *Profiles in Courage* wins the Pulitzer Prize.

September 26. The musical *West Side Story*, with music by Leonard Bernstein, lyrics by Stephen Sondheim, and choreography by Jerome Robbins, premieres in New York.

1958

Truman Capote's novel *Breakfast at Tiffany's*. *Selected Poems 1928–1958*, by Stanley Kunitz.

Peter Mennin's Piano Concerto.

April 11. Van Cliburn, a 23-year-old pianist from Texas, wins the Tchaikovsky competition in Moscow.

April 14. The Moiseyev Ballet premieres at the Metropolitan Opera, beginning a three-week tour of the country.

1959

Philip Roth's *Goodbye, Columbus*. D. H. Lawrence's novel *Lady Chatterley's Lover* is published in the United States after being banned for 30 years. Saul Bellow's *Henderson the Rain King*. John Updike's *Rabbit, Run*. The poet Anne Sexton's *To Bedlam and Part Way Back*.

Release of William Wyler's movie *Ben-Hur*; Marilyn Monroe stars in *Some Like It Hot*.

Lorraine Hansberry's *A Raisin in the Sun* becomes the first play by a black woman to appear on Broadway. *The Fantasticks*, a musical, begins its record-setting run in New York.

The Southern Christian Leadership Conference is founded under the Reverend Martin Luther King, Jr., to further the advancement of civil rights by Christian means.

Columbia University professor Charles Van Doren testifies before Congress that his victories on a TV quiz show were fixed (quiz show scandal).

May 22. Benjamin O. Davis, Jr., of the air force becomes the first black promoted to the rank of general.

October 21. The Solomon Guggenheim Museum opens in New York.

1960

Otto Preminger's film *Exodus.*

Pop Art, which takes everyday popular (Pop) objects as its subject, appears. Artists include Jasper Johns, Andy Warhol and Roy Lichtenstein.

The abstract painter Frank Stella's *Newstead Abbey.*

Folk music is popularized in the early 1960s by Pete Seeger, Joan Baez, Bob Dylan and other primarily young, rebellious artists.

Soul, black pop music, emerges in the 1960s.

The pioneering black choreographer Alvin Ailey's *Revelations.*

February 18–28. The Winter Olympic Games are held in Squaw Valley, California.

Chapter 25   1961–1963

JFK and the New American Dream

John Kennedy was 43 years old when he took office. Not only was he the youngest person ever elected president, he was also the first Catholic and the first to be born in the 20th century. He aroused widespread enthusiasm, especially among the young, by evoking a "New Frontier" in his Inaugural Address. He asked Americans to surpass themselves in every area of life. His administration sought to boost the economy, combat social injustice and improve the quality of life. Although Kennedy proposed to Congress a number of bills to enact his program, most became law only after his death, including a new civil rights bill. Blacks were more actively engaged in demanding equality, and violence became more frequent in the South.

Kennedy moved to develop a highly efficient armed forces with state-of-the-art weaponry. He shifted American forces from a military strategy of "massive retaliation," deemed impossible to apply, to a strategy of "flexible response." According to the seriousness of the threat, the United States was prepared to wage a counterinsurgency war, a conventional war, or a nuclear war.

Although Kennedy, in contrast to Eisenhower's secretary of state, John Foster Dulles, conceived of the Cold War in less religious and more pragmatic terms, and although he believed in "peaceful coexistence," he remained a staunch defender of the Free World against the Communist bloc. Key crisis spots included Berlin and Cuba. The United States emerged from the nuclear confrontation with the USSR over Cuba with a strengthened position in the East-West conflict. The situation in the Far East, however, was more alarming. Kennedy increased the number of military advisors in Vietnam, leading his country past the point of no return on the road to war.

Kennedy worked to create closer ties with America's allies. He wanted a militarily and economically stronger Europe. With the Latin American states, he developed the Alliance for Progress, a far-reaching aid and exchange program. In addition, he sought to provide more aid to underdeveloped countries.

Kennedy's life was brutally cut short on November 22, 1963, in Dallas, where he was assassinated by a 24-year-old man, Lee Harvey Oswald. The country was in a state of shock. As the historian Arthur Schlesinger, Jr., wrote, every person had lost a "leader, friend, brother."

Political and Institutional Life

1961

January 20. John Kennedy takes the oath of office as president. Lyndon B. Johnson is vice president.

January 25. A presidential press conference is televised live for the first time.

March 1. The Peace Corps, a program that will send young volunteers to Third World countries to help with development and training, is created.

March 29. The 23rd Amendment to the Constitution gives the citizens of the District of Columbia the right to vote for president and vice president.

1963

November 22. In Dallas, Texas, Kennedy is assassinated by Lee Harvey Oswald, who is arrested later in the day. Kennedy is pronounced dead at 1:00 P.M. At 2:30 P.M., Lyndon Johnson takes the oath of office in Dallas and becomes the 36th president.

November 24. While in police custody, Oswald is murdered by Jack Ruby.

November 25. Kennedy is buried in Arlington National Cemetery.

November 29. Johnson appoints a commission headed by Chief Justice Earl Warren to investigate Kennedy's assassination.

Foreign Policy

1961

January 3. The Eisenhower administration breaks diplomatic relations with Cuba.

March 26. In Key West, Florida, Kennedy meets with British prime min-

ister Harold Macmillan to discuss Laos, where Communist strength is steadily increasing.

April 17. Anti-Castro forces land at the Bay of Pigs, on Cuba's southern coast. Within 48 hours, the 1,200 Cuban exiles from the United States, whom the Central Intelligence Agency (CIA) had trained for the attempted overthrow of Castro, are defeated.

May. Vice President Johnson makes a fact-finding trip to South Vietnam; Kennedy sends U.S. special forces to the country.

May 16. Kennedy begins an official visit to Ottawa, Canada.

May 27. Congress appropriates funding for the Alliance for Progress, a 10-year program of economic assistance to 19 Latin American nations.

May 31. Kennedy meets with President Charles de Gaulle in Paris.

June 3–4. In Vienna, Kennedy meets Soviet leader Nikita Khrushchev for two days of talks. No agreement is reached on Berlin, which is a major irritant in East-West relations.

August 2. In the United Nations, the United States reaffirms its endorsement of membership for the nationalist Chinese government on Taiwan and its opposition to membership for the Chinese Communist government on the mainland.

August 13. East German troops backed by the Soviet Union begin building the Berlin Wall, dividing the city in two.

August 17. Nineteen Latin American nations sign the charter establishing the Alliance for Progress in Uruguay.

September 4. The Foreign Assistance Act creates the Agency for International Development to manage economic aid programs.

September 15. The foreign ministers of the United States, Great Britain, France and the Soviet Union meet in Washington to discuss Berlin.

December. The Kennedy administration promises aid to South Vietnam.

December 15. Kennedy begins an official visit to Puerto Rico, Columbia and Venezuela.

December 21–22. Kennedy meets with Macmillan in Bermuda; they agree to prepare for the resumption of atmospheric nuclear testing, which the Soviets resumed several months earlier.

December 22. The first American is killed by Communist Viet Cong guerrillas fighting the South Vietnamese government.

1962

January 29. The Geneva Conference on a nuclear test ban treaty between the United States, the USSR and Great Britain adjourns. Begun in October 1958, the talks stumble over the question of verifying compliance with an agreement.

February 3. Trade relations with Cuba are severed.

May 12 and 15. In response to a Communist offensive in Laos, Kennedy orders sea and ground units to Thailand. The 5,000 American servicemen deployed as of May 29 will remain there until July 27.

June 16. Two American officers are killed in an ambush north of Saigon, the South Vietnamese capital. Troops sent to Vietnam in an advisory capacity are authorized to open fire if attacked.

June 29. Kennedy begins an official visit to Mexico.

October 22. In a nationally televised speech, the president announces that the USSR is building bases for nuclear missiles in Cuba.

October 24. The U.S. Navy begins a blockade of Cuba to prevent Soviet ships from delivering missiles.

October 27. Khrushchev suggests that the Soviet missile sites in Cuba could be dismantled under UN supervision if the United States agrees to withdraw its missiles from Turkey.

A U-2 spy plane is shot down over Cuba.

October 28. The Cuban missile crisis is resolved when Khrushchev agrees to remove Soviet missile sites from Cuba in exchange for an American pledge not to attack the island.

November 2. Kennedy terminates the naval blockade of Cuba.

December 21. In Nassau, Bahamas, Kennedy and Macmillan meet to plan the creation of a nuclear arsenal for NATO.

December 23. Cuba frees 1,113 men captured during the Bay of Pigs invasion. In exchange, the United States will send $53 million worth of food and medicine to the island.

1963

March 18–20. In San Jose, Costa Rica, Kennedy confers with the presidents of Costa Rica, El Salvador, Honduras, Nicaragua, Panama, and Guatemala.

June 10. In a speech at American University in Washington, Kennedy announces the resumption of negotiations on a nuclear test ban treaty.

June 20. The USSR agrees to set up a "teletype hot line" link between Washington and Moscow; it will become operational on August 30, 1963.

June 23. Kennedy begins a 10-day trip to Europe. On June 26, in West Berlin, he gives a speech next to the Berlin Wall and declares "I am a Berliner."

August 5. The Limited Test Ban Treaty halting above-ground nuclear tests is signed by the United States, the USSR and Great Britain.

October 9. Four million tons of wheat are sold to the USSR.

November 1–2. In Saigon, President Ngo Dinh Diem and his brother Ngo Dinh Nhu are assassinated in a coup carried out by South Vietnamese military officers with U.S. acquiescence.

December. There are 16,300 American soldiers in Vietnam.

Economy and Society

1961

January 30. In his State of the Union Address, President Kennedy stresses the crisis in education and in particular the shortage of qualified teachers.

May 5. The Fair Labor Standards Act raises the minimum hourly wage to $1.15 in September and to $1.25 in September 1963.

June 30. A housing act funds the building of low-income housing.

1962

February 26. The Supreme Court rules that any law permitting segregated public transportation is unconstitutional.

April 11. The president denounces a 3.5 percent increase in the price of steel following agreements between the industry and the unions. The increase will be canceled on April 13.

May 25. George Meany, the president of the AFL-CIO, launches a national campaign for the 35-hour workweek.

May 28. Prices on the New York Stock Exchange fall $21 billion, their biggest decline since October 29, 1929. Stock prices will recover quickly.

June 25. The Supreme Court rules that prayer in public schools is unconstitutional under the 1st Amendment.

August 15. The national debt passes the $300 billion mark.

September 15. Legislation provides funding for public projects in disadvantaged areas.

September 21. The Department of Defense announces that military equipment will be sold to West Germany, France and Italy in order to increase gold reserves.

September 25. The governor of Mississippi, Ross Barnett, refuses to enroll a black student, James Meredith, in the state university.

September 28. The governor of Mississippi is indicted for contempt of the law and ordered to stop obstructing desegregation or face imprisonment.

September 30. Protected by federal marshals, James Meredith enrolls at the University of Mississippi. Demonstrations against his enrollment result in two deaths.

October 11. The Trade Expansion Act reduces some customs duties in an effort to revive international trade.

November 20. Kennedy orders an end to all forms of segregation in federally funded housing.

1963

April 12. Martin Luther King, Jr., is arrested during a demonstration in Birmingham, Alabama.

May 2. In Birmingham, several hundred blacks, including children, are arrested during a nonviolent demonstration.

May 12. After several days of violence and the arrest of several hundred demonstrators in Birmingham, President Kennedy sends federal troops to Alabama.

June 11. Alabama governor George Wallace physically blocks the entry of two black students to the University of Alabama. Wallace then abandons his resistance after President Kennedy federalizes the Alabama National Guard.

June 12. Medgar Evers, a black leader in the fight for racial equality, is murdered in Mississippi.

July 1. The Carpenters' Brotherhood, the main labor union in the building industry, bans segregation on its premises.

August 28. A march on Washington for civil rights draws 200,000 demonstrators and numerous black leaders. Martin Luther King, Jr., delivers his "I have a dream" speech in front of the Lincoln Memorial.

September 15. In Birmingham, Alabama, the bombing of a Baptist church kills four black girls and marks the beginning of a wave of violence in the city.

Science and Technology

1961

January 31. In Project Mercury, the manned space program, a chimpanzee orbits the Earth twice on a trial flight.

April 12. The Soviet cosmonaut Yuri Gagarin makes the first manned flight in space.

May 5. Alan Shephard, Jr., becomes the first American to fly in space during a sub-orbital flight lasting 15 minutes.

May 25. Kennedy proposes a space program whose goal is to land a man on the Moon before the end of the decade.

1962

February 20. John Glenn, Jr., becomes the first American to orbit the Earth.

October 3. Walter Schirra orbits the Earth nearly six times.

1963

May 15–16. L. Gordon Cooper orbits the Earth 22 times.

Civilization and Culture

1961

Books such as Gabriel Vahanian's *The Death of God: The Culture of Our Post-Christian Era* and Peter Berger's *The Noise of Solemn Assemblies* are part of an emerging reexamination of traditional theology.

Joseph Heller publishes his novel *Catch-22.* Henry Miller's *Tropic of Cancer* appears; first published in France in 1934, it had been banned in the United States for obscenity.

Release of the movie version of *West Side Story,* by Jerome Robbins and Robert Wise, and the black comedy *Dr. Strangelove,* by Stanley Kubrick.

May 9. The chairman of the Federal Communications Commission calls American TV "a cultural wasteland."

1962

Rachel Carson's *Silent Spring* focuses public attention on the deterioration of the environment.

Henry Miller's *Tropic of Capricorn* appears; it was first published in France in 1939.

Edward Albee's play *Who's Afraid of Virginia Woolf?*

Robert Mulligan's film *To Kill a Mockingbird.*

Aureole, by the choreographer Paul Taylor.

Pop artist Andy Warhol's *The Twenty Marilyns*.

Debut in the United States of the Soviet ballet dancer Rudolf Nureyev.

Eero Saarinen's TWA Terminal Building is completed at Idlewild Airport (later renamed JFK International Airport) in New York.

February 14. A tour of the White House, with the president's wife Jacqueline Kennedy as guide, is broadcast on TV.

May 8. An accord is reached with the USSR on cultural, scientific, technical and educational exchanges.

August 5. The actress Marilyn Monroe dies; she is generally considered a suicide.

September 23. In New York, Philharmonic Hall is dedicated; it is the first element of Lincoln Center, a complex devoted to the performing arts.

October 25. John Steinbeck is awarded the Nobel Prize for literature.

1963

Kurt Vonnegut, Jr., publishes *Cat's Cradle*. *Paterson, Books I–V*, by the poet William Carlos Williams. Betty Friedan's *The Feminine Mystique* helps launch the women's liberation movement.

The painter Roy Lichtenstein's *Whaam!*

Release of the movies *Cleopatra*, by Joseph Mankiewicz, and *How the West Was Won*, by John Ford, Henry Hathaway and George Marshall.

January 8–March 4. The portrait *Mona Lisa*, on loan from the Louvre, is exhibited in New York and then in Washington.

March 17. Elizabeth Ann Bayley (Mother) Seton, the founder of the Sisters of Charity of Saint Joseph in 1809, becomes the first native-born American to receive beatification from the Roman Catholic Church.

March–June. The first major exhibit of Pop Art is held at the Guggenheim Museum in New York.

The Great Society and America in Crisis

Lyndon Johnson was an experienced politician with a strong interest in domestic policy rather than foreign affairs. He continued John Kennedy's programs and launched numerous liberal reforms. In the presidential election of 1964, Johnson campaigned for an ambitious social program called the Great Society, which had two main thrusts: a "war on poverty" and the elimination of all forms of discrimination. He won the election by a huge margin, polling 43.1 million votes and 486 presidential electors against the Republican candidate Barry Goldwater's 27.1 million votes and 52 electors.

Despite the huge budgetary expenses of the Great Society, the program was supported by Congress and the public. From 1966 onward, however, black activism became more radical, and riots occurred in many cities. This was also the period in which the counterculture was born, with black activism providing a model for various protest movements, including those of students, women and other minorities.

In foreign affairs, the American military commitment to South Vietnam had political and ideological motives. As the non-Communist countries in Southeast Asia were deemed unable to resist Communist expansion, the administration was forced to give up "butter" for "guns," and the Great Society for the Vietnam War. In an atmosphere of growing protest at home against the fighting in Vietnam, the first televised war became increasingly difficult to comprehend for many Americans.

It was against this backdrop that the presidential election campaign of 1968 unfolded. Johnson soon decided against seeking another term, and in the spring both Martin Luther King, Jr., and Robert Kennedy, a Democratic presidential candidate, were assassinated. Richard Nixon, the Republican candidate, was elected with a razor-thin plurality of 31.8 million votes, or 43.4 percent of the total, and 301 presidential electors, against the Democrat Hubert Humphrey's 31.3 million votes (42.7 percent) and 191 electors. George Wallace, the candidate of the American Independent Party, polled 9.9 million votes (13 percent of the total) and 46 electors.

The 1968 election showed how deeply divided public opinion was at the time. Wallace appealed to disaffected Democrats resentful of federally mandated civil rights and welfare programs. He drew wide support not only in the South but in northern blue-collar areas as well. Nixon won by promising peace with honor, not peace at any price or defeat in Vietnam. He was also confident of his ability to reestablish law and order in the country, and he pledged to give voice to the "silent majority." His program was reassuring to an America in need of reassurance.

Political and Institutional Life

1964

January 23. The 24th Amendment to the Constitution prohibits the payment of a poll tax as a prerequisite for voting in presidential and congressional elections.

March 14. Jack Ruby is found guilty of murdering Lee Harvey Oswald in Dallas and is sentenced to death.

June 15. The Supreme Court rules unconstitutional the provision of the Internal Security Act of 1950 barring the granting of an American passport to any citizen belonging to the Communist Party.

September 27. The Warren Commission, in its report on the assassination of President Kennedy, concludes that Oswald acted alone, that there was no conspiracy, and that Jack Ruby did not know Oswald before killing him.

November 3. Johnson is elected president, defeating the Republican Barry Goldwater; Hubert Humphrey is elected vice president.

1965

January 20. Johnson takes the oath of office.

March 8. The Supreme Court rules that conscientious objectors are exempt from combat training and active military duty.

September 9. The Department of Housing and Urban Development is created.

November 15. The Supreme Court rules that the compulsory registration of Communists is unconstitutional.

1966

January 18. Robert C. Weaver, the first secretary of housing and urban development, becomes the first black member of a president's cabinet.

June 13. In *Miranda v. Arizona*, the Supreme Court rules that every suspect must be informed of his rights to remain silent and to have an attorney present before being interrogated by the police.

October 5. Jack Ruby's sentence is voided by the Texas Court of Appeals; he will die in prison of natural causes while awaiting a new trial in January 1967.

1967

February 10. The 25th Amendment to the Constitution provides for a successor to the president in the event of death, impeachment or resignation; should the office of vice president become vacant, the president will nominate a vice president who must be confirmed by a majority vote in both houses of Congress.

April 1. The Department of Transportation is created.

June 12. The Supreme Court rules that state laws banning racially mixed marriages are unconstitutional.

October 2. Following his nomination by Johnson and confirmation by the Senate, Thurgood Marshall is sworn in as the first black justice of the Supreme Court.

1968

January 25. John W. Gardner resigns as secretary of health, education and welfare because of his disagreement with Vietnam War policy.

March 12. The antiwar candidate Eugene McCarthy comes surprisingly close to defeating Johnson in the New Hampshire Democratic presidential primary.

March 31. Johnson stuns the nation by announcing at the end of a televised address on the Vietnam War that he will not seek reelection.

June 17. The Supreme Court rules that any discrimination in the sale or rental of property is illegal.

August 26. The national convention of the Democratic Party begins in Chicago. Violent demonstrations against the Vietnam War take place, and hundreds are injured.

November 5. Richard M. Nixon is elected the 37th president; Spiro T. Agnew is elected vice president. The Democrats retain their majorities in the Senate and the House of Representatives.

Vietnam War Chronology

1964

August 2 and 4. The U.S. destroyers *Maddox* and *Turner Joy* are allegedly attacked by North Vietnamese boats in international waters in the Gulf of Tonkin.

August 7. Congress overwhelmingly approves the so-called Gulf of Tonkin Resolution authorizing the president to "take all necessary measures to repel any armed attack against the forces of the United States and to prevent further aggression" in Southeast Asia; the vote in the House of Representatives is 416–0, and in the Senate 88–2.

December. American soldiers in Vietnam: 23,300.

1965

February 6. In South Vietnam, the Viet Cong attack an American base at Pleiku: 8 Americans are killed and 126 are wounded.

February 7. Johnson approves Operation Rolling Thunder, a bombing campaign against North Vietnam.

March 8–9. The first U.S. combat unit, including 3,500 Marines, arrives at Danang Air Base in South Vietnam.

April 2. At a press conference, the president announces an increase in military and economic aid to South Vietnam.

April 7. Johnson announces that the United States is ready to take part in peace talks with the Communist government of North Vietnam.

June 17. B-52 bombers flying from Guam carry out the first air raid against the Viet Cong 30 miles from Saigon.

August 4. The president asks Congress for an additional $1.7 billion for the war.

November 20. After a week of fighting in the Ia Drang Valley, U.S. casualties are 240 dead, 470 wounded and 6 missing.

December. American soldiers in Vietnam: 154,300.

1966

January 31. Following North Vietnam's rejection of a U.S. peace offer, the president announces that as of February 21, the bombing of North Vietnam, interrupted on December 24, 1965, will resume.

February 22. Operation Masher-White Wing involves more than 20,000 American, South Vietnamese and South Korean troops.

May 1. American troops shell Communist targets in Cambodia in the first U.S. combat operation against that country.

May 30. Three hundred U.S. bombers strike at targets in North Vietnam.

May 31. An important North Vietnamese arsenal is almost entirely destroyed.

June 3–13. American troops engage in a major battle in Kontum province.

June 29. For the first time, American bombers attack targets near Hanoi, the North Vietnamese capital, and Haiphong, in response to intensified North Vietnamese infiltration into South Vietnam. Approximately two-thirds of the North's oil reserves will be destroyed in a week.

July 30. American planes for the first time bomb the demilitarized zone (DMZ) between North and South Vietnam.

September 23. The U.S. Air Force begins defoliation operations south of the DMZ.

October 13. An air raid on the North is carried out by 173 U.S. bombers.

October 14. An air raid on the North involves 175 U.S. bombers.

December. American soldiers in Vietnam: 385,300.

1967

January 8–19. Operation Cedar Falls is carried out in the "Iron Triangle," 25 miles northwest of Saigon. Approximately 16,000 American and 14,000 South Vietnamese soldiers are engaged in the largest offensive against enemy positions thus far.

April 4. The U.S. Air Force has lost 500 planes since the beginning of bombing operations.

April 20. The North Vietnamese port of Haiphong is bombed; two electrical plants are destroyed.

May 19. Downtown Hanoi is bombed.

July 2–7. U.S. Marines suffer significant losses at Con Thieu during a North Vietnamese attack.

September 3. General Nguyen Van Thieu is elected president of South Vietnam.

November 22. The U.S. Army takes Hill 875 near Dak To after 19 days of fighting.

December. American soldiers in South Vietnam: 485,600.

1968

January 21–April 5. North Vietnamese and Viet Cong forces attack and besiege the U.S. Marine base at Khe Sanh.

January 30–February 24. Communist forces carry out a major offensive throughout South Vietnam during Tet, the lunar new year. The surprise offensive contradicts the Johnson administration's claims of an impending victory and undermines domestic popular support for the war effort.

March 16. A U.S. Army infantry division murders approximately 200 unarmed civilians during a search-and-destroy operation in the South Vietnamese village of My Lai. The American public will not learn of the massacre for more than one year.

March 22. General William Westmoreland, the U.S. commander in Vietnam, is appointed chief of staff of the army.

March 31. Johnson announces a halt to American bombing of most of North Vietnam.

April 8. In Operation Complete Victory, more than 100,000 U.S. and South Vietnamese troops attempt to expel the enemy from 11 provinces around Saigon.

May 10. Peace talks with the North Vietnamese begin in Paris.

October 31. The president orders a halt to bombing throughout North Vietnam.

December. American soldiers in Vietnam: 536,000.

Foreign Policy

1964

January 9–10. Panama severs diplomatic relations with the United States as violent demonstrations break out in the Canal Zone; Panama demands a revision of its canal treaties with the United States.

April 3. Diplomatic relations with Panama are reestablished.

1965

April 28. After a coup in the Dominican Republic, Johnson deploys a marine contingent to the Caribbean nation.

May 2. Johnson declares that a popular uprising in the Dominican Republic has come under the influence of Communists. He dispatches 20,000 troops to the island nation without consulting the Organization of American States.

September 4. The provisional government in the Dominican Republic is recognized by the United States.

1966

October 17. The president leaves on a 17-day trip to the Far East that will include stops in the Philippines, Australia, New Zealand, Thailand, Malaysia, South Korea and South Vietnam.

1967

April 12–14. Johnson attends the Conference of the American States in Punta del Este, Uruguay, where the heads of state of 18 nations agree to establish a Latin American common market by 1970, to improve communications and to reduce military expenditures.

June 23 and 25. Johnson and Soviet premier Alexei Kosygin hold talks in Glassboro, New Jersey.

July 23. In a referendum, Puerto Ricans decide to retain the status of their island as a U.S. commonwealth.

1968

January 23. North Korean patrol boats seize the navy intelligence ship *Pueblo* off the coast of North Korea. The crew will be freed on December 22.

July 1. The Nuclear Non-Proliferation Treaty is signed by 57 nations, including the United States and the USSR, after four years of negotiations.

Economy and Society

1964

California becomes the most populous state in the Union, replacing New York.

February 13. The secretary of the treasury announces that the United States will have to borrow from the International Monetary Fund (IMF) for the first time.

April 11. The Agricultural Act seeks to control surplus production by permitting farmers to let their land lie fallow.

May 22. In a speech at the University of Michigan, Johnson discusses his social program, the Great Society, for the first time.

July 2. In a live television broadcast, Johnson signs into law the Civil Rights Act of 1964. He describes it as "a challenge to all of us to go to work . . . to eliminate the last vestiges of injustice in our beloved country." Among its other provisions, the act creates the Equal Employment Opportunity Commission.

August 30. The Economic Opportunity Act provides funding for educational and training programs, and for loans to start small businesses. The Office of Economic Opportunity is established to oversee these programs.

October 14. Martin Luther King, Jr., is awarded the Nobel Peace Prize.

1965

The unemployment rate falls to 4.2 percent. The GNP reaches $672 billion.

February 21. In New York, Malcolm X, the former leader of the Black Muslims, is murdered by members of the group.

February 23. Arsonists burn the headquarters of the Black Muslims in New York and San Francisco.

March 11. The black minister James Reeb is murdered in Selma, Alabama.

March 21. Led by Martin Luther King, Jr., 3,200 blacks and whites begin a five-day march for civil rights from Selma to Montgomery, Alabama; the marchers will number 25,000 when they arrive in Montgomery.

July 30. The Medicare Act provides medical insurance coverage for the elderly and the handicapped. The legislation will take effect on July 1, 1966.

August 6. The Voting Rights Act removes all qualifying tests for voters.

August 11–16. Riots occur in the black district of Watts, in Los Angeles.

Arson and looting leave 34 dead and hundreds injured.

September 24. An executive order of the president asks businesses and institutions receiving federal funds to set aside a percentage of their job openings for nonwhite minorities and women.

October 3. The Immigration Act of 1965 abolishes the quota system based on national origin.

October 15–16. Demonstrations against the Vietnam War are held across the nation; draftees burn their induction notices.

October 19. The House Un-American Activities Committee (HUAC) opens an investigation of the Ku Klux Klan.

November 9–10. An electrical blackout in New York, New England and parts of New Jersey and Pennsylvania lasts up to 13 hours and affects 30 million people.

November 27. An antiwar demonstration is held in Washington.

December 5. The Federal Reserve Board increases its interest rate from 4 percent to 4.5 percent, the highest level in 35 years, in order to stabilize prices and avoid inflation.

1966

January 1. In New York, bus and subway workers go on strike. The city will be paralyzed for 13 days before drivers win a raise of 15 percent.

January 12. In his State of the Union Address, Johnson repeats his pledge to build the Great Society and declares that the United States is committed to aiding South Vietnam.

March 3. The Cold War GI Bill of Rights extends benefits to those who have spent at least 180 days in the armed forces since January 31, 1955; it is aimed primarily at Vietnam veterans.

March 25–26. Antiwar demonstrations take place in San Francisco, Chicago, Boston, Philadelphia and Washington.

April 6. Farm workers led by Cesar Chavez, on strike against California grape growers since September 8, 1965, achieve their first victory when one of the producers recognizes the farm workers' association as a union. Others will follow suit.

May 15. An antiwar demonstration takes place in Washington.

July 12. A riot occurs in the black district of the West Side in Chicago; it will be followed by riots in several other cities.

August 6. Antiwar demonstrations occur in Washington and New York on the anniversary of the bombing of Hiroshima.

September 6–7. Race riots occur in Atlanta, Georgia.

October 20. Legislation is passed for the rehabilitation of inner cities.

1967

Despite a declining birthrate, the population reaches 200 million.

April 15. Antiwar demonstrations take place in San Francisco and New York.

June 30. In Geneva, some 45 countries, including the United States, sign the General Agreement on Tariffs and Trade (GATT), which lowers international trade barriers. The treaty will come into force on July 1, 1968.

July 12–17. Race riots in Newark, New Jersey, leave 26 dead and 1,300 injured.

July 23–30. Race riots in Detroit leave 41 dead and 2,000 injured.

July 25. Blacks demonstrate in Cambridge, Maryland, following a speech by H. Rap Brown, a black-power activist.

Brown will be arrested and convicted for inciting violence (he had encouraged the crowd to burn the town).

August 17. The black leader Stokely Carmichael urges blacks to launch a general insurrection.

October 21–22. An antiwar demonstration in Washington turns into a riot in front of the Pentagon; demonstrators burn their draft cards.

November 14. The Air Quality Act provides a budget of $430 million over three years to fight atmospheric pollution.

November 29–30. Antiwar demonstrations occur at the University of California at Berkeley.

December 4–8. In New York, antiwar demonstrations and riots lead to 585 arrests. Other demonstrations in major cities will follow.

1968

January 17. In his State of the Union Address, the president asks for a tax increase of 10 percent to reduce the budget deficit and curtail inflation.

February 4–8. A race riot by students in Orangeburg, North Carolina, leaves three black students dead.

March 17. In Washington, the United States and six European countries agree to create a system with two price levels for gold. All gold transactions between governments will take place at the official price of $35 an ounce, but the market price will be allowed to fluctuate. Central banks pledge not to convert their dollars into gold. This conference marks the birth of a new international monetary system that replaces the one created by the Bretton Woods agreements in 1944.

March 28. In Memphis, Tennessee, demonstrations during a march led by

REGISTRATION OF BLACK VOTERS BEFORE AND AFTER THE VOTING RIGHTS ACT OF 1965

State	1960	1966
Alabama	66,000	250,000
Arkansas	73,000	115,000
Florida	183,000	303,000
Georgia	180,000	300,000
Louisiana	159,000	243,000
Mississippi	22,000	175,000
North Carolina	210,000	282,000
South Carolina	58,000	191,000
Tennessee	185,000	225,000
Texas	227,000	400,000
Virginia	100,000	205,000

SOURCE: U.S. Bureau of the Census, *Statistical Abstract of the United States, 1982–1983.*

Martin Luther King, Jr., result in one death.

April 4. In Memphis, James Earl Ray murders Martin Luther King, Jr. Riots in the black districts of large cities will follow.

April 10. A new civil rights act makes discrimination in housing illegal.

April 15. Richard Daley, the mayor of Chicago, orders his police to shoot in the event of riots.

April 23. At Columbia University in New York, student demonstrators protest against the school's participation in research projects linked to the military and seize several buildings. Most of the participants belong to the Students for a Democratic Society (SDS).

April 24. Black students at Boston University stage a revolt; they demand a program on Afro-American culture and increased financial aid.

May 2. A "march of the poor" is held in Washington; the event, planned by Martin Luther King, Jr., is led by another black minister, Ralph Abernathy.

June 6. In Los Angeles, Robert Kennedy dies of wounds he received in an assassination attempt on June 5, after his victory in the Democratic presidential primary in California. The assassin, Sirhan Sirhan, a Jordanian, will be sentenced to death on April 23, 1969 (his sentence will be commuted to life imprisonment in 1972).

June 8. James Earl Ray, who is wanted for the murder of Martin Luther King, Jr., is arrested in London. He will be sentenced to 99 years in prison on March 10, 1969.

July 15. Direct commercial flights between New York and Moscow are inaugurated.

August 7. In Miami, a race riot leaves three dead and several hundred wounded.

December 11. The national unemployment rate is 3.3 percent.

Science and Technology

1964

January 25. The satellite *Echo II* is launched into space; it is the result of the first cooperative program with the USSR in the exploration of outer space.

July 31. The lunar probe *Ranger* 7 transmits the first close-up pictures of the Moon before impacting the surface.

1965

April 6. Early Bird, the first commercial communications satellite, is put into orbit by the National Aeronautics and Space Administration (NASA).

June 3. Gemini 4 is launched into Earth orbit; Edward White becomes the first American to walk in space.

July 15. The first pictures of Mars taken by *Mariner 4* are received; the spacecraft has been traveling through space since November 1964.

November 21. The Verrazano Narrows Bridge, linking Brooklyn and Staten Island, is inaugurated; it is the longest suspension bridge in the world.

December 15. The first space rendezvous of manned craft is achieved by *Gemini 6* and *Gemini 7.*

1966

June 2. Surveyor 1 becomes the first spacecraft to successfully land on the Moon.

1967

R. M. Dolby develops a recording system that eliminates background noise.

The first multiple-warhead missiles (Multiple Independently Targetable Reentry Vehicles, or MIRVs) are built.

January 27. A fire on the launch pad at the Kennedy Space Center in Florida kills three astronauts, Virgil "Gus" Grissom, Edward White and Roger Chaffee, the first *Apollo* crew.

1968

The largest oil deposits in North America are discovered in Alaska.

The first heart transplant in the United States is performed by Dr. Denton Cooley.

January 22. Apollo 5, an unmanned flight testing the Lunar Excursion Module (LEM), is launched.

Civilization and Culture

1964

The musical *Fiddler on the Roof* opens on Broadway.

February 7. The Beatles arrive at Kennedy Airport in New York to begin their first U.S. tour.

April 19. Michelangelo's *Pieta,* which will be exhibited in the Vatican pavilion at the New York World's Fair, arrives in New York.

1965

Jerzy Kosinski's *The Painted Bird; The Autobiography of Malcolm X* (with Alex Halley); and *Ariel,* by the poet Sylvia Plath, are published.

The Salk Institute for biological research is established in La Jolla, California; Louis I. Kahn is the architect.

The Responsive Eye, an exhibit of Op Art, opens at the Museum of Modern Art in New York; it includes the sculptor David Smith's Cubi series (1961–1965) and the painter Jasper Johns's *Double White Map.*

March 30. The County Art Museum is inaugurated in Los Angeles.

April 9. The Houston Astrodome, a sports stadium, opens in Texas.

September 30. The Federal Aid to the Arts Act establishes the National Foundation on the Arts and the Humanities.

1966

Truman Capote's study of murder, *In Cold Blood,* is published.

Cabaret, starring Liza Minnelli, opens on Broadway.

September 28. The Whitney Museum, designed by the architect Marcel Breuer, opens in New York.

1967

Black Magic: Poetry 1961–1967, by Amiri Baraka (born LeRoi Jones), Richard Brautigan's *Trout Fishing in America* and William Styron's *The Confessions of Nat Turner* are published.

Release of the movies *Bonnie and Clyde,* by Arthur Penn, and *The Graduate,* by Mike Nichols.

John Kenneth Galbraith publishes *The New Industrial State.*

"Summer of Love" among the hippies in San Francisco, marking the emergence of an anti-establishment counterculture.

Robert Rauschenberg's painting *Revolvers.*

February 14. A retrospective of Andrew Wyeth's paintings opens at the Whitney Museum in New York.

February 28. Henry Luce, the founder of the weeklies *Time* and *Life,* dies.

April 21. Svetlana Alliluyeva, the daughter of Josef Stalin, arrives in New York after being granted political asylum.

1968

The complete works of the poet e. e. cummings, who died in 1962, are published, as are *Black Judgement,* by Nikki Giovanni, and James Dickey's *Poems.*

The Electric Kool-Aid Acid Test, a study of contemporary American culture by the journalist Tom Wolfe, and Eldridge Cleaver's *Soul on Ice,* on the tortuous black experience.

Films: *Planet of the Apes,* by Franklin Schaffner, and *2001: A Space Odyssey,* by Stanley Kubrick.

The Italian tenor Luciano Pavarotti makes his American debut at the Metropolitan Opera in *La Bohème.*

The rock musical *Hair* opens on Broadway.

Nixon and the Disengagement from Vietnam

In 1969, an exceptional event took place: an American became the first person to walk on the Moon. But the years of Richard Nixon's presidency were by and large a difficult period in American history. The economy began to experience inflation at the same time that a recession set in, a phenomenon later baptized "stagflation" by the experts. As unemployment grew, Nixon launched a program of economic recovery that seemed to be working by 1972. But the oil embargo imposed by the Organization of Petroleum Exporting Countries (OPEC) in October 1973, and the resulting increase in the price of oil, sent additional shocks through the economy.

As far as social programs and the management of the country were concerned, Nixon adhered to the traditional Republican ideology and sought to reduce governmental intervention. His doctrine of the "New Federalism" entailed a sharing of government revenues. State and local governments would receive from Washington funds to establish their own programs. The use of school busing, which involved transporting white students to predominently black schools, and vice versa, was intended to accelerate integregation. But Nixon, who did not favor busing, decided to slow the program's implementation. To broaden his political base, Nixon fashioned his so-called southern strategy, which emphasized law-and-order issues and patriotic values in order to draw the support of generally more conservative southern Democratic voters.

The nation's social fabric continued to unravel. Many groups had demands, but the Vietnam War attracted the most protest. Four years were required to complete America's disengagement from Vietnam. Nixon adopted a policy of Vietnamization, whereby South Vietnam assumed an increasing burden in the fighting, but the continued bombing by the U.S. Air Force and the incursion of American troops into Cambodia sparked new indignation and often violent demonstrations. In 1971, the publication of the "Pentagon Papers" revealed to the public the hitherto unknown history of America's involvement in Vietnam.

Still, Nixon achieved his greatest successes in foreign policy. He improved relations with Europe, began détente with the USSR and extended recognition to Communist China (he visited both countries in 1972), signed the first Strategic Arms Limitation Treaty (SALT) with Moscow and obtained a cease-fire in Vietnam. These accomplishments gave rise to hopes for improved relations between East and West, and Henry Kissinger, first the president's national security advisor and then his secretary of state, earned widespread recognition for his contributions.

Riding these successes, Nixon easily won reelection in 1972, polling 46 million votes, or 60.8 percent of the total, and winning 520 presidential electors, while the Democrat George McGovern received 28.5 million votes and 17 electors. During his second term, however, all of Nixon's accomplishments were overshadowed by Watergate, a scandal that stained the reputations of many of the top officials in the administration, including Nixon himself. Public opinion turned against a president who had violated the trust that had been placed in him, who had isolated himself from the people and from their representatives in Congress, and who had erected an "imperial" presidency. Forestalling at the last minute a procedure of impeachment, Nixon announced his resignation on August 8, 1974.

Political and Institutional Life

1969

January 20. Richard Nixon takes office as president, Spiro T. Agnew as vice president.

June 23. Earl Warren, the chief justice of the Supreme Court, retires. He is succeeded by Warren Burger.

September 24. Eight radicals, the so-called Chicago Eight, go on trial in Chicago on charges stemming from their involvement in the riots outside the 1968 Democratic National Convention. When Black Panther Bobby Seale's case is separated from the proceedings, the remaining defendants become known as the Chicago Seven.

November 21. Nixon's Supreme Court nominee Clement F. Haynsworth, Jr., is rejected by the Senate.

1970

February 18. Five of the Chicago Seven are found guilty of crossing state lines to incite a riot at the 1968 Democratic National Convention. The convictions are eventually overturned on appeal.

April 8. A second Nixon nominee to the Supreme Court, G. Harrold Carswell, is rejected by the Senate.

May 12. Nixon's Supreme Court nominee Harry A. Blackmun is confirmed unanimously by the Senate.

November 3. In congressional elections, the Democrats retain majorities in the Senate and the House of Representatives.

December 2. The Environmental Protection Agency (EPA) is established.

1971

January 22. In his State of the Union Address, Nixon presents his plan for revenue sharing.

July 5. The 26th Amendment to the Constitution lowers the voting age to 18.

1972

May 15. Alabama governor George Wallace, campaigning for the presidency, is shot and seriously wounded by Arthur Bremer in Laurel, Maryland. Bremer will be sentenced to 63 years in prison on August 4.

October 20. The State and Local Fiscal Assistance Act provides funding for revenue sharing.

November 7. In the presidential election, Richard Nixon defeats Democrat George McGovern and is reelected. The Democrats keep their majorities in both the Senate and the House of Representatives.

1973

January 20. Nixon begins his second term.

June 29. The Federal Energy Office is created to encourage energy savings and coordinate the search for new sources of energy.

October 10. Vice President Agnew resigns and pleads "no contest" to charges that he evaded paying taxes on payments made to him by contractors when he was governor of Maryland.

November 7. Overriding Nixon's veto, Congress approves the War Powers Act, which limits the power of the president to commit U.S. armed forces to combat: Troops cannot be committed for more than 60 days without congressional authorization.

December 6. Gerald R. Ford becomes vice president; he is the first person appointed to that office under the 25th Amendment.

1974

July. The Congressional Budget and Impoundment Control Act restricts the president's ability to impound (not spend) funds authorized by Congress. It creates the Congressional Budget Office and establishes in each of the two houses of Congress a committee to oversee the budget.

Watergate Chronology

1972

February 15. John Mitchell, the attorney general of the United States, resigns to become head of the Committee to Reelect the President (CRP, or CREEP).

June 17. In Washington, the police arrest five men who have broken into the headquarters of the Democratic Party in the Watergate Hotel office building. One of those arrested, James McCord, is a former employee of the CIA now working for the CRP. Another employee of the CRP, G. Gordon Liddy, and E. Howard Hunt, a former consultant to the White House and former CIA employee, will be implicated in the break-in. A police investigation is launched.

August 29. At a press conference, Nixon announces that his White House counsel, John Dean, has conducted an investigation of the Watergate break-in. Nixon states that "no one on the White House staff, no one in this administration, presently employed, was involved in this very bizarre incident."

September 15. The five men arrested in the Watergate break-in, together with Liddy and Hunt, are indicted for conspiracy, burglary and violating wiretapping laws.

October 10. The *Washington Post* reveals that John Mitchell, Nixon's former campaign manager, controlled a CRP-financed network for political spying.

1973

January 8. The trial of the seven men indicted in the Watergate break-in begins in Washington.

February 7. The Senate votes to create its own committee to investigate the 1972 presidential campaign. Democratic senator Sam Ervin of North Carolina is chosen as chairman of the "Watergate Committee."

March 23. Judge John Sirica sentences six of the seven Watergate conspirators to jail terms ranging from 6 to 40 years. The sentencing of James McCord is postponed.

April 5. Nixon withdraws his nomination of L. Patrick Gray to head the Federal Bureau of Investigation (FBI) after Gray admits he gave FBI files on Watergate to White House Counsel John Dean.

April 20. Patrick Gray admits having destroyed documents related to Watergate that he had received from John Dean. He says he acted on the advice of Nixon's advisors.

April 30. Nixon announces that he has accepted the resignations of top aides H. R. Haldeman, John Ehrlichman, John Dean and Attorney General Richard Kleindienst. He maintains that he had no prior knowledge of the Watergate break-in.

May 10. John Mitchell and Maurice Stans, a former secretary of commerce, are indicted for conspiring to arrange a secret $200,000 contribution to Nixon's campaign fund.

May 17. The Senate Watergate Committee begins televised hearings on the scandal.

May 22. Nixon admits that the White House tried to cover up some aspects of the Watergate scandal without his knowledge.

May 25. Attorney General Elliot Richardson appoints Archibald Cox as special prosecutor.

June 25–29. In testimony before the Senate's Watergate Committee, John Dean implicates Haldeman, Ehrlichman, Mitchell and Nixon in efforts to cover up the scandal.

July 16. Alexander Butterfield, a former aide to Haldeman, reveals that a tape-recording system was installed in the president's office to record conversations.

July 23. Nixon refuses to give up tapes of conversations relevant to the investigation.

August 3. Patrick Gray tells the Senate Watergate Committee that he destroyed papers formerly belonging to Hunt.

October 12. Nixon selects Gerald Ford to succeed Agnew as vice president; he will be sworn in on December 6.

October 20. In the "Saturday Night Massacre," the special prosecutor, Cox, is fired by Solicitor General Robert Bork for having rejected a summary of the tapes prepared by the White House. Elliot Richardson, the attorney general, and his assistant William Ruckelshaus resign rather than carry out Nixon's order to fire Cox.

October 23. Nixon announces that he is ready to give up the tapes. Congress takes up the question of impeachment.

November 1. A new special prosecutor, Leon Jaworski, is appointed by Robert Bork, the acting attorney general.

November 17. Nixon denies any personal involvement in Watergate and states: "I'm not a crook."

November 21. Judge Sirica is informed by the White House that an 18½-minute gap appears on a tape of a conversation between Nixon and Haldeman.

1974

January 2. The Internal Revenue Service (IRS) begins an audit of Nixon's tax returns.

January 4. Nixon refuses to release 500 tapes and documents to the Senate Watergate Committee.

January 15. A panel of experts appointed by Judge Sirica reports that the 18½ -minute gap was caused by erasures and re-recordings.

January 30. In his State of the Union Address, Nixon declares that he has "no intention whatever" of resigning.

February 19. The Senate Watergate Committee concludes its investigation.

March 1. Seven of Nixon's former assistants, including Mitchell, Haldeman, Ehrlichman and Charles Colson, are indicted for conspiracy to obstruct justice; Nixon is named an unindicted co-conspirator by the grand jury, but this fact is kept secret.

April 11. The House Judiciary Committee issues a subpoena for the White House tapes; Nixon will refuse to turn them over.

April 30. The White House releases edited transcripts of the subpoenaed tapes.

May 9. The House Judiciary Committee begins hearings on impeachment.

May 15. The Judiciary Committee again subpoenas Nixon for the tapes.

May 22. The president again refuses to relinquish the tapes.

May 24. In order to get the tapes and related documents, the special prosecutor appeals to the Supreme Court.

May 30. The House Judiciary Committee issues a third subpoena for the tapes.

June 10. The president again refuses to give up the tapes.

July 24. The Supreme Court unanimously rules in favor of the special prosecutor and directs Nixon to turn over the tapes. Transcripts of three conversations will show Nixon's involvement in the cover-up of the break-in.

July 27–30. The House Judiciary Committee adopts three articles of impeachment, including one alleging that the president engaged in a criminal conspiracy to obstruct justice.

August 5. The White House releases transcripts of three taped conversations revealing Nixon's participation in the cover-up.

August 8. In a televised speech, Nixon announces his resignation, effective at noon the following day. He becomes the first United States president ever to resign from office.

August 9. Vice President Gerald Ford takes the oath of office to become the 38th president.

September 8. President Ford pardons Nixon for crimes he may have committed in office.

Vietnam War Chronology

1969

January 18. In Paris, peace talks begin between delegations from the United States, South Vietnam, North Vietnam and the Viet Cong.

January 20. Henry Cabot Lodge replaces Averell Harriman as the U.S. representative at the Paris peace talks.

March–April. American planes bomb targets in Cambodia.

March 4. The Department of Defense admits sending tear and other incapacitating gases to Vietnam on a regular basis.

April 24. During an air raid near the Cambodian border northwest of Saigon, B-52s drop 3,000 bombs.

May 20. American and South Vietnamese troops retake "Hamburger Hill" after 10 days of fighting.

June 8. Following a meeting with South Vietnamese president Nguyen Van Thieu, Nixon announces the first withdrawal of American troops (25,000).

July 25. On the island of Guam, the president announces the "Nixon Doctrine." The United States will no longer provide massive numbers of troops to defend nations in Asia, but will look to those nations directly threatened to assume the primary burden of their own defense. The doctrine is an extension of Nixon's "Vietnamization" policy, which calls for South Vietnam to take over the role of U.S. forces in the war.

September 16. Nixon announces a plan to withdraw an additional 35,000 U.S. soldiers.

October 28. The Senate Foreign Relations Committee, chaired by J. William Fulbright, denounces the White House and the Pentagon for waging a "secret" war in Laos.

December. American soldiers in Vietnam: 475,000.

1970

April 30. Nixon announces that American and South Vietnamese troops have entered Cambodia to attack North Vietnamese bases in that country. The operation will end on June 30.

July 10. The Senate votes to repeal the Gulf of Tonkin Resolution.

November 12. Lieutenant William Calley, Jr., is court-martialed for the massacre of civilians that took place on March 16, 1968, in the village of My Lai, South Vietnam. The news media first reported the massacre on November 16, 1969.

December. American soldiers in Vietnam: 334,600.

1971

February 8. Protected by the U.S. Air Force, the South Vietnamese army attacks North Vietnamese sanctuaries in Laos.

March 29. Lieutenant Calley is sentenced to life in prison for the My Lai massacre. His immediate superior, Captain Ernest Medina, is found not guilty. Nixon will review the case, and on August 20, Calley's sentence will be reduced to 20 years; he will be released on parole in 1974.

June 13. The *New York Times* publishes the first excerpts from the "Pentagon Papers," a secret history of American intervention in Vietnam prepared by the Department of Defense. On June 28, Daniel Ellsberg, who once worked at the Department of Defense, will admit being responsible for the publication of the documents. The Supreme Court will at first restrain the media from publishing the history but then on June 30 permit its publication, citing the 1st Amendment.

June 16. The Senate votes 55 to 42 to reject an amendment withdrawing all funding for military operations in Vietnam as of December 30. The House of Representatives will reject the same amendment by a vote of 255 to 158 on June 17.

June 22. The Senate adopts an amendment calling for the withdrawal of

American troops from Vietnam within nine months.

October 3. Thieu is reelected president of South Vietnam.

December. American soldiers in Vietnam: 156,800.

December 26–31. The most intensive American bombing of North Vietnam since 1968 takes place.

1972

January 25. Nixon presents an eight-point peace proposal involving a cease-fire and the release of all captured U.S. soldiers in exchange for the withdrawal of American troops from South Vietnam. Nixon reveals that Henry Kissinger, his national security advisor, has been conducting secret negotiations with the Communists.

March 30. The North Vietnamese launch a major offensive across the demilitarized zone (DMZ). In five weeks of fighting, they will gain 21 miles. The United States will retaliate with air strikes against military targets near Hanoi and Haiphong.

May 8. The president orders the mining of North Vietnamese ports, in particular Haiphong.

June 27. By a vote of 244 to 152, the House of Representatives refuses to cancel all funding for the war as of September 1.

August 12. The last American ground-combat units leave Vietnam.

October 26. Returning from a visit to South Vietnam, Kissinger declares that peace is "at hand" two weeks before the U.S. presidential election.

November 1. Thieu denounces the cease-fire agreements prepared by Kissinger and the North Vietnamese as essentially surrendering South Vietnam to the Communists.

December. American soldiers in Vietnam: 24,200.

December 4. Kissinger and North Vietnamese negotiator Le Duc Tho resume their talks.

December 18–30. The U.S. resumes the bombing of North Vietnam and the mining of North Vietnamese ports.

1973

January 27. A cease-fire agreement is signed in Paris, to take effect the following day. Remaining American troops must withdraw within 60 days, all prisoners of war must be released, and North and South are to be reunited. In a key concession to the Communist side, North Vietnamese troops are allowed to remain in place in South Vietnam. In return, the North Vietnamese drop their demand for the removal of President Thieu. The American bombing of Cambodia will continue until August 14.

March 29. The last American prisoners of war are freed, and the last American combat forces leave Vietnam.

May 11. The espionage, theft and conspiracy trial of Daniel Ellsberg is stopped after it is revealed that White House operatives (the "plumbers") broke into the office of his psychiatrist in an attempt to find compromising documents.

October 16. Kissinger and Le Duc Tho are awarded the Nobel Peace Prize. Le Duc Tho will refuse to accept the award until peace is restored in Vietnam.

1974

March 7. John Ehrlichman, Charles Colson and G. Gordon Liddy are indicted for violating the civil rights of Ellsberg's psychiatrist; their trial will begin on June 26.

April 16. South Vietnam breaks off talks with the Viet Cong because of violations of the cease-fire.

July 30. Congress approves $1 billion in military aid for South Vietnam.

Foreign Policy

1969

March 14. Nixon unveils a plan to build an antiballistic missile (ABM) system.

July 26–August 3. The president visits South Vietnam and other Asian countries as well as Romania.

November 17. In Helsinki, Finland, U.S. and Soviet delegations begin the Strategic Arms Limitation Talks (SALT) aimed at limiting offensive and defensive nuclear weapons.

1971

June 10. The 21-year-old trade embargo against Communist China is relaxed.

July 15. Nixon announces that he has accepted an invitation to visit China.

October 12. Nixon announces that he will visit Moscow in 1972.

October 25. The People's Republic of China is admitted to the United Nations with the support of the United States.

November 5. Grain worth $136 million is sold to the USSR.

1972

February 21–28. Nixon becomes the first U.S. president to visit China. In Shanghai, a joint communiqué announces that both nations will work toward normalizing relations.

May 22–30. Nixon visits the Soviet Union. On May 26, he and Soviet leader Leonid Brezhnev sign the ABM Treaty and the Interim Agreement limiting strategic nuclear arms (SALT I agreements).

July 8. The United States agrees to sell the USSR $750 million worth of grain.

1973

June 16–25. Leonid Brezhnev visits the United States. On June 22, he and Nixon sign an agreement on the prevention of nuclear war.

September 22. Henry Kissinger is appointed secretary of state.

October 6. The Arab-Israeli "October War" begins when Egypt and Syria attack Israel.

October 13. Washington begins sending military equipment to Israel; the Soviet Union had already begun sending weapons to Egypt and Syria.

October 19–21. Arab members of the Organization of Petroleum Exporting Countries impose an embargo on shipments of oil to the United States; the embargo will not be rescinded until March 18, 1974.

October 24. After the Soviet Union threatens to intervene in the Arab-Israeli conflict, the United States puts its military forces on alert to deter such intervention.

1974

June 12. Nixon begins a trip to the Middle East, visiting Egypt, Saudi Arabia, Syria, Israel and Jordan.

June 25–July 3. Nixon visits the USSR. On July 3, he and Brezhnev sign a treaty limiting underground nuclear weapons tests.

Economy and Society

1969

April 9. At Harvard University, a demonstration organized by the Students for a Democratic Society results in 45 injuries and 184 arrests.

July 23. The consumer price index has risen 6.4 percent since January 1, the largest increase since 1951.

October 15. A nationwide moratorium against the Vietnam War includes prayers, vigils and silent marches.

October 29. The Supreme Court rules in *Alexander v. Holmes Company* that desegregation of schools must take place immediately.

November 15. In Washington, 250,000 demonstrators march against the war.

November 20. Seventy-eight Indian activists seize control of the former prison island of Alcatraz, in San Francisco Bay; they demand that the island be given to the Indians. The Indian occupation of the island will end in June 1971

December 30. The Tax Reform Act reduces the income tax by 5 percent while exempting 9 million of the poorest citizens from the tax altogether.

April 22. Earth Day is marked by demonstrations against pollution.

1970

May 4. At Kent State University, in Ohio, a demonstration against the war turns violent when National Guard troops open fire and kill four students and wound eight. A wave of demonstrations will follow.

May 9. A large demonstration against the war is held in Washington.

May 14–15. At Jackson State College, in Mississippi, a demonstration

against the war results in the deaths of two students and the wounding of 12.

June 13. The president appoints a commission to investigate campus unrest.

August 12–November 11. Approximately 350,000 members of the United Auto Workers union go on strike against General Motors plants in the United States and Canada. It is the largest strike in 20 years.

December 31. The Clean Air Act strengthens regulations on atmospheric pollution and mandates a 90 percent reduction in automobile pollution by 1975.

1971

April 20. The Supreme Court unanimously rules that busing to achieve racial integration in public schools is constitutional.

April 23–24. Demonstrations are held against the war.

May 3. A huge demonstration against the war is held in Washington. Thousands are arrested when demonstrators attempt to disrupt the operations of the federal government.

August 15. Phase I of Nixon's program for economic recovery is unveiled. Wages, prices and rents are frozen for 90 days, government expenditures are cut, and a 10 percent surcharge is imposed on imports subject to duties or quotas. The president also announces that the dollar will no longer be convertible into gold and that its value will be allowed to fluctuate. The Economic Stabilization Act will enable this program to come into force.

September 9–13. An uprising by prisoners in Attica, New York, leaves 43 dead; 9 guards taken hostage are executed.

October 7. Phase II of the president's economic program is unveiled. Flexible ceilings are set for wages and prices, in order to reduce the inflation rate by 2.5 percent.

December 18. The dollar is devalued by approximately 8.0 percent.

1972

March 17. Nixon proposes to Congress a moratorium on school busing and the improvement of conditions in public schools.

June 8. A law on education postpones school busing for 18 months. Funding is provided to help schools achieve desegregation.

October 18. A law is passed to control water pollution.

October 30. Legislation increases social security payments for senior citizens.

November 8. Five hundred Indians stage a sit-in at the Bureau of Indian Affairs; they demand the enforcement of treaties with the government and the cancellation of decisions concerning the use of natural resources on Indian lands. These demands will be rejected in January 1973.

November 14. The Dow-Jones stock market index passes 1000.

November 28. The presidential staff is reorganized.

1973

The inflation rate reaches 6.2 percent.

January 11. Phase III of the president's economic program is unveiled. Controls on wages and prices are lifted except for foodstuffs, pharmaceutical products and building materials.

January 22. In *Roe v. Wade*, the Supreme Court rules that state laws restricting abortions during the first six months of a pregnancy are an unconstitutional infringement of a woman's right to privacy.

February 12. The dollar is devalued by 10 percent.

February 28. The Indian reservation town of Wounded Knee, South Dakota, is occupied by members of the American Indian Movement (AIM). They will give themselves up on May 8 after being promised that their demands will be considered.

March 1. The birth rate in the second half of 1972 was 1.98 per couple. A rate of 2.1 per couple is equivalent to zero population growth.

June 13. A price freeze is announced by President Nixon.

July 18. In Phase IV of the president's economic program, all price controls will be lifted on September 12.

October 16. In Atlanta, Georgia, Maynard Jackson becomes the first black elected mayor of a large southern city.

October 17, 1973–March 17, 1974. An oil embargo by the Arab members of OPEC causes widespread shortages and a rapid quadrupling of oil prices, fueling inflation in the U.S. and other Western economies. During the energy crisis, Americans experience brownouts and long gas lines.

November 7. Nixon announces that the United States will seek to become self-sufficient in energy by 1980. He imposes restrictions on the consumption of electricity and gasoline, and he reduces the speed limit on the nation's highways.

November 16. Legislation authorizes the construction of the Alaska oil pipeline, despite the opposition of environmentalists.

1974

The inflation rate reaches 11 percent.

April 8. Legislation enables 8 million additional workers to receive the minimum wage, which is increased to $2.30 an hour.

Science and Technology

1969

April 4. The first implant of an artificial heart is performed by Dr. Denton Cooley. The patient will die on April 8.

July 20. Neil Armstrong becomes the first person to walk on the Moon. *Apollo 11*, launched on July 16, will return to Earth on July 24.

December 2. The Boeing 747, a widebody passenger airliner, makes its first commercial flight, traveling from Seattle to New York.

1971

July 26–August 7. *Apollo 14*, the third mission to land on the Moon, returns to Earth with 98 pounds of minerals from the lunar crust. One stone, called Genesis Rock, is 4 billion years old.

1972

Acupuncture is used for the first time in the United States to anesthetize a patient during a surgical procedure.

January 5. The president authorizes NASA to build a reusable space shuttle.

July 23. The satellite *ERTS 1* (Earth Resources Technology Satellite) is launched; it will send back to Earth photographic data on the resources of the planet.

1973

Two American scientists perform the first genetic engineering.

May 25. *Skylab 2*, the first American space station, is launched into orbit around the Earth.

November 3. *Mariner 10*, the first American space probe to observe two planets (Venus and Mercury), is launched.

1974

July 12. The National Research Act sets limits on the kinds of research that can be performed on human beings.

Civilization and Culture

1969

Dennis Hopper's film *Easy Rider* celebrates the anti-establishment counterculture.

Randall Jarrell's *The Complete Poems* and Mario Puzo's *The Godfather* are published.

Pop sculptor Claes Oldenburg completes *Lipstick on Caterpillar Tracks*.

The *Saturday Evening Post* ceases publication.

March 27. The Black Academy of Arts and Letters is established.

October 18–20. A rock music festival is held in Woodstock, New York; 500,000 attend.

1970

Erich Segal's *Love Story*, Joan Didion's *Play It as It Lays*, Kate Millet's *Sexual Politics* and Alvin Toffler's *Future Shock* are published.

Robert Altman's movie *M*A*S*H* is released.

Yale University's Mathematics Building is designed by Robert Venturi.

Concerto for Orchestra, by Elliot Carter.

September 13. The first New York City marathon is run.

1971

The Book of Daniel, by E. L. Doctorow; James Wright's *Collected Poems.*

April 10–14. The American table tennis team visits China, symbolizing an easing of tensions in Sino-American relations.

1972

John Barth's *Chimera;* A. R. Ammons's *Collected Poems 1951–1971.*

Release of Francis Ford Coppola's movie *The Godfather.*

The architect Louis I. Kahn's dramatic style is evident in the library at Exeter Academy in New Hampshire.

1973

Erica Jong's *Fear of Flying,* Joyce Carol Oates's *Do With Me What You Will,* Thomas Pynchon's *Gravity's Rainbow* and Gore Vidal's *Burr* are published.

George Lucas's film *American Graffiti.*

September 12. The Philadelphia Orchestra begins a 12-day tour of China.

1974

All the President's Men, a book about the Watergate scandal, is published by the journalists Carl Bernstein and Robert Woodward, who broke the story in the *Washington Post.*

David Mamet's play *Sexual Perversity in Chicago.*

Roman Polanski's film *Chinatown.*

January 21. The Supreme Court mandates English as a second language of instruction for students for whom it is not their native tongue.

After Watergate

Gerald Ford, who became president upon Richard Nixon's resignation on August 9, 1974, was well-liked by his former colleagues in Congress for his open-mindedness and honesty, and for his conciliatory nature. Given the crisis of confidence that then prevailed in America, his main objective was to restore the public's faith in government. Ford chose former New York governor Nelson Rockefeller as his vice president, and the Senate approved the nomination. On September 8, in perhaps his most controversial decision, Ford granted Nixon an official pardon.

The economy remained the most pressing issue. The inflation rate remained high and, aside from a slight decline in 1976, continued to increase. But a recession accompanied the inflation. Prices rose, the trade deficit grew, and unemployment spread. Those economic woes were all tied to the nation's rising oil bill.

In foreign policy, Secretary of State Henry Kissinger continued his efforts to establish peace in the Middle East. In South Vietnam, the last Americans hurriedly left Saigon as a Communist offensive seized the entire country. In Asia as a whole, Ford and Kissinger sought to create a new balance of power by continuing the process of normalizing relations with Communist China.

In the 1976 presidential election, Ford was narrowly defeated by the Democratic candidate, Jimmy Carter, who received 40.8 million votes and 297 presidential electors to Ford's 39.1 million votes and 241 electors. Carter, a former governor of Georgia, was not well known by most Americans, but he presented himself in the campaign as a man of principle who was concerned with moral values, and he promised he would "never lie" to the American people. Hoping to further the cause of human rights throughout the world, he corresponded with Andrei Sakharov and received the Soviet dissident Vladimir Bukovsky at the White House. At the same time, he cut economic aid to countries where democracy was not respected. But Carter was unable to hold entirely to this commitment to human rights, and as a consequence his foreign policy was inconsistent. Nonetheless, he achieved some noteworthy successes, including the Camp David Accords between Israel and Egypt, the ratification of the Panama Canal Treaty—both agreements marked the end of lengthy conflicts—and the establishment of diplomatic relations with Communist China. But his presidency was also marred by several crises, including the rise to power of the Sandinistas in Nicaragua, the Soviet invasion of Afghanistan, and the Islamic revolution in Iran, which led to the taking of hostages in the American embassy in Teheran.

Carter's failure to deal adequately with these crises explains the magnitude of Ronald Reagan's victory in the 1980 presidential election. The former governor of California carried 44 states and received 42.8 million votes and 489 electors to Carter's 34.4 million votes and 49 electors. Undoubtedly misperceived and misunderstood, Carter became yet another victim of a turbulent period in American history.

Political and Institutional Life

1974

August 9. Richard Nixon resigns the presidency at noon. Gerald Ford becomes the 38th president, taking the oath of office before the chief justice of the Supreme Court, Warren Burger.

August 20. Ford selects Nelson Rockefeller to become vice president. Rockefeller will take the oath of office on December 19.

October 15. The Federal Election Campaign Act limits the expenditures of candidates for president and congress as well as private contributions to such candidates.

November 5. In the midterm elections, the Democrats increase their majorities in the Senate and the House of Representatives.

November 21. Over President Ford's veto, Congress approves amendments to the Freedom of Information Act that provide for greater public access to government records.

1975

January 5. Ford appoints a commission headed by Vice President Rockefeller to investigate alleged misdeeds of the CIA. A Senate committee headed by Frank Church of Idaho will launch its own investigation.

June 10. The Rockefeller commission reports that the CIA had placed 300,000 individuals and organizations, including antiwar, black and political groups, under illegal surveillance.

September 5 and 22. Lynette "Squeaky" Fromme and Sarah Jane Moore fail in separate attempts to assassinate President Ford in California.

1976

July 4. The Bicentennial of the United States is celebrated.

November 2. Democrat James Earl (Jimmy) Carter is elected the 39th president; Walter Mondale is elected vice president.

1977

January 20. Carter is sworn in as president.

March 16. In Clinton, Massachusetts, Carter speaks at a town meeting and is housed overnight by a local family.

August 4. The Department of Energy is created.

1978

June 6. California voters adopt Proposition 13, reducing their property taxes; the measure will spark a nation-wide "taxpayer revolt."

1979

October 17. The Department of Education is created.

1980

April 26. Secretary of State Cyrus Vance resigns after opposing an attempted rescue of American hostages in Iran. He will be succeeded by Senator Edmund Muskie.

November 4. Republican Ronald Reagan is elected the 40th president; George Bush is elected vice president. Republicans also gain a majority in the Senate for only the second time in 50 years.

Foreign Policy

1974

September 4. Diplomatic relations are established with the German Democratic Republic (East Germany).

November 23–24. Ford holds a summit meeting with Soviet leader Leonid Brezhnev at Vladivostok, in the Soviet Far East. They agree on a framework for limiting offensive strategic weapons until 1985.

1975

The United States and the Soviet Union step up their covert military assistance to rival factions in Angola's civil war; Cuba sends combat troops to assist Angola's Marxist government.

April 17. The Communist Khmer Rouge seize Phnom Penh, the capital of Cambodia.

April 28. The last Americans are evacuated from Saigon as the capital of South Vietnam is attacked by the Communists.

April 29. The government of South Vietnam surrenders to the Communists.

May 12. The American merchant ship *Mayaguez* is seized by Communist Cambodian forces. On May 14, Ford will order a rescue operation that results in the deaths of 15 American soldiers and the wounding of 50 others. The ship will be freed on May 14.

August 1. Ford signs the Helsinki Accords, in which 35 nations formally recognize the post-World War II territorial boundaries in Europe and pledge to uphold certain human rights.

October. The Japanese emperor Hirohito visits the United States.

December 1–5. President Ford visits China, Indonesia and the Philippines.

December 7. In Honolulu, Ford unveils a new doctrine for the Pacific: American influence will be reasserted in the region, with Japan as one of the cornerstones of this strategy. Closer relations will also be established with China.

1976

March 26. A military agreement with Turkey is renewed for four years: American bases, closed in July 1975, will reopen. The United States pledges military and economic assistance.

May 28. In their respective capitals, Ford and Brezhnev sign a treaty limiting the yield of underground nuclear explosions carried out for peaceful purposes.

June 16. In Beirut, the American ambassador to Lebanon is murdered.

July 27. The U.S. Navy evacuates 160 Americans and 148 foreigners from Beirut.

November 15. The United States vetoes the admission of Vietnam to the United Nations.

1977

February 24. Carter's secretary of state, Cyrus Vance, announces that U.S. foreign aid will be linked to the observance of human rights in other countries.

March 1. Carter receives the Soviet dissident Vladimir Bukovsky at the White House; the president had personally written to Andrei Sakharov, another Soviet dissident, in February.

May. In Paris, the United States and Vietnam begin unsuccessful talks aimed at normalizing relations.

May 4. The United States announces it will no longer oppose the admission of Vietnam to the UN but refuses to give it any economic aid.

May 22. At the University of Notre Dame, Carter defines three goals of his foreign policy: defending human rights, limiting arms sales to foreign countries and strengthening America's influence in black Africa.

June 3. An agreement is reached with Cuba on the opening of diplomatic missions in Washington and Havana.

September 7. Two treaties are signed with Panama concerning the canal: Control of the Canal Zone will be transferred to Panama at the end of 1999, and the canal must remain neutral and open to ships of all nations. The treaties will be approved by the Senate on March 16 and April 18, 1978.

1978

February 8. Anwar Sadat, the president of Egypt, arrives for a six-day visit.

March 9. Marshal Josip Tito, the president of Yugoslavia, begins a visit to the United States.

May 15. The Carter administration announces controversial sales of jet fighter planes to Egypt, Saudi Arabia and Israel.

September 5–17. Carter mediates peace talks between Sadat and Israeli prime minister Menachem Begin at Camp David, Maryland. On September 17, at the White House, the three leaders sign an agreement providing for a peace treaty between Israel and Egypt within three months and a "Framework for Peace in the Middle East."

November 27. The United States increases its quotas for immigrants from Southeast Asia.

1979

January 1. Diplomatic relations are established with the People's Republic of China. Diplomatic relations with Taiwan are severed, although the U.S. will continue its existing commercial and cultural relations with the island.

February 8. Military aid to the government of Nicaraguan strongman General Anastasio Somoza is suspended.

February 14. The U.S. ambassador to Afghanistan is kidnapped and murdered in Kabul.

March 26. A peace treaty between Egypt and Israel is signed in Washington.

April 27. The Soviet dissident Alexander Ginzburg is freed in an exchange of prisoners between the United States and the USSR.

June 8. Carter approves the deployment of the MX intercontinental ballistic missile (ICBM).

June 16–18. Carter and Brezhnev hold a summit meeting in Vienna, Austria. On June 18, they sign the SALT II treaty limiting offensive strategic nuclear weapons.

June 28. The Organization of Petroleum Exporting Countries (OPEC) announces a 16 percent increase in the price of oil. In the past year, the price of oil has increased by 50 percent.

June 29. The seven major industrial nations, meeting in Tokyo, announce a plan to limit oil imports until 1985; the United States will import a maximum of 8.5 million barrels a day (President Carter will reduce this quota to 8.2 million barrels on July 16).

November 4. The U.S. embassy in Teheran is occupied by Iranian Muslim fundamentalists who are followers of Ayatollah Khomeini; 66 Americans are taken hostage. The fundamentalists demand the return of the former shah of Iran, who is undergoing medical treatment in the United States. Thirteen hostages will be released shortly.

November 12. Carter bans the importation of Iranian oil and freezes Iranian assets in the United States.

November 21. The American embassy in Islamabad, Pakistan, is attacked and destroyed by a mob.

December 2. The American embassy in Tripoli, Libya, is attacked.

December 26–27. The Soviet Union invades Afghanistan.

1980

January 4. An embargo is imposed on the sale of grain and high-technology items to the USSR in retaliation for the Soviet invasion of Afghanistan.

January 23. In his State of the Union Address Carter warns the Soviet Union that the United States will use military force to defend the route along which oil is conveyed in the Persian Gulf.

January 24. Carter announces that the United States is ready to sell military equipment to Communist China.

March 17. The Refugee Act broadens the definition of refugees eligible to enter the United States and increases the annual quota.

April 7. Diplomatic relations with Iran are severed, exports to that country

are prohibited, and Iranian diplomats are expelled from the United States.

April 21–22. Cuba announces it will allow relatives of Cuban-Americans to leave for Florida from Mariel Harbor; over the next few months, more than 100,000 Cubans will arrive in the United States (Mariel boatlift).

April 24. A military mission to rescue the 52 Americans held hostage in Iran ends in failure; eight U.S. servicemen are killed.

Economy and Society

1974

September 2. The Employee Retirement Income Act establishes criteria for more than 300,000 pension plans managed by private companies.

September 16. Vietnam War deserters and draft evaders are offered an amnesty. They must take an oath of loyalty to the country and fulfill two years of community service.

October 8. In order to bring inflation under control, President Ford proposes a plan that includes voluntary energy savings and a tax surcharge of 5 percent on business profits and personal incomes of more than $15,000.

December 18. Layoffs occur in the auto industry.

December 31. The ban on gold purchases by private individuals is lifted.

1975

The inflation rate rises to 9.1 percent.

Congress approves the admission of women to the army, navy and air force academies.

January 4. The unemployment rate is 7.1 percent; it will rise to 9.2 percent in May, the highest in 33 years.

March 11. The Civil Rights Commission announces that schools in southern states are more racially integrated than schools in northern states.

June 30. Social benefits for the unemployed are extended to 65 weeks.

October 20. The Supreme Court upholds corporal punishment for students.

November 29. Federal legislation requires states to provide free education for the handicapped.

1976

The inflation rate rises to 5.8 percent.

January 8. A new international monetary system is created. The system of fixed exchange rates is abandoned in favor of flexible exchange rates valued against the dollar; the gold standard is abandoned once and for all.

1977

The inflation rate rises to 6.5 percent.

January 21. Carter grants a pardon to Vietnam War draft evaders.

April 18. Carter calls for energy savings.

April 30. A huge demonstration against the use of nuclear reactors to generate electricity takes place in Seabrook, New Hampshire: 1,400 demonstrators are arrested when they occupy the site of a future nuclear power plant.

November 1. Legislation raises the minimum wage to $3.35 an hour by 1981.

December 10. A nationwide farmers' strike begins.

1978

The inflation rate rises to 7.7 percent.

January 13. Japan agrees to open its borders to more American products.

April 6. Legislation enables a majority of workers to retire at age 70 rather than at 65.

June 28. In a case involving the University of California, which had rejected the application of Allen Bakke, a white student, while accepting comparable applications of minority students, the Supreme Court rules against rigid quotas in affirmative-action plans.

July 15. The "Longest Walk," a march from Alcatraz Island, California, to Washington, organized by the American Indian Movement (AIM), ends on the steps of the Capitol.

October 20. The Dow Jones index of stock prices drops 59.08 points in one week.

October 31. The Federal Reserve raises the interest rate on loans granted to banks to 9.5 percent.

October 15. Several laws aimed at reducing the consumption of energy are passed by Congress, including one deregulating the price of natural gas.

November 1. Carter announces that the United States will sell gold. The dollar rises.

The Dow Jones index gains 35.34 points in a single day.

November 18. In Jonestown, Guyana, nearly 1,000 American members of a religious cult led by Jim Jones commit mass suicide after cult members murder Representative Leo Ryan of California.

1979

The inflation rate rises to 11.3 percent.

The consumption of petroleum drops 1.8 percent, the first decline since 1975.

February 13. The Civil Rights Commission announces that 25 years after segregation was ruled unconstitutional,

46 percent of minority children still attend racially segregated schools.

April 5. Carter orders a progressive lifting of controls on oil prices.

October 6. The Federal Reserve raises its interest rate to 12 percent.

October 17–19. Opponents of school busing riot in Boston.

November 1. The federal government announces a $1.5 billion loan guarantee for Chrysler Corporation, the nation's third largest automaker, after the company reported a huge loss in revenue.

1980

The inflation rate rises to 13.5 percent.

Auto sales have declined by 20 percent since the beginning of 1979.

The Federal Reserve raises its interest rate to 13 percent.

The unemployment rate climbs to 7.1 percent.

April 2. The Crude Oil Windfall Profits Tax Act imposes a tax on the excessive profits of oil companies.

May 17–19. In Miami, race riots follow the acquittal by a white jury of four white policemen who had killed a black man.

May 18. In the state of Washington, Mount St. Helens begins a series of volcanic eruptions that will kill approximately 60 people.

June 27. A "standby" draft law is enacted, requiring the registration of all men of eligible age.

Science and Technology

1974

Ultrasonic diagnostic technology is developed.

1975

July 17. In the first joint Soviet-American space mission, *Apollo 18* links up with *Soyuz 19* in Earth orbit.

December 11. Legislation provides for the voluntary conversion to the metric measurement system within ten years.

1976

May 24. Inaugural flight of the supersonic Concorde linking London, Paris and Washington.

July 20 and September 3. The *Viking I* and *Viking II* spacecraft make successful landings on Mars.

1977

The enhanced radiation or "neutron" bomb is developed.

July 28. The Trans-Alaskan Pipeline is opened.

1978

January 16. NASA selects 35 future astronauts for the space shuttle program, including six women, three blacks and one Asian.

April 7. Carter postpones deployment of the neutron bomb.

July 6–10. An American scientific delegation visits China.

1979

March 28. In the nation's most serious nuclear accident, a reactor at Three Mile Island, near Harrisburg, Pennsylvania, releases clouds of radioactive steam into the atmosphere.

1980

February 14. The Solar Maximum Observatory, a satellite that will study radiation from the Sun, is launched into orbit.

Civilization and Culture

1975

Release of Steven Spielberg's movie *Jaws*.

The Bolshoi Ballet tours the United States for the first time.

August 29. A five-year agreement is reached with the USSR on the exchange of works of art.

1976

Alex Haley's *Roots*, the saga of an Afro-American family, is published.

April 22. Barbara Walters becomes the first anchorwoman of a nightly television newscast.

October 21. The Nobel Prize for literature is awarded to Saul Bellow.

1977

Marilyn French's *The Women's Room* and Walker Percy's *Lancelot* are published.

Films: Woody Allen's *Annie Hall* and Steven Spielberg's *Close Encounters of the Third Kind*.

Roots, a weeklong television miniseries based on Alex Haley's book, attracts 130 million viewers.

July 13–14. A 25-hour electrical blackout occurs in New York City.

August 16. The singer Elvis Presley dies.

November 18–21. The First National Women's Conference, the most important feminist gathering since the Seneca Falls Congress of 1848, is held in Houston, Texas.

1978

John Irving's novel *The World According to Garp*.

Isaac Bashevis Singer, a Polish-born author of Yiddish fiction, is awarded the Nobel Prize for literature.

Films: John Carpenter's horror classic *Halloween* and Michael Cimino's *The Deer Hunter*.

The new National Gallery of Art building, designed by the architect I. M. Pei, opens in Washington, D.C.

1979

Norman Mailer's *The Executioner's Song*, about the execution of the murderer Gary Gilmore, is published.

Release of Francis Ford Coppola's film *Apocalypse Now*.

September. The Dalai Lama, the spiritual leader of Tibetan Buddhists, visits the United States.

October 1–7. Pope John Paul II visits the United States.

1980

John Kennedy Toole's novel *A Confederacy of Dunces* is published.

The Lithuanian-born poet Czeslaw Milosz, who writes in Polish, is awarded the Nobel Prize for literature.

In New York, a retrospective exhibit of Picasso's work opens at the Museum of Modern Art. The painting *Guernica* is then bequeathed to Spain in accordance with the will of the artist.

February 12–24. The Winter Olympic Games are held at Lake Placid, New York.

April 12. At the request of President Carter, the U.S. Olympic Committee decides that American athletes will boycott the Summer Olympic Games in Moscow to protest the Soviet invasion of Afghanistan.

December 8. John Lennon, a former member of the Beatles, a British rock group, is shot and killed outside his apartment building in New York.

Chapter 29   1981–1988

The Reagan Revolution

Ronald Reagan was elected president on an economic program that called for less government intervention and more private initiative. But "Reaganomics" went further. Inspired by economists such as Arthur Laffer, the Reagan team sought to overcome the economic crisis by stimulating supply instead of demand. The tax rate was lowered to encourage investment and production and thus to create jobs. The government also reduced regulation in order to increase competition. At first, the Federal Reserve maintained high interest rates to avoid a revival of inflation, but the rates were progressively lowered in 1983 and 1984.

The results of this policy were not immediately forthcoming. In 1981, a short-lived but painful recession began. In 1983, there was a discernible recovery that continued into 1984. The upswing was felt first in the construction industry. The dollar rose steadily in value and foreign capital flowed into the economy, which was growing, but at a rate of 2.3 percent a year. Two problems remained unsolved: the budget deficit continued to increase and farmers found themselves in dire straits.

In foreign policy, Reagan adopted a hard-line stance toward the Soviet Union, which he characterized as an "evil empire." He increased the defense budget and initiated a major buildup of U.S. conventional and nuclear forces. Relations between the United States and Communist China continued to improve, and in 1982 Vice President George Bush traveled to China. The visit marked the beginning of an era of expanded trade. Reagan himself made an official visit to China in May 1984.

The Middle East remained tense. On October 6, 1981, Egyptian president Anwar Sadat was murdered. In Lebanon, a civil war worsened, while a war between Iraq and Iran intensified. In September 1982, Reagan decided to send peacekeeping troops into Beirut after the assassination of Lebanese President-elect Bashir Gemayel (the troops were withdrawn in February 1984). In Central America, the United States moved to counter the installation of Soviet- and Cuban-backed regimes. Aid to the leftist Sandinista government in Nicaragua was cut off, while the Contras, or anti-Sandinista guerrillas, received unofficial help through the CIA. In El Salvador, after having sent military advisors, the United States backed a moderate, José Napoléon Duarte, who took power. In October 1983, after the murder of the prime minister, U.S. forces invaded Grenada to safeguard American lives and prevent a possible Communist takeover on the island.

By November 1984, Reagan, the "Great Communicator" who could articulate simple, traditional values, had succeeded in rebuilding American confidence. He was reelected by a huge margin over his Democratic opponent, Walter Mondale. For the first time, a woman, Geraldine Ferraro, a Democratic U.S. representative from New York, was chosen to run for vice president. Reagan took 49 states and won 54.3 million votes and 525 presidential electors against Mondale's 37.5 million votes and 13 electors.

The coming to power of Mikhail Gorbachev in the USSR in March 1985 ushered in a period of rapidly improving U.S.-Soviet relations. Reagan and Gorbachev held four summit meetings, eased the East-West confrontation in Europe, and signed the landmark Intermediate-range Nuclear Forces Treaty in 1987. Reagan capped this remarkable turnaround in superpower relations by traveling to Moscow in 1988. U.S. efforts to help negotiate an end to Arab-Israeli hostilities in the Middle East, however, were unsuccessful. Relations with Communist China continued to improve, but tensions remained high in Central America.

Reagan's second term was marked by a steady improvement of the economy. Massive federal deficits, however, raised concerns across the political spectrum, and the White House and Congress were unable to agree on a remedy. Reagan advocated cutting domestic spending while Democrats favored trimming the defense budget. Politically, Reagan's final years as president were tarnished by the Iran-Contra scandal, which involved the sale of arms to Iran in exchange for the release of American hostages held in Lebanon, in violation of Reagan's stated policy of not dealing with terrorists. In turn, the arms sale proceeds were diverted to the Contras, circumventing a congressional ban on U.S. aid to the guerrillas.

In the presidential election of 1988, Vice President Bush won with 53 percent of the votes and 426 presidential electors against Democrat Michael Dukakis's 112. Still, the Democrats would have a 56-seat majority in the Senate and 262 seats to the Republicans' 173 in the House of Representatives.

Political and Institutional Life

1981

January 20. Ronald Reagan takes the oath of office as president.

March 30. Reagan is wounded by a bullet in an assassination attempt by John Hinckley in Washington.

September 21. The Senate confirms Sandra Day O'Connor as the first female Supreme Court justice.

December 4. An executive order allows the CIA to conduct limited intelligence-gathering operations in the United States.

1982

June 25. Secretary of State Alexander Haig resigns. He will be replaced by George Shultz.

November 2. In the midterm elections, the Republicans retain a majority in the Senate with 54 seats, but win only 166 seats in the House against the Democrats' 269.

1983

October 9. Secretary of the Interior James Watt resigns after making a racist remark. He will be replaced by William Clark, the president's national security advisor.

1984

November 6. Ronald Reagan is re-elected president in a landslide, winning 49 states against former vice president Walter Mondale, the Democratic candidate.

1985

January 20. Reagan begins his second term as president.

1986

May 13. A special commission of the Justice Department issues a report on pornography. It calls for strict measures against those producing and distributing pornography.

June 17. The chief justice of the Supreme Court, Warren Burger, retires. Reagan nominates Associate Justice William Rehnquist to become chief justice and Antonin Scalia to become associate justice. The Senate will approve both nominations on September 17.

The appointments strengthen the conservative wing on the Court.

November 4. In the midterm congressional elections, the Democrats regain a majority in the Senate with 55 seats and retain their majority in the House of Representatives with 258 seats to the Republicans' 177.

1987

February 27. Donald Regan, the White House chief of staff, resigns. He is replaced by former senator Howard Baker.

July 1. Reagan nominates Robert Bork to replace the retiring Lewis Powell on the Supreme Court.

October 23. The Senate rejects the nomination of Robert Bork to the Supreme Court.

October 29. Reagan nominates Douglas Ginsburg to fill Lewis Powell's seat on the Supreme Court.

November 5. Secretary of Defense Caspar Weinberger resigns. He will be replaced by National Security Advisor Frank Carlucci.

November 11. After admitting he had smoked marijuana, Douglas Ginsburg withdraws his name from consideration for a seat on the Supreme Court. Reagan nominates Anthony Kennedy to the Court; Kennedy will be confirmed by the Senate on February 3, 1988.

1988

November 8. George Bush is elected the 41st president, defeating Democrat Michael Dukakis, the governor of Massachusetts; Dan Quayle is elected vice president.

July 18. Attorney General Edwin Meese announces that he will resign after he is accused of financial wrongdoing.

Foreign Policy

1981

January 20. Minutes after Reagan is inaugurated, Iran frees the 52 hostages held in captivity for 444 days in the American embassy in Teheran. Jimmy Carter will welcome the hostages in Wiesbaden, West Germany, the following day. The United States pledges to unfreeze Iranian assets in the United States and freeze those of the former shah. The United States also pledges not to interfere in Iran's internal affairs and to lift the trade embargo.

March 2. Reagan announces that he plans to send 20 additional military advisors to El Salvador as well as $25 million in military equipment.

April 21. A sale of arms worth $1 billion to Saudi Arabia is announced. Israel will protest the sale, which will be approved by the Senate on October 28.

April 24. The embargo on wheat sales to the USSR, imposed by President Carter after the Soviet invasion of Afghanistan, is lifted.

May. Libyan diplomats are expelled after a Libyan terrorist is implicated in a murder in Chicago.

June 16. The United States agrees in principle to sell arms to China.

August 10. Reagan authorizes the production of the neutron bomb.

August 19. Two Libyan fighter planes are shot down after attacking U.S. Navy planes over international waters in the Gulf of Sidra.

October 2. Reagan proposes to build 100 B-1 strategic bombers and 100 MX intercontinental ballistic missiles (ICBMs).

October 18–19. French president François Mitterrand takes part in the commemoration of the bicentennial of the victory over the British at Yorktown during the Revolutionary War. In Williamsburg, Virginia, Mitterrand and Reagan discuss the strengthening of nuclear forces in Europe.

October 22–23. A North-South conference of rich and poor nations meets in Cancún, Mexico: 22 states, including the United States, take part in the economic summit.

November 18. Reagan proposes his "zero option" plan for limiting intermediate-range nuclear forces in a televised speech broadcast live in Europe. The United States pledges to give up its plan to install Pershing II and ground-launched cruise missiles in Europe if the USSR dismantles its SS-20 missiles targeted on Western Europe.

December 28. Following the Soviet-instigated imposition of martial law in Poland and the suppression of the independent trade union Solidarity, Reagan announces sanctions against the Polish military government and Moscow, including an embargo on high-technology equipment to be used in the construction of a pipeline for conveying Soviet natural gas to Europe, and a ban on Aeroflot flights to the United States. The embargo will be lifted on November 13, 1982, when Lech Walesa, the leader of Solidarity, is freed by Polish authorities.

1982

March 10. Economic sanctions are imposed on Libya in retaliation for its support of international terrorism. The sanctions include an embargo on the export of high-technology equipment and a ban on imports of Libyan oil.

May 21. Following Argentina's invasion of the Falkland Islands, a British colony, the United States lends support to the British military operation to retake the islands.

August 25. Approximately 800 U.S. Marines land in Beirut as part of a multinational force overseeing the withdrawal of Palestinian soldiers. The marines will be withdrawn on September 10 and then sent back into Beirut on the 29th following the massacre by Christian militiamen of hundreds of Palestinians in the camps of Sabra and Shatila. On the 30th, one marine will be killed and three wounded.

December. The president visits Latin America.

1983

January. Arms are sold to Guatemala, and aid to El Salvador is increased.

March 23. Reagan announces that the United States will develop weapons to defend against a ballistic missile attack—the Strategic Defense Initiative (SDI), or "Star Wars" program.

April 18. Terrorists explode a car bomb at the U.S. embassy in Beirut; 63 are killed, including 17 Americans.

May. High-technology equipment is exported to China.

July. A treaty is signed with China, permitting the export of Chinese textiles to the United States.

July 28. Exports of grain to the USSR are increased by 50 percent under a new five-year agreement.

September 1. One U.S. congressman and 60 other Americans are among the 269 persons killed when the Soviet Air Force shoots down a South Korean Boeing 747 passenger plane that had strayed into Soviet airspace in the Far East. The Reagan administration will condemn the Soviet action and suspend negotiations on the opening of an American consulate in Kiev.

October 23. A truck bomb destroys the marine barracks in Beirut: 241 marines are killed.

October 25. American military forces land on the Caribbean island of Grenada. The operation to rescue American students and forestall a leftist takeover is a success.

November 11. The first American intermediate-range missiles arrive in Great Britain; 572 are scheduled to be deployed in Europe.

November 23. Retaliating against the deployment of American missiles in Europe, the USSR walks out of the negotiations on intermediate-range nuclear forces (INF). On December 8, Soviet negotiators will suspend the Strategic Arms Reduction Talks (START).

December 4. American bombers attack Syrian positions near Beirut.

December 28. The United States announces its intention to withdraw from the United Nations Educational, Scientific and Cultural Organization (UNESCO) at the end of 1984; it will reaffirm its decision on December 19, 1984, citing the organization's mismanagement and political bias.

1984

January 10. Diplomatic relations with the Vatican are reestablished after a 116-year lapse.

February 7. American troops are withdrawn from Lebanon.

April 10. The Senate condemns the mining of Nicaraguan ports by the CIA; the World Court will also condemn the mining in June 1986.

April 26–May 1. President Reagan visits China. Agreements on scientific and cultural exchanges, economic cooperation and nuclear energy are signed.

May 28. A solemn ceremony is held to commemorate the Unknown Soldier killed in Vietnam.

June 6. In Normandy, Reagan attends ceremonies marking the 40th anniversary of D Day.

September 20. An explosion at the American embassy in Beirut kills two Americans.

1985

February 21. The United States begins returning to Cuba more than 2,500 criminal and mentally ill refugees who entered the country in 1980 in the Mariel boatlift.

May 5. In West Germany, Reagan tours the former Nazi concentration camp at Bergen-Belsen and makes a controversial visit to the military cemetery at Bitburg, where 49 German SS soldiers are buried.

June 14. In Athens, a TWA passenger plane is hijacked by 2 Shiite terrorists.

July 23. During a visit to Washington by the president of the People's Republic of China, Li Xiannian, an agreement on the sale of nuclear equipment for nonmilitary purposes is signed.

September 9. Limited economic sanctions are imposed on South Africa to protest its policy of racial apartheid.

October 10. U.S. Air Force planes intercept an Egyptian airliner carrying four Palestinian terrorists who had hijacked the Italian cruise ship *Achille Lauro* and killed an American passenger. The Egyptian plane is forced to land in Sicily, where the Palestinian terrorists are taken into custody.

November 19–21. In Geneva, Reagan holds a summit meeting with Mikhail Gorbachev, the new Soviet leader.

November 22. The United States extends financial assistance to UNITA, an anti-Marxist group fighting the Cuban-supported government of Angola.

1986

January 1. Reagan extends New Year's greetings on Soviet television while Gorbachev does likewise on American television.

January 7 and 8. Economic sanctions are imposed on Libya, which is held responsible for bombings at airports in Rome and Vienna on December 27, 1985. Libyan government assets in the United States are frozen, and American citizens are ordered to leave Libya.

January 23. A war of nerves with Libyan leader Muammar Qaddafi begins. American bombers complete a series of flights near Libya.

March 14. Speaking to Congress, Reagan declares that his administration will help "democratic revolutions" in countries ruled by right-wing regimes even when those governments are allied with the United States.

March 24. During American naval maneuvers in the Gulf of Sidra, Libyan forces attack several American planes; in retaliation, U.S. forces sink two Libyan patrol boats and destroy a Libyan missile radar.

March 25. Reagan approves $20 million in emergency aid for Honduras, claiming that Nicaraguan troops had crossed into that country to attack the Contras.

April 2. A bomb in a West Berlin nightclub kills an American soldier and wounds 50 others; Libya is held responsible for the act of terrorism.

April 14. In retaliation for the bombing in West Berlin, the U.S. Air Force attacks five Libyan military bases and training camps in Tripoli and Bengazi.

May 27. Reagan announces that the United States will no longer consider itself bound by the SALT II treaty, which was never ratified.

June 5. Ronald Pelton, a former employee of the National Security Agency, is found guilty of espionage on behalf of the USSR.

June 19. Richard Miller, a former FBI agent, is found guilty of espionage on behalf of the USSR.

October 2. Overriding President Reagan's veto, Congress approves harsher economic sanctions against South Africa, including a ban on new American investments in that country.

October 11–12. Reagan and Gorbachev hold a summit meeting in Reykjavik, Iceland. They tentatively agree on sweeping reductions in nuclear arsenals, but they fail to complete an agreement when Reagan rejects Gorbachev's demand for restrictions on the development of SDI.

October 21–22. Reagan and West German chancellor Helmut Kohl meet in Washington.

November 2. The American hostage David Jacobsen, a prisoner of the Shiite Muslims in Lebanon for 17 months, is freed.

November 13. In a televised speech, Reagan admits that the United States has secretly sold arms and military equipment to Iran but denies that the sale was in exchange for the release of hostages held in Lebanon.

November 19. Reagan defends the decision to sell arms to Iran.

November 25. John Poindexter, the national security advisor to the president, resigns after the White House reveals that profits from the sale of arms to Iran were secretly used to aid the Nicaraguan Contras. Reagan dismisses marine lieutenant colonel Oliver North, a member of the National Security Council staff, for his role in the diversion of profits to the Contras. Reagan also appoints former Texas senator John Tower to head an investigative commission.

December 19. Judge Lawrence Walsh is appointed special prosecutor to investigate the "Iran-Contra scandal." In Congress, a special investigative committee is established in each house.

1987

January 19. The *Washington Post* reports that the Reagan administration had solicited aid for the Contras from six nations in recent years.

January 28. A ban is imposed on travel to Lebanon following the kidnapping of three Americans in Beirut. The U.S. government asks the 1,500 Americans living there to leave the country within 30 days. The American military presence in the Middle East will be strengthened.

February 2. CIA director William Casey resigns for reasons of health; the CIA has been implicated in the Iran-Contra affair.

February 27. The Tower Commission concludes that President Reagan was uninformed about the Iran-Contra affair; the commission faults several key present and former aides to the president as well as Reagan's management style.

March 4. In a televised speech, Reagan admits that the trading of arms for hostages was an unfortunate mistake. His public approval rating will fall substantially.

May–August. Senate and House committees investigating the Iran-Contra affair hold public hearings, some of which are televised.

May 17. An Iraqi warplane attacks the frigate *Stark* in the Persian Gulf; 37 sailors are killed in the incident, which Iraq claims was an accident.

June 17. The journalist Charles Glass is kidnapped in Beirut, becoming the ninth American hostage. He will escape on August 18.

July 22. The U.S. Navy begins escorting neutral shipping in the Strait of Hormuz and the Persian Gulf during the Iran-Iraq war.

August 1–3. An American team visits Vietnam to search for 2,400 G.I.s declared missing in action (MIA) during the war.

August 7. In Guatemala City, the presidents of Guatemala, Costa Rica, Nicaragua, El Salvador and Honduras sign a regional peace plan.

August 21. In Los Angeles, Reagan meets with the political and military leaders of the Nicaraguan Contras and guarantees them his support.

August 24. Marine sergeant Clayton Lonetree, a guard at the U.S. embassy in Moscow, is found guilty of espionage on behalf of the USSR.

August 26. In a speech given in Los Angeles, Reagan encourages the USSR to make progress with its policy of openness (*glasnost*).

September 17–19. Pope John Paul II visits the United States.

September 21. In the Persian Gulf, an American helicopter attacks an Iranian boat laying mines; the boat's crew is captured.

September 29. The Senate unanimously approves an embargo on imports from Iran, to come into effect on October 26.

October 8. American helicopters attack four Iranian patrol boats during the night in the Persian Gulf.

October 16. An oil tanker flying the American flag is attacked by an Iranian missile within the territorial waters of Kuwait; 18 are wounded.

October 19. American warships shell an Iranian oil platform in the Persian Gulf.

November 18. The final report of the House and Senate committees investigating the Iran-Contra scandal accuses administration officials and the president of having hidden facts and of deceiving the American people.

December 8–10. Reagan and Gorbachev hold a summit meeting in Washington. Arms control, regional conflicts, bilateral relations, human rights and Jewish emigration from the USSR are among the topics raised. On December 8, the leaders sign the Intermediate-range Nuclear Forces (INF) Treaty, which bans all such missiles throughout the world.

December 26. Gorbachev is named *Time* magazine's "Man of the Year."

1988

January 1. New Year's greetings are exchanged: Reagan appears on Soviet TV and Gorbachev on American TV.

January 25–29. Egyptian president Hosni Mubarak visits Washington, seeking to advance peace in the Middle East.

February 8. Mikhail Gorbachev announces that the USSR will begin withdrawing its troops from Afghanistan on May 15.

February 17. U.S. Army Lieutenant Colonel William Higgins, a United Nations observer in Lebanon, is kidnapped near Tyre.

February 21–22. In Moscow, Secretary of State George Shultz and his Soviet counterpart Eduard Shevardnadze hold the first in a series of monthly meetings.

February 25. The USSR dismantles 30 medium-range SS-12 missiles on two

East German bases and sends them back to the Soviet Union.

March 14–17. Israeli prime minister Yitzhak Shamir visits Washington.

March 16. Reagan orders 3,200 soldiers into Honduras after accusing the Nicaraguans of having invaded the country; the soldiers will leave Honduras on March 28.

A federal grand jury indicts Oliver North and John Poindexter on Iran-Contra charges of conspiring to defraud the government.

March 16–17. Secretary of Defense Frank Carlucci and Soviet defense minister Dmitri Yazov meet in Bern, Switzerland.

March 23. In Nicaragua, a cease-fire is signed by the government and the Contra rebels; 25,000 have died since 1981.

March 25. In a speech, Reagan defends North and Poindexter against accusations of conspiracy.

March 31. Congress approves $48 million in humanitarian aid for the Contras.

April 5–7. An additional 1,300 soldiers are sent to Panama to defend American bases because of political turmoil in that country.

April 8. Approximately 800 marines arrive in Panama for training.

April 18. In the Persian Gulf, American forces sink six Iranian ships and shell two oil drilling platforms after U.S. naval vessels are attacked.

May 29–June 2. Reagan and Gorbachev hold a summit meeting in Moscow. Nine agreements are signed, dealing with exchange programs and bilateral cooperation.

July 3. The American cruiser *Vincennes* mistakenly shoots down an Iranian passenger airliner in the Persian Gulf; 290 persons are killed. On July 11,

Reagan will announce that the United States will offer compensation to the victims' families.

November 5. A U.S.-mediated settlement in Namibia is announced; the African nation will receive it independence, and Cuban troops will be withdrawn from neighboring Angola.

December 21. A terrorist bomb destroys Pan Am flight 103 over Lockerbie, Scotland, during a flight from London to New York; all 259 passengers and 11 persons on the ground are killed.

Economy and Society

1981

The inflation rate is 14 percent, and the unemployment rate is 7.4 percent.

January 7. The Dow Jones stock market index loses 23.8 points; the market will stabilize on January 19.

February 17. Automakers announce major losses in 1980, due to foreign competition.

February 18. In his State of the Union Address, Reagan outlines his economic program, which includes a $41 billion cut in the federal budget for the coming fiscal year, a 10 percent cut in the individual income tax in each of the next 3 years, and $5 billion in additional defense spending. The projected deficit is $45 billion.

July 29. Congress approves a program to cut income taxes by 5 percent on October 1, by 10 percent on July 1, 1982, and by 10 percent on July 1, 1983; it is the largest tax cut in the nation's history.

August 3. An illegal nationwide strike is begun by 13,000 air traffic controllers. Reagan orders them back to work, and on August 5 he will fire those who have not complied.

POPULATION OF THE UNITED STATES, 1880–1980

	Population (in millions)	Increase (in percent)	Urban Population (in percent)	Rural Population (in percent)
1880	50.1	26.0	28.2	71.8
1890	62.9	25.5	35.1	64.9
1900	75.9	20.7	39.6	60.4
1910	91.9	21.0	45.6	54.4
1920	105.7	15.0	51.2	48.8
1930	122.7	16.1	56.1	43.9
1940	131.6	7.2	56.5	43.5
1950	150.6	14.4	64.0	36.0
1960	179.3	19.1	69.9	30.1
1970	203.3	13.4	73.5	26.5
1980	226.5	11.4	73.7	26.3

SOURCE: Mary B. Norton, et al., *A People and a Nation: A History of the United States*, 2nd ed. (Boston: Houghton Mifflin, 1986), vol. II.

1982

The inflation rate for the year falls to 6 percent; the consumer goods price index increases by 3.9 percent, the smallest rise since 1972. The gross national product (GNP) declines 1.8 percent. The unemployment rate for the year is 9.7 percent.

January 26. In his State of the Union Address, Reagan proposes transferring $47 billion in federal programs to state and local governments.

February 28. The United Auto Workers union negotiates a new contract with Ford. Guaranteed employment is granted in lieu of wage hikes. A similar agreement will be signed on March 21 with General Motors.

June 12. Nearly 500,000 people demonstrate in New York against nuclear weapons.

June 15. The Supreme Court rules that any child of school age is entitled to a free education, even if the child's parents are illegal immigrants.

July 19. The poverty rate reaches 14 percent, its highest level since 1967 and 7.4 percent above its level in 1980. Poverty is defined as an annual income of $8,414 or less for a four-person household.

September 8. The president announces that he supports a bill introduced by Senator Jesse Helms of North Carolina that would allow prayer in public schools.

October 26. The federal budget deficit for Fiscal Year 1982 reaches $110 billion, a new record.

December 16. The nation's factories are estimated to be producing at 67.8 percent of their capacity.

December 27. The Dow Jones index reaches 1070.55 points.

1983

Consumer prices increase by 3.8 percent. Incomes increase by 6.3 percent. Automobile production increases by 10.2 percent.

April 12. Voters in Chicago elect their first black mayor, Democrat Harold Washington.

April 20. Reagan signs into law a bill designed to save the Social Security System from bankruptcy.

April 26. A federal report on education discloses that 23 million Americans are functionally illiterate.

May. AIDS, a disease of the immune system, begins receiving priority attention from the federal government.

June 16. Congress approves compensation for Japanese-Americans interned during World War II.

August 27. In Washington, 250,000 demonstrators commemorate the 1963 civil rights march led by Martin Luther King, Jr.

1984

Consumer prices increase by 4 percent. Incomes increase by 6.8 percent.

The trade deficit climbs to $107.6 billion.

According to a census, the United States has 236,158,000 inhabitants.

1985

Consumer prices increase by 3.8 percent. Incomes increase by 5.95 percent. The unemployment rate is 6.8 percent.

The federal budget deficit reaches $211.9 billion. For the first time since World War II, the United States is a debtor nation.

January 2. Reagan meets with Japanese prime minister Yasuhiro Nakasone in an effort to balance trade relations with Japan.

January 11. The national association of chiefs of Indian tribes rejects the proposals made in November 1984 by a presidential commission to close the Bureau of Indian Affairs, integrate the businesses managed by the tribes into the free market, increase external investment on the reservations, and link tribal judicial systems to the federal courts.

September 22. In New York, the finance ministers and the heads of the central banks of the United States, Great Britain, West Germany, France and Japan meet to discuss reducing the value of the dollar on international markets.

December 11–12. The Gramm-Rudman-Hollings bill is approved by Congress and signed into law by the president. Federal spending will be cut automatically if the budget is not balanced within five years.

December 16. The Dow Jones sets a new record: 1553.10 points.

1986

January 8. The Dow Jones drops 39.10 points.

February 21–22. In Paris, the finance ministers of the leading industrial nations meet to stabilize their currencies at their present rates.

March 7. The Federal Reserve lowers its interest rate to 7 percent. The rate will fall to 6.5 percent on April 18, and to 6 percent on June 10.

May 4–6. At an economic summit in Tokyo, the leaders of seven major industrial countries conclude agreements on closer economic cooperation and on antiterrorist measures.

May 25. In "Hands Across America," 5 million Americans form a human chain from the Atlantic to the Pacific in order to alert the public about hunger and homelessness in the United States.

August 4. Reagan calls for a "war on drugs."

October 22. Reagan signs a tax reform law, the most comprehensive since World War II. The number of tax brackets is reduced, as are the opportunities for fraud.

October 31. Treasury Secretary James A. Baker and Minister of Finance Kiichi Miyazawa of Japan announce an agreement on economic cooperation.

1987

January 8. The Dow Jones index passes the 2000 point mark.

January 9. The unemployment rate in December 1986 was 6.6 percent, the lowest since March 1980; the rate was 7 percent for the entire year.

January 14. According to a report by the National Urban League, blacks are falling further behind whites economically. A black worker in 1985 earned an average of $6,840 per year, 44 percent less than a white worker, whose average income was $11,671; in 1975, a black earned 38 percent less than a white. The poverty rate among blacks in 1985 was 31.3 percent.

January 15. The value of the dollar against the German mark decreased by 5 percent in the first two weeks of 1986.

March 27. Reagan announces a tariff that will double the price of some Japanese electronic components, in retaliation for Japan's failure to fulfill its agreement in 1986 to open its market to U.S. semiconductors. The dollar's value against the yen is at its lowest level since World War II.

April 25–27. Demonstrations against Reagan's policies toward Central America and South Africa take place.

April 29–May 1. Japanese prime minister Yasuhiro Nakasone visits Washington in an effort to resolve economic disagreements between the two countries.

June 7. In Greensboro, North Carolina, the Ku Klux Klan holds a demonstration, the first since 1979.

August 25. The Dow Jones index reaches 2722.42, a record high.

October 3. The United States and Canada agree to eliminate all customs duties between their countries within 10 years.

October 14–16. The Dow Jones falls 95.46 points, then 108.36 points on the 16th.

October 19. On "Black Monday," the stock market crashes: the Dow Jones drops 508.32 points (22 percent).

December 31. The Dow Jones hovers around its January 1987 level. The dollar has lost 23 percent of its value against the yen and 18 percent against the mark.

1988

The unemployment rate is 5.7 percent.

January 8. The special commission headed by Nicholas Brady that the president appointed to study the circumstances surrounding the stock market crash releases its report: The financial system came within a heartbeat of total collapse on Tuesday, October 20. Radical changes are proposed.

The professional journal of the American Medical Association publishes an anonymous article entitled "It's All Over, Debbie," in which a physician describes how he helped euthanize a 20-year-old woman suffering from cancer. The article sparks serious debate.

January 13. Noboru Takeshita, the new Japanese prime minister, visits Washington to discuss ways of reducing the U.S. trade deficit with Japan.

January 27. In 1987, the GNP increased by 3.8 percent.

February 5. In the first housing legislation of the Reagan administration, $15 billion in 1988, and $15.3 billion in 1989, are earmarked for the building of low-income housing. A program to help the neediest is also planned.

February 10. The secretary of education reports that racial integration, prescribed by the civil rights law of 1964, is still not entirely enforced in the universities of six southern states.

February 12. The trade deficit for 1987 was the largest ever, $171 billion. Exports increased 11.4 percent over 1986, reaching $253 billion, but imports increased 10.7 percent and totaled $424 billion.

March 7. Crisis: Heterosexual Behavior in the Age of Aids is published. The authors, Masters and Johnson, assert in a press conference that the AIDS virus is also spreading uncontrollably among heterosexuals. A wave of panic ensues.

March 22. The Civil Rights Restoration Act protects the civil rights of individuals with contagious diseases, especially those with AIDS. Such individuals are considered handicapped and therefore protected by law.

August 23. President Reagan signs the Omnibus Trade Act, providing for sanctions against countries employing unfair trade practices.

September. Unemployment edges down to 5.3 percent.

Science and Technology

1981

April 12–14. The space shuttle *Columbia*, the first reusable spacecraft, orbits the Earth 36 times during its first flight.

1982

December 2. A permanent artificial heart is implanted in a human for the first time. The patient, Barney Clark, will live 112 days.

1983

June 18–24. Sally Ride becomes the first American woman in space; she is a member of the crew of *Challenger*, the nation's second space shuttle.

1984

February 13. A six-year-old Texas girl is the recipient of the first heart and liver transplant.

April 23. The AIDS virus is identified.

October 11. Kathryn D. Sullivan becomes the first woman to walk in space during the sixth flight of the *Challenger* shuttle.

October 16. The heart of a monkey is implanted in a newborn baby, who will survive until November 15.

December 12. In Florida, human bones and skulls 7,000 years old are discovered; a sample of DNA is extracted from brain tissue.

1986

January 24. The *Voyager 2* spacecraft passes near Uranus.

January 28. The space shuttle *Challenger* explodes 74 seconds after lift-off from Cape Canaveral, killing all seven crew members.

April 1. The first "test tube" baby is born in Cleveland, Ohio.

May 4. A Delta rocket malfunctions after lift-off and must be destroyed. The space program will be revamped to take into account the recent series of failures.

June 18. Reagan signs a code regulating research and applications in the field of genetic engineering.

1987

June 1–5. The third international conference on AIDS is held in Washington.

October 26. A Titan 34-D military rocket with a secret payload becomes the nation's first space launch in two years.

December 29. The launching of the space shuttle is postponed indefinitely.

1988

March. Scientists report a vast hole in the ozone layer over the Arctic, similar to the hole over the Antarctic discovered in 1982.

September 29–October 3. Discovery flies the first space shuttle mission since the 1986 *Challenger* explosion.

Civilization and Culture

1981

June 6. A 21-year-old architecture student, Maya Yang Lin, wins the design competition for a monument in Washington to commemorate Americans killed in the Vietnam War.

1982

Jonathan Schell's *The Fate of the Earth* and Alice Walker's novel *The Color Purple* are published.

Release of Steven Spielberg's movie *E.T., the Extraterrestrial.*

1983

William Kennedy's novel *Ironweed* is published.

Michael Jackson's album *Thriller* breaks all sales records.

November 20. The made-for-TV movie *The Day After* dramatizes the results of a nuclear attack on the United States.

1984

The Fact of a Doorframe, by Adrienne Rich, is published.

In New York, "Van Gogh in Arles," an exhibit, opens at the Metropolitan Museum of Art.

The Methodist Church bars the ordination of noncelibate homosexuals.

June 9. Donald Duck, the Walt Disney character, is 50 years old.

July 28–August 12. The Summer Olympic Games are held in Los Angeles; Soviet-bloc countries boycott the games.

1985

Larry McMurtry's novel *Lonesome Dove* is published.

Sam Shepard's play *A Lie of the Mind.*

Conservative Judaism approves the ordination of women rabbis.

October 2. The actor Rock Hudson dies of AIDS.

1986

From Courbet to Cézanne: A New XIXth Century, an exhibit of 130 paintings from the Orsay Museum, is shown at the Brooklyn Museum in New York.

July 3. Reagan rekindles the flame of the newly restored Statue of Liberty.

July 27. The racing cyclist Greg Lemond becomes the first American to win the Tour de France.

1987

Allan Bloom publishes *The Closing of the American Mind,* a rebuke of anti-intellectualism in the U.S.

March 11. The exhibit *An American Eye: The Wyeths, Three Generations of Painters* opens in Leningrad; it will later travel to Moscow.

1988

Toni Morrison's Pulitzer Prize-winning novel *Beloved* is published.

Barry Levinson's *Rain Man* wins the Academy Award for best motion picture.

Chapter 30   1989–1992

America in a Changing World

George Bush took office on the eve of extraordinary international developments. The process of political and economic liberalization set in motion by Mikhail Gorbachev in the Soviet Union brought about the collapse of communism in Eastern Europe in 1989. Within a year, Germany, divided since World War II, was reunified. By the end of 1991, the USSR itself had disintegrated and been replaced by Russia and the other newly independent former Soviet republics.

The Bush administration received high marks for its handling of foreign affairs. With the specter of nuclear war receding as Washington and Moscow concluded a series of historic arms control agreements, Bush worked to fashion a "new world order." In the 1991 Persian Gulf War, the United States led an international coalition that reversed Iraq's invasion of Kuwait. But the uncertain parameters of the U.S. military deployment to a starving Somalia in December 1992 underscored the difficulties of defining American foreign policy in a changing world.

With the end of the Cold War, Americans focused their attention on domestic issues. As Bush struggled to articulate a domestic agenda, burgeoning federal budget deficits and economic recession raised widespread concern about the nation's future. In the 1992 presidential election, Democrat Bill Clinton, governor of Arkansas, campaigned on the need for vigorous new programs to revitalize the economy and redress America's failing education, health care and welfare systems. Independent candidate Ross Perot mounted a surprisingly strong populist challenge by stressing the issues of deficit reduction and political reform. Clinton won the presidency with 43 percent of the popular vote and 370 electors to Bush's 38 percent and 168 electors, and Perot's 19 percent and no electors.

Political and Institutional Life

1989

January 20. George Bush is sworn in as the 41st president; Dan Quayle becomes vice president.

February 10. Ronald Brown, elected chairman of the Democratic National Committee, becomes the first black to head a major American political party.

March 9. The Senate rejects Bush's nomination of former senator John Tower as secretary of defense. The president will nominate Wyoming congressman Dick Cheney, who will be confirmed on March 17.

May 4. Former National Security Council staff member Oliver North is convicted on three counts in the Iran-Contra scandal.

May 31. The Speaker of the House of Representatives, Jim Wright, facing serious ethical charges, resigns.

August 10. Army general Colin Powell becomes the first black to be selected chairman of the Joint Chiefs of Staff.

November. Democrats win most of the major offices at stake in off-year elections.

1990

April 7. Former national security advisor John Poindexter is convicted on five counts in the Iran-Contra scandal.

April 23. Bush signs the Federal Hate Crimes Statistics Act.

July 20. Justice William Brennan retires from the Supreme Court. On July 23, the president will nominate David Souter to replace Brennan.

July 26. The Americans with Disabilities Act protects the rights of the disabled.

August 10. Mayor Marion Barry of Washington, D.C., is convicted on one count of possession of cocaine.

October 2. David Souter is confirmed by the Senate as a justice of the Supreme Court.

November 6. In the midterm elections, the Democrats retain their majorities in both houses of Congress.

1991

July 1. President Bush nominates Clarence Thomas to succeed the retiring Thurgood Marshall on the Supreme Court.

October 11–13. In televised hearings, the Senate Judiciary Committee explores Anita Hill's charges that Clarence Thomas engaged in sexual harassment when they worked together at a federal agency. Thomas denies the allegations.

October 15. Thomas is confirmed by the Senate as a justice of the Supreme Court.

November 5. Robert Gates is confirmed as head of the CIA.

November 20. William Barr is confirmed by the Senate as attorney general.

December 3. John Sununu resigns as White House chief of staff.

1992

March 1. Senator Brock Adams announces his retirement amid allegations of sexual misconduct.

April. More than 300 members of the House of Representatives are identified as having overdrawn their checking accounts at the House bank.

May. "Family values" become a major topic of debate in the presidential election campaign.

June 16. Former secretary of defense Caspar Weinberger is indicted in the Iran-Contra scandal.

July 15–16. Arkansas governor Bill Clinton becomes the Democratic Party's nominee for president. Senator Albert Gore of Tennessee is chosen as Clinton's running mate.

Independent candidate Ross Perot of Texas drops out of the presidential race.

October 1. Perot reenters the presidential campaign.

November 3. Bill Clinton is elected the 42nd president. The Democrats retain their majorities in the Senate and the House of Representatives. Women increase their numbers in the Senate from 2 to 6, and in the House from 29 to 48.

December 24. President Bush pardons Caspar Weinberger and five other Iran-Contra figures.

Foreign Policy

1989

January 4. U.S. Navy warplanes shoot down two Libyan jet fighters in the Gulf of Sidra.

February 2. Japanese prime minister Noboru Takeshita meets with President Bush in Washington.

February 10. In his first trip abroad as president, Bush confers with Prime Minister Brian Mulroney in Canada.

February 14. The presidents of five Central American nations agree on a plan that will lead to the disarming and repatriation of the Contras.

July. President Bush visits Poland and Hungary amid the tide of democratic reform sweeping through the two Soviet satellites.

July 31. Terrorists in Lebanon announce they have executed Marine lieutenant colonel William Higgins, whom they abducted in 1988.

November 9. East Germany opens the Berlin Wall, effectively ending the post–World War II division of Europe. By the end of the year, non-Communist governments will emerge throughout Eastern Europe.

December. U.S. air support helps defeat an attempted coup against the government of President Corazon Aquino in the Philippines.

December 2–3. Bush and Soviet leader Mikhail Gorbachev hold their first summit meeting on the Mediterranean island of Malta. Discussions center on the political changes taking place in Eastern Europe.

December 20. In Operation Just Cause, U.S. military forces invade Panama to safeguard American lives and interests and to depose Panamanian strongman General Manuel Noriega, who was indicted in the United States in February 1988 on drug trafficking charges.

1990

January 3. Noriega surrenders to U.S. forces and is flown to Miami to face trial. He will be convicted in April 1992.

February 15. President Bush attends the Drug Summit in Colombia, where he and the leaders of Peru, Bolivia and Columbia agree to cooperate against drug trafficking.

February 25. The U.S.-favored National Opposition Union led by Violeta Chamorro defeats the Sandinistas in national elections in Nicaragua. President Bush will lift economic sanctions against Nicaragua on March 13.

May 31–June 3. Bush and Gorbachev hold a summit meeting in Washington. The two leaders sign a major trade agreement and accords on reducing strategic nuclear arsenals and ending the production of chemical weapons.

June 20. Black South African leader Nelson Mandela, freed in February after 27 years in prison, begins an 11-day visit to the United States.

August 5. U.S. Marines evacuate foreigners from a civil war in Liberia.

August 6. The United States votes in favor of a United Nations Security Council resolution imposing mandatory economic sanctions on Iraq, which invaded Kuwait on August 2; Bush had frozen Iraqi and Kuwaiti assets in the United States on August 2.

August 7. President Bush orders Operation Desert Shield: U.S. troops and warplanes are sent to the Persian Gulf at the request of Saudi Arabia to defend that country and its vast oil reserves against a potential Iraqi attack.

August 25. The UN Security Council authorizes U.S. and allied ships to use force to uphold an embargo on trade with Iraq.

September 9. Bush and Gorbachev confer in Helsinki on the Persian Gulf crisis. They issue a joint statement condemning Iraq's invasion of Kuwait.

September 12. The Final Settlement with Respect to Germany, providing for German reunification on October 3, is signed by the United States, Great Britain, France, the Soviet Union and the two Germanys in Moscow.

November 8. President Bush deploys another 200,000 troops to the Persian Gulf, doubling U.S. forces in the region, to bolster the United Nations' demands that Iraq withdraw from Kuwait.

November 19. The Conventional Forces in Europe Treaty, cutting NATO and Warsaw Pact conventional arsenals on the continent, is signed in Paris. On November 21, Bush, Gorbachev and other European leaders sign the Charter of Paris, proclaiming an end to the military division of Europe.

November 21–22. Bush holds talks in the Middle East with the leaders of Saudi Arabia, Kuwait and Egypt. He will meet with the president of Syria in Geneva on November 23.

November 26. The UN Security Council authorizes the use of "all means necessary" to expel Iraq from Kuwait. A January 15, 1991, deadline is set for Iraq to withdraw peaceably.

December. The U.S.-led multinational coalition finalizes preparations for military action to force Iraq from Kuwait.

1991

January 5. U.S. Marines evacuate American embassy personnel from war-torn Somalia.

January 9. Secretary of State James Baker and Foreign Minister Tariq Aziz of Iraq meet in Geneva in a final unsuccessful effort to end the crisis in the Persian Gulf.

January 17. Coalition forces launch Operation Desert Storm, a massive military campaign to liberate Kuwait. For the next six weeks the allies will wage a punishing air war against Iraq.

February 24–27. In a 100-hour ground war, the U.S.-led coalition forces rout the Iraqi army and free Kuwait.

February 27. President Bush declares a cease-fire in the Persian Gulf War effective at midnight.

April 6. Iraq accedes to UN terms, bringing the Persian Gulf War to an official end.

April 15. The United States and its allies establish a "safe zone" in northern Iraq to protect the Kurdish people from Iraqi attack.

May 12. A U.S. naval task force deploys to Bangladesh to aid in that nation's recovery from a devastating hurricane.

July 30–31. Bush and Gorbachev hold a summit meeting in Moscow. They sign the Strategic Arms Reduction Treaty (START), under which the United States and the Soviet Union will reduce their long-range nuclear arsenals by 30 percent over seven years. The two leaders also announce that they will co-sponsor a Middle East peace conference.

August 19–21. President Bush throws America's support behind Russian president Boris Yeltsin during the abortive hard-line coup against Gorbachev.

September 27. In a move intended to draw a corresponding Soviet response, Bush offers additional reductions in U.S. strategic and tactical nuclear weapons. On October 5, Gorbachev will offer similar Soviet reductions.

October 30. Bush and Gorbachev attend the opening of the Middle East Peace Conference in Madrid. The conference, jointly sponsored by the United States and the Soviet Union, is aimed at resolving the Arab-Israeli conflict.

November 14. A U.S. court indicts two Libyan intelligence officers for the December 1988 bombing of Pan Am Flight 103. Libya will refuse U.S. requests for the extradition of the officers.

December 4. Terry Anderson, the last American held hostage in Lebanon, is freed after almost seven years of captivity.

December 25. With Mikhail Gorbachev's resignation as president, the Soviet Union officially ceases to exist. The United States recognizes Russia, headed by Boris Yeltsin, as the successor state.

1992

January 31. At the United Nations, Bush and the leaders of Russia, Great Britain, France and China hold a summit meeting of the five permanent members of the Security Council.

February 1. The Coast Guard begins returning Haitian refugees picked up at sea to Haiti.

June 16–17. Meeting in Washington, Bush and Yeltsin agree on the framework for a START II agreement that will further cut strategic nuclear arms.

August 27. The United States and allied nations establish a "no-fly zone" in southern Iraq to protect Shiite Muslims from Iraqi air attack.

September 2. President Bush announces the sale of 150 F-16 jet fighters to Taiwan.

December 9. Approximately 28,000 U.S. troops begin arriving in Somalia to protect international relief efforts to feed the starving populace of that war-ravaged country.

Economy and Society

1989

January 24. Serial killer Theodore Bundy is executed in Florida.

February 10. Major banks raise their prime lending rate to 11 percent, the highest level since 1984.

March 10. The jobless rate dips to 5.1 percent, a 14-year low.

May 25. President Bush identifies Brazil, India and Japan as unfair trading partners.

July 14–16. The heads of government of the seven major Western industrialized powers meet in Paris; economic aid to Eastern Europe, air pollution and drug trafficking are among the topics discussed.

August 9. Bush signs legislation to rescue the failing savings and loan industry. The bill provides $166 billion over a 10-year period to close insolvent banks.

October 17. The Commerce Department reports that the U.S. trade deficit continues to increase.

December 29. On the New York Stock Exchange, the Dow Jones index closes at 2753.20, up 27 percent for the year.

1990

January 18. Secretary of Health and Human Services Louis Sullivan deplores the targeting of cigarette advertising to blacks.

February 13. The American Bar Association announces its support for a constitutional right to abortion.

The Wall Street securities firm Drexel Burnham Lambert, known for its trading in "junk bonds," files for bankruptcy.

April 12. Major tuna-canning companies announce they will no longer buy tuna caught in nets that also trap dolphins.

June 4. A "suicide machine" developed by Dr. Jack Kevorkian is used for the first time.

July 9–11. The leaders of the seven major industrial democracies meet in Houston; they agree to study the feasibility of extending economic aid to the Soviet Union.

July 16. The Dow Jones index rises above 3000 for the first time.

October 24. Secretary of Labor Elizabeth Dole, the highest-ranking woman in the Bush administration, resigns to accept the presidency of the American Red Cross.

December 26. The Census Bureau releases the official 1990 census figures. The U.S. population is 249,632,692.

1991

January 2. Major banks cut their prime lending rate to 9.5 percent to stimulate demand.

February. Unemployment rises to 6.5 percent; 450,000 jobs are lost.

March 15. Four white Los Angeles policemen are indicted in the beating of the black motorist Rodney King.

April 2. The minimum wage, earned by an estimated 3 million workers, increases 45 cents to $4.25 per hour.

April 26. The Commerce Department reports that the economy is in recession, ending eight years of expansion since the 1981–1982 downturn.

June 5. An openly homosexual woman is ordained an Episcopal minister in Washington, D.C.

July 17. Soviet president Mikhail Gorbachev attends the economic summit of the Group of Seven industrial democracies in London; technical and other assistance is extended to the Soviet Union.

August 15. The Congressional Budget Office announces that the federal deficit will reach a record $360 billion in the coming year.

August 26. The College Board releases figures showing that the scores on the Scholastic Aptitude Test taken by college-bound students continue to decline.

October 16. Congress fails to override President Bush's veto of a bill extending benefits to those who have lost their jobs in the recession. A revised measure will be enacted in November.

December 4. Pan American World Airways ceases operation.

December 31. A recession-induced cut in interest rates spurs a stock-buying rally on Wall Street; the stock market closes the year at 3168.83, an all-time high.

1992

January. Unemployment rises to 7.1 percent, the highest level in five years.

January 27. The R.H. Macy Company, which operates a chain of retail stores, files for bankruptcy.

January 28. In his State of the Union Address, Bush proposes new measures to deal with the recession.

April 14. A five-month United Automobile Workers strike at the Caterpillar Tractor Company ends without a settlement.

April 29. A violent riot erupts in Los Angeles after the acquittal of four white policemen on trial for the beating of black motorist Rodney King. President Bush will send federal troops to restore order; 52 are killed and more than 600 buildings are destroyed.

June 11. An amendment that would require the federal budget to be balanced is defeated in the House of Representatives.

July. Unemployment rises to 7.8 percent, the highest level in eight years.

Russian president Boris Yeltsin attends the Group of Seven economic summit in Munich.

August 12. The United States, Canada and Mexico conclude the North American Free Trade Agreement.

October 3. Congress overrides President Bush's veto of a bill regulating the cable television industry.

Science and Technology

1989

January 11. The Surgeon General reports that cigarette smoking claimed 390,000 lives in 1985.

March 24. The *Exxon Valdez*, an oil tanker, runs aground in Alaska's Prince William Sound, resulting in the largest oil spill in U.S. history.

June 4. The *Titan 4*, the largest unmanned U.S. rocket, is launched for the first time.

November 2. A computer "virus" spreads through university, military and corporate computers. A Cornell University graduate student will later be found responsible.

1990

April 22. Earth Day is celebrated worldwide.

June 27. The Hubble Space Telescope, launched into earth orbit in April,

is found to have a serious design flaw in one of its mirrors.

September 14. A four-year-old girl suffering from a rare immune deficiency becomes the first person to receive human gene therapy.

1991

January 9. Climatologists report that 1990 was the warmest year since measurements began in 1880, reinforcing fears of global warming.

August 30. Neurobiologists at the Salk Institute in California report finding differences in the brain physiologies of heterosexual and homosexual men.

1992

January 14. Two rare California condors are released into Los Padres National Forest in an effort to restore the almost extinct birds to their natural habitat.

May 13. The crew of the space shuttle *Endeavour* captures and repairs a satellite that had gone off course.

May 14. The Bush administration opens to logging 1,700 acres of federal land identified as a habitat of the spotted owl.

June. President Bush attends the Earth Summit in Rio de Janeiro.

June 28. The strongest earthquake in 40 years, measuring 7.4 on the Richter scale, strikes southern California.

August 24–25. Hurricane Andrew devastates southern Florida and coastal Louisiana.

Civilization and Culture

1989

Taylor Branch's *Parting the Waters: America in the King Years, 1954–1963,*

James McPherson's *Battle Cry of Freedom: The Civil War Era* and Richard Wilbur's *New and Collected Poems* win Pulitzer Prizes.

Steven Soderbergh's movie *Sex, Lies and Videotape*.

Digital audio tape recorders are marketed in the United States.

March 4. The media companies Warner Communications and Time, Inc., agree to merge.

August 24. Pete Rose is banned for life from major league baseball for betting on games.

1990

Oscar Hijuelos's novel *The Mambo Kings Play Songs of Love* wins a Pulitzer Prize.

March 18. Art valued at $100 million is stolen from the Isabella Stewart Gardner Museum in Boston; it is the largest art theft in history.

April 7. A controversial exhibit of sexually explicit photographs by the late Robert Mapplethorpe opens in Cincinnati.

1991

Neil Simon's play *Lost in Yorkers* wins a Pulitzer Prize.

Oliver Stone's film *J.F.K.* puts forth the theory that the late president was the victim of an assassination conspiracy.

Natalie Cole wins a Grammy Award for "Unforgettable," in which she sings a duet with the taped voice of her late father, Nat "King" Cole.

November 7. Basketball star Earvin "Magic" Johnson announces he has tested positive for the AIDS virus and will retire from the Los Angeles Lakers.

1992

A Thousand Acres, by Jane Smiley, and James Tate's *Selected Poems* are published.

Spike Lee's movie *Malcolm X*.

The Toronto Blue Jays become the first foreign team to win the World Series of major league baseball.

May 22. Johnny Carson retires after 29 years as host of television's "Tonight Show" and is replaced by Jay Leno.

INDEX

The index headings are filed letter by letter. Some entries are filed by date to reflect the chronology. Maps are indicated by "*m*" following the page number; tables by "*t*" and glossary items by "*g*".